DEFENDING THE FLOCK

A Security Guide for Church Safety Directors

Kris P. Moloney

Dedications and Acknowledgements

The author would like to thank the following individual for her tireless assistance, commitment and dedication:

Malene A. Little

Malene earned a Master of Arts in English and a Master of Public Administration with a nonprofit management specialization. She works with USD Head Start, has two children in K12 and volunteers with their organizations when she can, and is an adjunct instructor at the University of South Dakota. Dedicated to advancing education at all levels and especially enthusiastic about using her skills to serve God, Malene contributed substantially to the research, writing, and editing of this project.

Thank you for all your contributions, so we can serve God by making churches safe.

Your loyal companion in Christ,
Kris P. Moloney, Owner at Sheepdog Church Security

Contents

An Overview of This Manual

Welcome to the Sheepdog Church Security training manual! Thank you for investing in the safety and security of your church. The material found within this book will help you train church staff and volunteers to perform the duties of a Church Safety Team member. Hundreds of churches across the US have already used the material within this book effectively.

This manual contains best practices in church security built on the work of nationally-recognized subject matter experts (SMEs). After completing the book, you'll be encouraged by how easily you have become the security expert for your congregation.

Within this book, we will teach you:

- Background information about specific church vulnerabilities
- How to conduct a security assessment
- The purpose of a Church Safety Team
- How to select and train your Church Safety Team members to serve your church's unique needs
- How to prevent crime at your church
- How to stop criminals as necessary
- How to prepare for natural disasters

All this information will enable you to keep your church members and property safe.

Each unit provides an overview of the information found within individual chapters contained in that unit. Within each chapter, you'll find material explaining and exploring the topic, as well as explanations on how to use that information in real life and step-by-step instructions about sharing this knowledge with your Church Safety Team members.

Within the appendices, you will find numerous tools and resources, such as checklists, sample forms and sample protocols that can be modified and printed to meet your specific needs.

Note that the training and resources made available within this book originate from professionally-recognized sources, but it is your church's responsibility to consult with a licensed attorney and insurance agent within your location while developing policies and procedures specifically for your church.

Sheepdog Church Security assumes no civil or criminal Liability for Application of our training by your church employees and/or volunteers who may have received no other training for serving on a Church Safety Team. This waiver of liability includes any foreseen or unforeseen consequences or outcomes of an emergency.

If you have questions, please call 612-470-7364, or email Kris@SheepdogChurchSecurity.net. You are not alone. I am here to help you succeed, and will answer any questions you might have.

Your loyal companion in Christ,

Kris P. Moloney Owner Sheepdog Church Security

Introduction

Church security may seem to be an absurd topic. Some people are convinced that bad things can't happen in churches. Other people believe that church security is somehow a sign of lack of faith. In a survey of 4,000 churches, more than 75% did not have emergency or security plans (Hawkins, 2012). This information is directed toward Christian churches, but all religious organizations can benefit from the information in this book.

The irony is that God has always used his people to accomplish his tasks. Pastors preach the word of God. Deacons assist the pastor and take care of the flock. Of course, God could accomplish all these tasks by himself, but instead, he chooses to allow his followers to help him.

This is true for every function of the church. Some Christians have the gift to take care of children. Some teach Bible studies. Some work as ushers to welcome members and help first-time visitors. Others work in administrative positions.

Like all Christians, Church Safety Team members use their gifts to serve the church. Just as all Christians face tasks that need to be completed during the week, Church Safety Team members have tasks that need to be accomplished during the week, too, including preparing for medical emergencies, criminal activity, natural disasters, and technological disasters.

Sheepdog Church Security has worked for years to help churches around the nation to improve their ability to provide safe and secure places for worship and fellowship.

The reason that Church Safety Teams are needed to prevent criminal activity is best explained by Lieutenant Colonel (U.S. Army retired) Dave Grossman, an internationally recognized expert on violence. Grossman wrote about the now-famous metaphor a Vietnam veteran shared with him (Killology Research Group, 2016). Grossman and Christensen (2004) explained it in their book, *On Combat: The Psychology and Physiology of Deadly Conflict in War and in Peace* (2004).

There are three types of people in the world:

- Sheep, who are "kind, decent people who are not capable of hurting each other, except by accident or under extreme provocation" and who may even be unable to accept that there is evil in the world
- Wolves, who "feed on the sheep without mercy"
- Sheepdogs, who "live to protect the flock and confront the wolf" (Killology Research Group, 2016)

Grossman and Christensen also argued that people exist on a continuum and may sometimes act as sheep and other times as sheepdogs (Killology Research Group, 2016). Every day, we make choices that determine where we exist on the continuum.

Kris P. Moloney further extended this metaphor and Christianized it by explaining that sheep are generally kind and gentle followers of the Good Shepherd (Christ) and exist to serve the Church. Sheep want to live a life pleasing to God by serving others and practicing righteousness.

Wolves, on the other hand, continuously look for opportunities to steal from, molest, destroy, and even kill the sheep. Wolves may even pretend to follow the Shepherd to deceive the sheep. However, they exhibit neither mercy nor grace.

Sheepdogs are both companions to the Shepherd and protectors of the sheep. Sheepdogs live and die for Christ and His Church. God has called and equipped sheepdogs to defend the sheep from wolves.

There are many aspects of security that we will cover in this book. To determine which issues you should focus on first, you must conduct a security assessment to discover where your church is most vulnerable. A security assessment includes evaluating the following questions:

- Does the church have a system in place to deal with medical emergencies?

- Are our finances vulnerable to attack?
- Are our children protected from abuse or neglect?
- Is church property safe from vandalism?
- Do we have systems in place to deal with bomb threats or violent intruders?
- Are we prepared for fires?
- Are we prepared for severe weather?

Using Sheepdog Church Security's General Security Assessment can help you answer these questions so you know where to concentrate your efforts.

Sheepdog Church Security will help your Church Safety Team members become sheepdogs!

Unit 1 Overview: Why Church Security and Safety Matter

In Unit One, we will discuss the need for church safety as a whole, including startling statistics concerning the growth of crime and vandalism against churches across the United States, the impact of natural disasters, and more.

The point of this chapter is to illustrate the significant and increasing need for vigilance on the part of sheepdogs (you and your Church Security Team), and the growing number of threats the Church as a whole faces in today's world.

This chapter can be shared with your Church Security Team members in whole or in part, but I recommend that all members read and understand the statistics concerning crime, violence, vandalism and other threats individual churches face. My recommendation is that you address this initial chapter in a group meeting setting so that as many team members as possible are exposed to this information.

Chapter 1:
The Need for Church Security and Safety Solutions

Throughout history, churches have been both places of safety and the targets of vandalism, anger, violence, and even outright hatred. When the Vikings first invaded England in AD 793, it was the churches and monasteries that initially attracted their rapacious interest. Priests were put to the sword. Church treasures were stolen. Buildings were burnt to the ground.

Today, things have not changed all that much. The Charleston Bible study slaughter by Dylan Roof in 2015 is possibly the most visible proof of this, but the story goes much, much deeper. In fact, violence against the Church is on the rise as the bonds that hold society together inevitably decay and break.

Those threats are not just outside the church. Wolves lurk within the congregation, as well, masquerading as sheep and seeking to devour and destroy. As sheepdogs, it is our responsibility to be vigilant, to stand guard, to identify wolves both without and within, and safeguard the sheep so that they may serve God.

Not convinced? Just consider a few headlines from recent years:

"CHURCH SHOOTINGS HAPPEN OFTEN ENOUGH THAT THERE'S A NATIONAL CHURCH SHOOTING DATABASE" – *THE PACIFIC STANDARD*, **JUNE 19, 2015**

"CHURCHES BOOST SECURITY AS VIOLENT INCIDENTS GROW" – *USA TODAY*, **JULY 7, 2013**

"VIOLENT HISTORY: ATTACKS ON BLACK CHURCHES" – *THE NEW YORK TIMES*, JUNE 18, 2015

"VIOLENT INCIDENTS AT CHURCHES ARE RISING" – *CHRISTIANITY TODAY*, JUNE 7, 2016

These are just a handful of examples. In truth, church violence is among the most common in the country. Church shootings are actually much more common than school shootings, although schools tend to see the most press coverage.

Startling National Statistics

The rise in church-related violence is seen in more than simple article headlines and news stories. Hard statistics back up the increase in violent incidents within houses of worship across the United States.

According to the National Church Shooting Database (http://www.icpsr.umich.edu/icpsrweb/DSDR/studies/25561), which only tracks church shootings from 1980 through 2005, there were 139 shootings in US churches in that 15-year period. Within those shootings, 185 people were killed. 36 of those were children.

Carl Chinn (http://nebula.wsimg.com/dd349bdc053330df2c77c85ee-591b805?AccessKeyId=16B07A2D0672906279DB&disposition=0&allow-origin=1), a security consultant and Christian, has tracked church-related violence across the US in greater detail, though. From his collected deadly force incident statistics, we gain a much more accurate view of the situation.

Note that these statistics only involve situations in which deadly force was used. Thus, they do not contain information about vandalism, robberies in which deadly force was not utilized, thefts in which deadly force was not used, or any type of natural disaster. Also note that these statistics cover all houses of worship, not only Christian churches.

- From 1999 through August 2017, there were 1617 "deadly force incidents" within churches across the United States.

Of those, the breakdown as to motive/trigger for the event is as follows:

- 203 were due to domestic violence that spilled over to the church
- 323 were robbery related
- 169 were personal conflicts involving two or more people not from the same household
- 141 were directly related to mental illness
- 42 incidents were related to drugs
- 75 incidents stemmed from bias against a specific type of religion
- 112 of the incidents were gang related
- 187 events were categorized as "random"

The weapon(s) involved in these incidents can be broken down as follows:

- 275 incidents used a weapon other than a gun, knife, automobile or explosive, including poison, hanging, and beating/physical abuse
- 945 incidents involved firearms
- 260 incidents involved knives/stabbing
- 97 incidents involved automobiles
- 90 incidents involved fire and/or explosives

In all, there have been 1617 deadly force incidents at houses of worship across the country since 1999, as of the time of this writing. 759 individuals lost their lives during those incidents, and countless others were wounded.

As you can see, there is a very real need for security and improved safety within your church. Your denomination does not matter. Your geographic location does not matter. Your congregation makeup does not matter. Violence against churches exists and is increasing. It is your responsibility to take the safety and security of your congregation seriously, and to build the best Church Safety Team possible.

Unit 2 Overview: Building and Training Your Church Safety Team

Within this unit, we will cover the aspects involved with building and training your Church Safety Team. We will look at the purpose, need and training required for both medical and security teams, as well as other aspects, such as team ethics and conduct, team duties and responsibilities, and how to build your team.

The information presented within this unit is primarily designed for team leaders and/or organizers, rather than for individual team members. I will outline the sources of training needed, such as CPR training from a local emergency response unit, but the majority of the training for individual team members will come from outside sources.

This unit primarily provides guidance, advice and help for organizers interested in learning why a Church Safety Team matters in the first place, how such teams should be constructed, how to prepare their teams for training and service to the congregation, and how to create a training plan for their teams in the first place.

Chapter 2:
The Value of a Church Safety Team

Before we dive into how to go about building a Church Safety Team, it's important to understand why such a team is vital to today's body of believers. As mentioned in the previous chapter, the number of deadly force attacks within churches has grown significantly over the years, and today are more common than school violence.

Obviously, a Church Safety Team can help to mitigate the significance of those events, or even prevent them from happening in the first place. However, there are other benefits here that should be understood.

A Church Safety Team is more than a mere security force – they can be vital assets in the church's employ, helping to streamline processes, improve visitor experiences, increase overall safety for everyone on property at all times, and more.

Some of the benefits your church could see by creating, managing and growing your Church Security Team include the following:

- Preventing the exploitation of vulnerabilities by aggressors, robbers, attackers, and others, including:
  - Potential kidnappers
  - Thieves
  - Those motivated by religious bias/intolerance
  - Terrorists
  - Armed attackers
  - Those involved in family disputes
- Assistance with security and protection for vehicles and contents within vehicles
- Assistance for congregation members with medical conditions who are likely to experience health emergencies on property
- Assistance with congregation members who suffer from phys-

ical and/or mental disabilities that may require help while on church property
- Assistance with vetting and ID processing for adults, guardians or siblings with child pickup from youth services/children's church
- Assistance with ensuring playground equipment is properly maintained, and that dangerous situations are noticed immediately
- Assistance with ensuring that all lights are working properly throughout the church grounds to ensure visibility in low-light or nighttime situations
- Assistance with identifying and eliminating environments and situations that invite crimes of opportunity (piles of cardboard waste that could be easily set aflame, for instance)

These are just a few examples of the value that a well-managed, motivated Church Safety Team can provide. It's about ensuring security, safety and peace of mind for everyone on the church property, from the youngest child in the nursery, to the oldest congregation member sitting on a pew during Sunday morning service.

It's about preventing all sorts of threats, from those stemming from attackers motivated by a desire for infamy or out of hatred, to those created by congregation members themselves within their day-to-day lives and relationships.

Ultimately, it's about following God's commands.

1 Peter 5:8-10
Be of sober spirit, be on the alert. Your adversary, the devil, prowls around like a roaring lion, seeking someone to devour. But resist him, firm in your faith, knowing that the same experiences of suffering are being accomplished by your brethren who are in the world. After you have suffered for a little while, the God of all grace, who called you to His eternal glory in Christ, will Himself perfect, confirm, strengthen and establish you.

Chapter 3:
Building a Security and Safety Solution

In this chapter, we will discuss the organizational structures that need to be in place to support your Church Safety Team. Without these in place, your team will not have the foundation it needs for success. In fact, disorganization may take its toll, and your team might crumble into disarray.

However, do note that all of these bodies should be analyzed and then customized to meet your specific church's needs. These are meant to be modified options, not cookie-cutter solutions to your needs. At Sheepdog Church Security, we're ready to help you.

How to Implement a Church Safety Ministry

To be successful, your church must develop proactive strategies. Working diligently with your church, Sheepdog Church Security will help with each step of the way. We will:

- Propose a Church Safety Ministry to church leadership
- Conduct a security assessment
- Assemble a Church Safety Ministry
- Create response plans and procedures (based on your security assessment and information throughout this book)
- Develop training for staff and volunteers
- Hire and train Church Safety Team members

Proposing a Church Safety Ministry

The Church Safety Ministry must be fully supported by church leadership and other ministry leaders (children's ministry, etc.). If church leadership and ministry leaders are not committed to providing support, then it will be much more difficult to create and enforce policies. You can share the information in this book with church leadership to help convince them that a Church Safety Ministry is not only beneficial but essential to the church.

Once the leadership approves the ministry, conduct a security assessment and determine your specific areas of vulnerability. Once the areas of vulnerability have been identified, modify the example policies and procedures to meet your church's needs, create and submit a budget and form a Church Safety Ministry.

Assembling a Church Safety Ministry

After a Church Safety Ministry has been approved by church leadership, it is important to start choosing people who can serve as members of that body. The Church Safety Ministry serves the wider organization by adding layers of protection to the church's primary mission and supporting activities by mitigating risk to people, property, and assets. The Church Safety Ministry consists of three to four entities:

- The Church Safety Committee
- The Director of Church Safety and Security
- The Assistant Director of Safety and Security (optional)
- The Church Safety Team

Note that we have provided complete example job descriptions for all positions.

The Church Safety Committee members administer the entire safety ministry program and report to the lead minister. The committee members:

- Develop policies and procedures.
- Assess church activities for risks.
- Negotiate and have oversight on the part of the ministry budget used for capital improvements, training, and equipment: Example Budget Request.
- Facilitate training for staff and volunteers.

- Act as the liaison between church leadership and the church safety director.

The Director of Safety and Security reports to the Church Safety Committee and the lead minister. A short description of his/her duties include the following:

- Develop emergency response plans.
- Ensure Church Safety Team members' compliance with policies.
- Manage the budget, including purchasing equipment.
- Lead the Church Safety Team, which includes recruitment, training, and scheduling.
- Oversee practice drills

If the organization is large and there are enough resources, an Assistant Director of Safety and Security may be hired. He/she reports to and is responsible for helping the Director of Safety and Security fulfill all the duties described above.

The Church Safety Team members (who are most likely volunteers) report to the Church Director of Safety and Security. They must:

- Comply with all policies and procedures.
- Report and correct procedural violations by other members.
- Conduct patrols.
- Respond to emergency situations.
- Conduct safety and security inspections.
- Participate in all training.
- Monitor church facilities.
- Maintain equipment.

Chapter 4:
Building Your Safety Teams

A Church Safety Team should consist of two sub-teams: a security team and a medical team. If your church does not have resources for two teams, then all Church Safety Team members should be trained for both types of problems.

Before beginning work as a Church Safety Team member, an individual must successfully complete and submit an application, a reference check, and a background check. The forms are available in the appendices listed. See information below about information for choosing Church Safety Team members.

After a Church Safety Team member has been hired, he/she must successfully complete all training required by the church before working his/her first shift. The following procedures are written as examples for Church Safety Team members to follow and are in the perspective of information for them.

Safety Team – Medical

The medical portion of your Church Safety Team is a crucial element when dealing with emergency responses to attacks, violence, accidents and more. You should attempt to build your medical team of individuals with experience in related fields. For instance, doctors, nurses and EMTs should be considered for these positions. At a bare minimum, your medical team will need to complete training in the following areas:

CPR – CPR is a vital lifesaving technique that should be taught to both medical and safety team members. Free training can be found from any number of outlets, ranging from local medical clinics to your area fire department. Arrange to have certification classes held at your church, and then track certification expiration so that recertification classes can be held at regular intervals.

AED – AED stands for automated external defibrillator. Training with this device can help save lives for patients who go into cardiac arrest as the result of injuries, accidents, heart attacks and other conditions. Note that AED and CPR training can often be arranged together from specific training providers, such as the American Red Cross and the American Heart Association.

Basic First Aid – All Safety Team – Medical members should be well versed in basic first aid. This ranges from the proper way to bandage a wound to knowing how to splint a broken bone, and a great deal more. Basic first aid courses can often be provided by local first responders and emergency response units in your local area (fire departments, EMT teams, etc.).

Safety Team – Security

Just as you want medical team members with relevant real-world experience and backgrounds, the same applies to your security specialists. Source your Safety Team – Security members from congregants with backgrounds in law enforcement, armed forces, or professional security.

The members who make up your Safety Team – Security sub-team should have experience and knowledge in a number of different areas, including the following:

- Access control
- Patrol techniques
- Emergency response
- Perimeter control

Training can be sourced from employment organizations (for team members with backgrounds in law enforcement, professional security and the armed forces), and can be provided to other team members by those with relevant experience.

Just as important as experience and/or security training is the background of each team member, which we'll discuss below.

Qualities of Church Safety Team Members

Church Safety Team members should have the same qualities as other church leaders: every member must be "above reproach, faithful to his [or her spouse], temperate, self-controlled, respectable, hospitable, [and] able to teach" (1 Timothy 3:2). In addition, every Church Safety Team member must:

- Be a member and/or a regular attendee of the church.
- Have no physical limitations that prevent the person from doing what is required for the job.
- Be able to demonstrate good character, honesty, and integrity.

To emphasize my point once more, it is beneficial if Church Safety Team members have backgrounds in a medical field (e.g., nurse, doctor, emergency technician, paramedic, etc.) or backgrounds in security (police officer, security guard, has armed forces training, etc.). No one can serve who:

- Has a disqualifying criminal conviction.
- Has committed a crime.
- Knowingly provides the church with false information.

Note that if the person is already a Church Safety Team member and such an infraction occurs, then he/she will should be immediately dismissed from the team.

Team Ethics and Conduct

There are several practices expected from members of the Church Safety Team. They're outlined and explained below, and it will fall to the members themselves, as well as the Director of Safety and Security to ensure that everyone adheres to these ethics and upholds the code of conduct specified. Of course, you may modify these instructions so they best fit your church.

- Honor others above yourself.
- Perform all duties completely, correctly, and on time.
- Be an example for others.
- Be faithful.
- Be wise.
- Be discrete.

Honor Others Above Yourself

Be courteous, conscientious, and professional in the church. Be respectful to other members of the congregation. Be examples of Christ-like behavior by educating people instead of reprimanding them.

It is ineffective and inappropriate to "scold" people or punish them into acting safely. People come to church to worship and serve the Lord. It's not the place of Church Safety Team members to cause them any emotional heartache, so educate rather than reprimand. Tell people what behavior concerns you, how that behavior might harm people or property, and (if possible) how they can engage in the activity more safely.

Perform All Duties Completely, Correctly, and on Time

Attend church safety training. Your actions reflect your training (and lack thereof). Be good representations of the church's training programs.

There are certain circumstances that might require immediate reporting to either a pastor or to the supervisor on the Church Safety Team. Make sure that you're reporting in a timely fashion so your leadership can fix the problem (if it's something that can be fixed immediately) or can put together a plan to resolve the issue later. For timely reporting of incidents, complete and submit reports before ending your shift.

Be an Example for Others

Show people what proper safety looks like by always being safe and addressing safety risks as soon as you see something that is (potentially) harmful. Take immediate actions to fix it.

Be Faithful

Fulfill your commitments to the church. Work your scheduled services and events. You may be permitted to swap with other people, but it's your responsibility to call people on the team to see if they will switch shifts.

Be Wise

Keep security information confidential. Security plans are on a need-to-know basis, so don't tell people what your plans are. You can give them some general idea, some general guidance, but don't give them specifics. That's a clue that somebody may be planning a dangerous act: they're asking questions about how you would respond to certain situations.

Be Discrete

Keep information private; don't gossip or spread rumors. As a Church Safety Team member, you may learn private information such as that people are going through a divorce or a child custody battle. There might be a suspicion of misconduct on the part of someone at the church. This information is given to you so you can watch the situation and be alert, not so you can share it with others in the congregation.

Team Priorities

There are several priorities for members of the Church Safety Team. As with the instructions on ethics and conduct, we've outlined these below for easier understanding and access to each point. Of course, you may modify these instructions so they best fit your church.

The Church Safety Team's priorities are:

- Attend church services.
- Spend time with families.
- Participate in training.
- Serve at Sunday services.
- Serve at large events.

Attend Church Services

This is an extremely important rule. As examples to the rest of the congregation, you are expected to make your relationship with Christ a priority. It's hard to be an example of Christ if you're not regularly plugged into his Word, so take time to be in church services with your family when off duty so you can pray, worship, read the Bible, and be fed spiritually. If you are being scheduled to work every Sunday, talk to the person in charge of scheduling as he/she probably did not realize that issue.

Spend Time with Your Families

Remember to spend time with your families. Any time you volunteer for the church, there are sacrifices being made by yourself and by your family. Don't volunteer so much that your families can't handle that sacrifice. Talk to the scheduler about taking time off when you need it to be with your family.

Participate in Training

One of the most important parts of being on this team is that you make it to the training and you are able to complete all that applies to you and your position. If you're not trained to respond to an emergency, you can't help anyone. Participating in training will require a time commitment – you must be physically present during the times that training is provided, and you must engage in the training sessions and follow the instructor's guidance.

Serve at Sunday Services

Sunday is the most challenging and taxing time because it's when the most people are at church, including children and the general public. The maximum number of people need to be working on Sundays, with the most focus on Sunday morning services, as well as children's church, Sunday school classes, and the rest. Sunday evening services are also important, although most churches have lower attendance for nighttime services, so your staffing should be adjusted to your specific attendance trends.

Serve at Large Events

A lot of churches thrive by hosting programs and events, and some churches always have something going on. You don't need to work every single event, but many team members should serve at large events when there are a lot of members and/or a lot of the public.

Remember that these events will see the largest influx of general public visitors to the church – even Sunday morning services will not have as many non-congregation members in attendance. Take the time needed to create an accurate forecast of turnout and schedule staff appropriately.

Sample Policies and Procedures

The following information can start the conversation about how your church creates policies and procedures to ensure the safety of the congregation and church property. As with all other information within this book, you should modify these instructions so they best fit your church's needs.

Identifying Apparel

Church Safety Team—Security members will wear gray shirts with the church logo and the words "Church Security Team" embroidered above the left breast area. Church Safety Team—Medical team members will wear the same style shirt but in a maroon color with the words "Church Medical Team" embroidered on the shirt. To identify the team members to the public, Church Safety Team ID cards (which are personalized to include an individual team member's name, picture, and whether he/she is Security or Medical) will be worn with clip-on holders.

Staffing

Basic staffing per service should include one Church Safety Team member on each floor and one person at the children's entrance. Another member should be on standby and monitor the radio during service. As necessary, a member may be stationed in the sanctuary during the service.

Schedule

Each church has its own calendar system. Make sure you understand your church's system. Know which services and events you are scheduled to work. Work your scheduled services and the services for which you volunteered. If you have a conflict, find a Church Safety Team member who can work for you and notify the scheduler of the change.

Supporting Ministry

Church Safety Team members should introduce themselves to ministry leaders and volunteers at least the first three times they are on duty. Every Church Safety Team member should get to know ministry leaders and volunteers, so they feel confident contacting the Church Safety Team if they have an incident.

Remember to introduce yourself and communicate only after the person has finished with the ministry. Ministries are the primary mission of the church, so you should never interrupt them while in progress to introduce yourself.

Immediately fix minor issues such as icy sidewalks or people not checking into the children's area correctly. Reassure the staff and guests that they are not in trouble, but you are there to help them do it correctly. Whatever the issue is, address it. If you cannot solve the issue yourself, immediately report it to your supervisor.

Reporting for Duty

Identify yourself to all church areas (e.g., the information desk, parking lot team) at the start of your shift. Wear the appropriate identifying apparel (as described previously). Read the patrol log, so you know what's going on and what has been done or needs to be done. Draw your equipment (handheld radio and flashlight). Finally, connect with other Church Safety Team members who are already working.

If enough Church Safety Team members are working, you may be asked to serve in the children's area, welcome area, or parking lot. Other Church Safety Team members will be asked to patrol the facilities.

Patrolling Campus

Get the big picture of the event. Walk around and see what's going on. Observe what you can, and see where the foot traffic is, where it is flowing, and whether any bottlenecks exist. The flow of people can give you an idea of problems that need to be addressed.

Handle safety issues that you discover along the way. Check empty rooms, utility closets, hallways, stairwells, etc. A lot of unfortunate things have happened in locked and dark areas, especially during events with many teenagers or visitors.

Patrol the parking lot and the exterior the building. You don't necessarily need to spend the whole shift outside walking the parking lot and exterior of the building, but at least randomly go out there a few times to prevent any vandalism or theft from vehicles. While there, watch for other issues, including the following:

- Does the playground equipment look safe (e.g., is any equipment broken or are there nails sticking out)?
- Are the lights working?
- Are there any signs of vandalism?
- Are there any potential burglary tools (such as cinderblocks) lying around outside the building that could be picked up and thrown through a window?
- Is anything inviting arson, such as an overflowing trash can?

Responding

Respond to all safety and security issues that are called out on the radio as soon as you become aware of them. Follow your training and the law. Notify proper authorities—that may be the Director of Safety and Security, church leadership or ministry director, or local law enforcement. If you're unsure, contact your Director of Safety and Security, and then talk to the pastor.

In emergency situations, contact civil authorities at 911. Tell the dispatcher what's going on and where you are in the building. Be sure you stay on the line until the dispatcher hangs up. In an emergency, call 911 first.

Note that when calling 911 from a cellphone, the dispatcher's system will request your location from the cellular network. This can take seconds, minutes, or not occur at all. For this reason, consider calling 911 from a landline rather than a cellphone whenever possible.

Once you have called 911, reported the situation and the dispatcher has hung up the call, report the situation. Tell your team leadership about what you did and why you did it.

Help first responders if they require it. Complete necessary report forms. Fully cooperate with any investigation by civil authorities and/or the church leadership. If it's a larger event and there is media response, don't talk to the media. You don't need to be rude to them; just refer them to a person of responsibility at your church.

Ending Shift

At the end of every shift, assist in clearing and securing the building. Turn in reports. If leadership is not present, send a text or an email to let him/her know that there's a report waiting. Add pertinent information to the patrol log. Turn in equipment. Check the schedule, and sign up for required training or events you want to work.

Communication Policies

Every Church Safety Team member will carry the following equipment while on duty: a handheld radio, and a flashlight. First-aid kits should be stationed around the church, although personal kits can also be used as carried equipment. Church Safety Team member will be stationed in areas such as parking, children's area, and the greeting area.

The Church Safety Team members who patrol must be capable of contacting other safety ministries including safety, parking, and greeting, so it is vital these members have operational radios. Each Church Safety Team member on standby will carry a radio either with an earpiece or a silent-vibrating feature. If any situation should arise in which the Church Safety Team member on duty needs additional help, he/she should immediately contact the other Church Safety Team members by radio.

Church Safety Team members must be aware of all locations within the church so he/she can contact local police and be sufficiently knowledgeable of the church's location to direct local police or other emergency personnel to the church.

If feasible, Church Safety Team members will carry a cell phone for quick calls to the local police. However, when using a cell phone do not use 911 because it will not connect to the correct location in all instances. Instead, dial the direct number to the police department, or call 911 from a landline.

On-duty Church Safety Team members should always be aware of the head usher's location. If a situation should arise that requires notification of personnel on the platform, the Church Safety Team member will immediately inform the head usher of the situation and the desired response.

Radio Procedures

Radios can be expensive but are essential for all Church Safety Teams. Motorola's TALKABOUT® MT350R is a reasonable radio with a good range that will suit most churches. The only problem is that the sound quality can be poor, so when people get excited and start to yell a little bit, their voices get garbled.

There are also many expensive radios you can purchase. The Black Diamond CE450 is recommended. These are considered better than the Motorola mentioned above because the quality is higher and the operational range is appropriate with this model. Make sure to read the user's guide for any radio your church purchases.

Communication is extremely important. Sheepdog Church Security recommends that all team members use earphones or earbuds. They will work with all radios. Using earphones ensures that radio-based communication will not disturb the congregation during service, or during other activities, and calls about minor emergencies will not alarm the congregation unduly, thereby creating a panic.

Expectations

Radios need to be worn and turned on at the beginning of each shift and used throughout the shift. Radios must remain on campus unless there's an off-campus event. Radios are to be maintained per manufacturer's instructions.

Defending the Flock

Etiquette

Radios are regulated and can be heard throughout the campus and beyond, so casual conversations, profanity, inappropriate remarks, and music should be prohibited for your team members. All violators should be subject to disciplinary measures.

Keep transmissions short. For a long conversation, use the telephone. If you need to discuss something with a specific person, begin your transmission with the name of the person you are calling followed by your name. An example would be, "Pete, this is Kris." Pete's response would be, "Go ahead, Kris."

When you're done with your conversation, sign off. An example would be "Kris out." That's how we clear all transmissions, even unanswered ones. This way, if somebody else is on the radio and they're waiting to get to say something, they can hear that you are done. Of course, only interrupt transmissions in the case of an emergency.

Plain English

Use plain English with the radios except for codes discussed below. The more you listen and use the radio, the more familiar you will become with codes, usage methods and more. To help you start the familiarization process, here are a few basic codes and what they mean:

- "Go ahead," = "Send your message."
- "Copy," = "The message was received and understood."
- "Say again," = "Retransmit your message." Perhaps you were doing something else and didn't clearly hear the message.
- "Stand by," = "I heard your message but please wait."
- "Affirmative," = "Yes."
- "Negative," = "No."
- "Do you copy?" = "Do you understand?"
- "Unreadable," = you can't understand the person who transmit-

ted the message (i.e., you don't know what was said because the message was garbled due to a technological problem).
- "Disregard," = "Don't pay any attention to the last message."

Approved Codes

There are approved codes that are exceptions to the plain English rule and are used to protect the congregation. If you have a minor fire and say over the radio, "There's a fire in the kitchen," people may hear that and understandably become alarmed. You may alter these codes, so they are unique to your church:

- "Code Red" means there is a fire emergency.
- "Code Blue" is a medical emergency.
- "Code Pink" is a missing or lost child.
- "Code Orange" is an actively disruptive or combative person.
- "Code Yellow" is a suspicious person.
- "Code Green" is a cash or offerings escort.

As a note, "911" is an enhancement code that means respond quickly and call local law enforcement. (In using this code, you would include the primary code that describes the situation. For instance: "911 Code Orange 911" would mean there is a combative person and 911 should be called.)

Do not have too many codes because people may forget what each means and have delays in their responses. In emergencies, delays can be costly.

Chapter 5:
Preparing for Team Building and Training

I mentioned previously in this book that God works through His people – pastors preach, and deacons help to care for the body of believers. The Church Security Team also does God's work by providing safety, assistance and peace of mind to those on church property.

However, building a team and then training those individuals is not a process that you can approach without any preparation. Yes, God will lead you, but remember that God also helps those who help themselves. You must take an active role in participation.

Build Your Team

Step one is perhaps the simplest sounding, yet most challenging. You need to start building your team. It's pretty normal for church organizations, committees and other bodies to essentially accept all comers. This can be due to a number of reasons, but low turnout/low volunteerism is probably the most common issue.

Let me say this very clearly so that there can be no misunderstanding.

DO NOT DO THAT.

Got that? Don't accept all comers. You cannot afford to simply allow anyone and everyone who applies to be a member of the Church Safety Tem onboard. Why is that? Well, think of it this way:

- Would you trust a thief to watch your home for you while you're away on vacation?
- Would you trust a drug abuser not to use drugs if given access to a limitless supply?
- Would you trust an alcoholic not to take a drink if you poured them one?

- Would you trust a murderer to watch your sleeping children, after you'd given that murderer a gun?

The answer to all of these questions is "no". Now, I'm not trying to sow discord or mistrust between believers. The world does enough of that on its own without any need for help from me. What I'm trying to point out is that the body of the Church is made up of people.

People sin. People have problems. People face challenges, many of which are completely unknown to those outside their inner circle, or even to anyone else at all. We also need to face the facts – a significant number of the crimes we discussed previously in this book were committed not by outside actors or agents, but by church members themselves. Suicides, murders, theft, vandalism – the body of believers you are safeguarding can be just as large a threat as those lurking outside the church doors.

From that, we can draw this meaning – you MUST be choosy when building your team. You MUST be thorough when vetting your potential team members. You MUST do your due diligence when assembling your team, and that begins well before you even start to think about training.

What process should you follow here? What procedures should be used when vetting potential Church Safety Team members? Actually, several critical steps should be followed with every single applicant.

The Application

Every single would-be Church Safety Team member should submit an application. This should include all pertinent personal information, including:

- Full name (first, middle and last)
- Current physical and mailing address
- Age, gender and other demographic information
- Social Security number
- Background/experience information (if possible – it's not neces-

sarily a deal breaker if they lack medical or security experience, but such experience is very beneficial)

The Background Check

Every applicant should provide you with the information needed to conduct a criminal background check. In most instances, this will require that they sign and submit a background release forms. However, in some jurisdictions, the individual themselves will have to obtain the background check information from the local sheriff's department. Know what situation applies in your geographic area and ensure that no one is added to the team without a criminal background check being conducted.

Full References

All applicants should be able to provide a list of at least four or five references. These should speak to the individuals' character, morality and trustworthiness. Note that almost any type of reference can be acceptable, including:

- Managers and other bosses
- Coworkers
- Business partners
- Employees, if the applicant is a business owner
- Spouses
- Parents
- Grandparents
- Other family members

Note that while you are welcome to accept family members as references, you should take their recommendation with a grain of salt. It's also important that you actually follow through and contact each of those references. Speak with them about the applicant's desire to be part of the Church Safety Team, and learn as much as possible about whether or not the applicant would be a good fit. Document the responses from all references, as well.

The Interview

Every applicant who wants to be part of the Church Safety Team must sit for a full interview. Obviously, not showing up for the interview is a bad sign, and if the person doesn't have a good excuse, you should consider this as a disqualification.

The interview is also your best chance to vet them yet further. What do you think of them? How do they carry themselves? Do they seem honest, upright and moral? Do they seem to be a good addition to your team? Trust your intuition – that's God's voice leading you.

Training Completion

The final hurdle to joining the Church Safety Team is completing the training required. Some training will apply to both your Safety Team – Security members, and your Safety Team – Medical members. For instance, everyone can benefit from basic first aid training and even CPR training. However, some training will be team-specific.

In order to officially become a member, everyone must fully complete (and pass) the training. If they do not complete the training, they should be disqualified, unless there is a compelling reason to offer them the chance to make it up. If they do not pass the final exams during the training course, they should be disqualified.

Store and Secure All Documentation

Once an applicant has gone through all the steps above, they can be allowed on the team and can be issued their shirts or uniforms. Note that you must now take steps to store and secure all the documentation and data generated during the onboarding process. This should include:

- The completed application
- Notes/data on interviews with references
- The background check release form (signed and dated)
- Any pertinent health information (for instance, medical conditions that might preclude an individual from specific duties)
- Notes on interview performance/experience
- Records of training completion

Preparing to Train

We'll deal with training specifically in the next chapter, but for now, you need to get prepared for the reality. Training is vital for the performance of your team members, and the safety of the church congregation in the face threats. It's critical that you ensure that you have the right training materials and training sources lined up before forming your team.

Many of these individuals and experts could actually be part of your existing congregation. Others are available within your community. Some of the training resources available to you include:

- CPR and first aid instructors
- Crime prevention officers
- Fire marshal/fire chief
- County human services
- Self-defense instructors
- Firearms instructors

In addition, Sheepdog Church Security delivers a very wide range of crucial courses designed to improve and enhance church safety through our website, including:

- Safety Team Academy
- Fire safety and evacuations
- Disruptive persons and verbal de-escalation
- Child protection

- Use of force and citizen's arrest
- Active shooter response and lockdown drills

Note that while we will cover these topics in detail within this book, our online video courses provide a dynamic, immersive learning experience that is a better fit for visual learners.

In addition to the sources we've listed above, you'll also find a host of church security seminars held across the country each year. Some of the names you should know include Carl Chinn and Lieutenant Colonel David Grossman (both of whom should be familiar from previous mentions within this book), Tina Lewis Rowe and Jimmy Meeks.

We should also point out that if there is one single thing that derails most efforts, it is this – feeling like you need to accomplish everything at once. You don't. In fact, you need to get over that idea. Start with step one, and then move to step two. Progress as you can. There is no need to rush into the process.

While it is important that you make steady progress, there is nothing saying that you need to finish instantaneously. The most important step is creating the safety ministry in the first place, and then onboarding and training Church Safety Team members. Sheepdog Church Security can help you with every step along the way.

Chapter 6:
Creating a Church-Specific Training Plan

Creating a church-specific training plan is vital. The fact is that every church is different. Some are located in far-flung rural areas. Others are in the heart of urban areas. Some are mega-churches with thousands of members. Others are small churches, with 100 or fewer members.

Obviously, one church's needs will be radically different from another when it comes to security, safety and medical assistance. In this chapter, we'll discuss creating a training plan specific to your church.

Every church is different. The only thing we all share is a love and commitment to Jesus Christ. Everything else is variable, including:

- The size and layout of our buildings or meeting places
- The size of our congregations
- The number of visitors we have every week
- The average ages of our attendees
- The laws that govern our operations
- The basic attitudes about church safety and security

The list can go on and on… As the Church Safety / Security Director or the one responsible for training, you may want to modify the content of this course to fit your church's uniqueness.

Course Customization Considerations:

- Local and state laws governing the course topic
- Church policies and procedures
- Current practices in relation to the course topic

General Attitude about Church Safety and Security:

- It is sometimes more beneficial to target progress over perfection. You can always come back to this course to increase the standards every year until you reach your goal.

Step One – Your Security Assessment

Without a full security assessment of your church and its grounds, you cannot create a customized training plan. We'll deal with the assessment in the next chapter, but for now, understand that you cannot progress before that has been handled. The assessment will cover virtually every aspect of your church, from the parking lot to your security system, and will provide essential information on which to build your training plan.

Step Two – Assess Your Congregation Size and Needs

To create a customized training plan, you'll need to know how large or small your Church Safety Team should be. That is based on the size of your congregation, as well as the number and scope of events held throughout the year. You need to have enough team members to handle regular weekly needs, as well as reserves on which you can draw for larger events, such as church yard sales, bake sales, plays, musical performances and the like.

Step Three – The Physical Structure

The physical structure of your church will have a definite impact on your training plan. For instance, how many entrances are there to the building? How many are open during each service? Are there services where certain entrances are kept locked? How many floors are there in your church? How often are those floors occupied? These are a few of the many questions you'll need to answer during the assessment regarding the physical structure of your church.

Step Four– Your Congregation

In many instances, your church's congregation will constitute the single most prevalent risk. What do they do that puts them at risk? Are you located in an area known for drug use? Is domestic abuse a problem, or do many families in the church struggle with domestic violence?

Is there a specific culture within the church that leads to gaps in safety preparedness and preparation? For instance, churches in very rural areas may have congregations unused to even locking the doors of their homes, which makes it difficult to ensure constant protection within the church.

Step Five – Conduct Drills Regularly

You'll need to conduct training drills on a regular basis to ensure that your team members (and the congregation as a whole) are prepared for whatever threats they might face. Some of the drills you should conduct include the following:

- Fire drills
- Severe weather drills
- Lockdown drills

These drills should be reviewed and conducted on an annual basis once the Church Safety Team is in place. New employees and volunteers should be instructed on these drills during orientation. All other employees and volunteers should have an annual review of these procedures. The youth should practice each of these drills on an annual basis as should the entire church.

Note: Never conduct a surprise drill. Always communicate with church members and staff well in advance, so everyone knows what's going on. Also, make sure church staff and the Church Safety Team are well trained and have practiced what to do many times so there is no confusion.

Fire Drills

Consider it a best practice to conduct regular fire drills for youth during Sunday school. There should also, however, be full drills that include both adults and children at least once a year. One way to accomplish this is to hold drills after the last service of the day.

Ensure participation by turning the drill into an event with lunch and other activities. Invite the fire department so the children can see the trucks. This also gives the local fire department an opportunity to see the inside of the church and develop a plan of how they might respond to an emergency there.

Severe Weather Drills

A best practice for severe weather drills is to invite the local Emergency Manager. He or she will be able to give you some valuable insight on your severe weather drills. Before conducting the drill, figure out where your entire congregation will take shelter and how you will communicate with members before, during, and after the drill.

Lockdown Drills

Lockdown drills must be handled with sensitivity so that people —especially children— are not frightened, yet everyone accepts the importance of learning what to do.

- Discuss the drill with parents and youth beforehand.
- Include local law enforcement in the planning, as they can be of valuable assistance.
- Make sure your Church Safety Team is well trained and knows exactly what to do (The Safety Team should have a number of drills with just Safety Team members before conducting any church-wide drills).
- Teach members to close shades, turn off lights, barricade doors, and keep silent until they receive an all-clear signal.

Unit 3 Overview: Security Assessments and Your Church

In the following chapters, we will discuss conducting a security assessment of your church. This assessment will be wide-ranging and will cover everything from the physical structure of the building itself to the grounds, to the potentially essential resources available to you. Key takeaways from this section include:

- **Plan, Prep and Research:** Work with authorities, government agencies and other resources in your local area to create a plan to safeguard your church and the congregation. These can include the local police or sheriff's department, the Child Protective Services office, your local fire marshal or fire chief, and even national organizations, such as OSHA.
- **Know Your Risks:** What are the most likely threats your church will face? When will they occur? How long will the effects of those threats last? How much warning might you have before the threat occurs? Answer these questions and more to prepare correctly.
- **Follow the Principles:** Follow the six CPTED principles during your assessment of your church. Know where you stand in terms of access control, surveillance, territoriality, image and maintenance, activity support and target hardening. Then, create a plan that builds on your strengths and remedies your weaknesses.

In the end, your security assessment will help you create a blueprint for improvements that can be made immediately, and over time. It should also grow as your church grows and as your needs change. Assess your safety and security regularly to ensure that you are safe from new and emerging threats, and to handle safety issues that might arise over time (age/maintenance related, for instance).

Chapter 7:
Conducting a Safety and Security Assessment, and Understanding Your Specific Vulnerabilities

Conducting a safety and security assessment is an important first step to protect churches and the people in them. Assessments should include identifying threats, developing goals and objectives, developing possible courses of action, planning, implementation, and review (United States Department of Homeland Security et al. [DHS], 2013, p. 4). Assessments include planning for fires, natural disasters, and crime prevention.

<u>Know Your Church's Risk</u>

Depending on their locations, churches are vulnerable to different types of severe weather and natural disasters. Churches are also targeted by criminals. The American Crime Prevention Institute (ACPI, 2012) explained that, "Crime is the result of the desire or wish to commit the crime, the ability or knowledge how to commit the crime and the opportunity to commit the crime" (p. 7).

Churches are as likely to be criminally victimized as other locations but may be more vulnerable due to misperceptions that criminals will not attack a sacred space, despite ministering to high-risk populations and being high-profile sites for hate crimes (ACPI, 2012, pp. 513-514). Churches are also underprepared. OneNewsNow surveyed 4,000 churches in 2008 and found that more than 75% did not have security or emergency plans (Hawkins, 2012; Sullivan, 2009).

The United States Department of Homeland Security et al. (DHS) (2013) outlined six steps for emergency operations plans (DHS, 2013, p. 4):

- Form a collaborative planning team
- Understand the situation

- Determine goals and objectives
- Plan development
- Plan preparation, review, and approval
- Plan implementation & maintenance

These steps are explained in further detail below.

First, create a planning team to consult community partners including emergency management and first responders (DHS, 2013, p. 4). Sheepdog Church Security recommends that the Church Safety Committee work with community resource providers for the planning team. Consider community resources such as the following:

- Ask the local Child Protective Services office for a checklist to consult in assessing the children's areas and workers.
- Contact your local police department or sheriff's office to see if they have a crime prevention officer. Crime prevention officers are great sources for information on crime trends and simple steps to prevent crime.
- Talk to your local fire marshal or fire chief. He/she can help with fire safety and evacuation planning.
- Consult the Occupational Safety and Health Administration (OSHA) to ensure the church is safe for all workers.

If possible, invite representatives from these community resources to be members of the planning team or a more significant part of the assessment process.

Work with local resource providers. Use the tools available in your community. Make your community part of your preparedness.

Second, the planning team should conduct an assessment to understand the situation. For each threat, the team should identify the following (DHS, 2013, p. 7):

- The likelihood the threat can occur

- The frequency with which the threat might occur
- The expected severity of the threat
- The time available for warnings
- How long the threat will last
- The ongoing effects

There are several steps in identifying the likelihood of threats. You should review past incidents and assessments, assess current policies and procedures, assess current threats, review emergency response plans, conduct a detailed walkthrough of the facilities, and interview key personnel.

Can it happen? How often? When? How long? What will it affect?

There are also actions to avoid when conducting the assessment, such as the following:

- Do not ignore any risks, even those that most congregation members know about and avoid.
- Do not focus on only one type of hazard or threat. Some safety teams are initially drawn to church security because of the threat of active shooters. While this is an extremely important threat to solve, don't stop there. Also, plan for threats with higher probabilities (e.g., vandalism or theft).
- Do not use the same assessment team each year. People can get complacent and start to overlook threats. A fresh set of eyes is always best.
- Do not accept risk on behalf of others. Just because you think "everyone" knows to avoid a long-standing risk doesn't mean it should be ignored. A long-standing risk that has not been addressed is a huge liability issue.

   For instance, most people might be aware that paint cans are stored under a specific stairway and exercise caution there.

However, this remains an active threat and MUST be addressed, not ignored.

After the likelihood of each type of threat as well as the possible effects of that threat are understood, the team should prioritize its planning for each type (DHS, 2013, pp. 6-7).

When the team has decided which threats are a priority, the third step is to determine goals and objectives:

- A **goal** is a general statement about the desired outcome (e.g., prevent fires in the church) (DHS, 2013, p. 8).
- An **objective** is a step taken to achieve a goal (e.g., provide fire prevention training to all people who cook in the church) (DHS, 2013, p. 8).

The fourth step is plan development. The team needs to create specific scenarios based on the threats it identified were priorities (e.g., tornados or active shooters). The team should determine how long it will take to respond to each threat, who should make decisions during the emergency, and possible courses of action.

As you are developing your plans, read the chapters in this book for specific threats your team has identified (e.g., "preparing for natural disasters" or "preventing financial attacks") so you can utilize our research and implementation information.

Know your response time for each threat. Know who's in charge. Know your outcomes.

The fifth step is plan preparation, review, and approval. After determining several courses of action for each threat, the team should compare costs and benefits to decide which plan is best for each situation (DHS, 2013, pp. 9-10). The team should then present the plan to the church leader so he/she can approve it or request changes (DHS, 2013, p. 13).

Prepare your plan. Review the plan. Approve the plan.

The sixth step is plan implementation and maintenance. The team should share the plan with emergency responders and community partners, post information throughout the building, train stakeholders, hold practice drills, and update the plan at least every two years and when there are changes to buildings, policies, or personnel (DHS, 2013, pp. 13-16).

> *Involve the community. Share and spread information. Most of all – don't be complacent. All plans should be dynamic and change as needs evolve.*

How to Implement

Depending on the areas where you decided first to concentrate your efforts, read the units in this book that relate to those areas (training for emergencies and disasters, preventing criminal activity, and preparing to stop violence). Crime Prevention Through Environmental Design (CPTED) is beneficial for preventing crime and general safety information.

CPTED (pronounced sep-ted) is the use of "physical design, citizen participation and law enforcement strategies in a comprehensive way to protect facilities or neighborhoods" (ACPI, 2012, p. 23).

There are six principles of CPTED (van Soomeren, n.d., p. 7):

- Access control
- Surveillance
- Territoriality
- Image and maintenance
- Activity support
- Target hardening

Use these principles together to achieve the best results. They are explained in detail below.

Access Control

Access control limits people's ability to enter or leave settings unnoticed. It is the use of "entrances, exits, signs, fencing, landscaping and lighting" to hinder unseen access to the environment (ACPI, 2012, p. 23). An easy way of thinking about this principle is imagining that these items serve as a corral which dissuades people from going into areas they should not enter. Although the best access control measures cannot always deter a determined individual, access control is the first step in preventing crime.

Access control can also be one of the hardest issues for churches. There must be a balance between a secure entrance and a welcoming one. Honestly, the lack of solid access control in churches often comes down to convenience.

Finding the right balance between staff and volunteer expectations of safety with the public's image of a church is difficult, but the priority is to control access to the church and/or monitor everyone who goes in and out. Church security begins at the main entrance.

No one has time to monitor the door fulltime for delivery people and visitors. The best way to change behavior is to create improved awareness of the importance of securing access to the church. It will be necessary to engage and empower staff to implement access control procedures so that the worship and work areas are consistently safe.

One of the steps in determining access control is asking, "Is access to the church necessary for everyone?" There are options.

- Staff members and volunteers can prearrange meeting appointments.
- Visitors can meet at the office and be escorted to meeting rooms or offices.
- If the staff does not recognize the person, there is no reason to grant entry.
- If the staff cannot get a visual of the person or if he/she tries to

get in based on another visitor's access (i.e., a "piggyback" entry), access can be denied.

Access should definitely be denied if the person is being difficult, has no acceptable reason for requesting entry, is acting suspiciously, or is verbally combative. This is one of the most important steps in maintaining the security of the church. Staff will need to be trained in verbal de-escalation and conflict resolution to address these situations, as well.

Control access to your grounds. Period. This is the most crucial consideration for protecting against most threats.

Surveillance

Surveillance includes natural surveillance by residents; formal surveillance by police or hired personnel; semi-formal surveillance done by postal workers, housekeepers, etc.; and technical surveillance from equipment such as mobile phones, cameras, or closed-circuit television (van Soomeren, n.d., p. 7).

Natural surveillance is the ability to observe activity without having to take special measures. For any surveillance to occur, there must be clear lines of sight in the areas of the property that need to be monitored. Large trees, bushes, and privacy fences are discouraged. However, this also applies to the design and construction of new buildings on the church grounds, new churches, etc.

Know what's going on, when and where.

Territoriality

Territoriality establishes authority over the environment to identify who belongs, who is in charge, and who may be up to no good. It is important because people are motivated to protect what they perceive as "theirs." Therefore, it is important to design places that indicate ownership:

- Signs
- Colors
- Building materials
- Gates

These are all ways to visually specify places as separate from the public (van Soomeren, n.d., p. 7). An example is using signs and landscaping to discourage people from walking across church property or using it for unsanctioned activities.

Set your church and its grounds apart – claim ownership.

Image and Maintenance

The principle of image and maintenance is based on the broken windows theory that a property that is not well maintained is more vulnerable to vandalism and theft. Thus, it is important to keep the space clean and well maintained (van Soomeren, n.d., p. 8). This principle is the most often overlooked even though it's the easiest to implement.

A well-maintained building creates a sense of ownership, whereas unkempt areas attract unwanted people and activities. Any area that exudes an "abandoned" feel is far more likely to see trespassers, vandals, and criminals, regardless of whether or not the area actually is abandoned.

Even a minor amount of maintenance can make an immense difference in how your property is perceived.

Activity Support

Activity support is about facilitating positive use and encouraging a broad mix of people to enjoy the property. A group that is solely young men is more dangerous than a mixed group that includes people of all ages and both genders (van Soomeren, n.d., p. 8). One strategy is to encourage different activities throughout the day and week.

Perhaps your church can host a high school group on Monday nights, a Mothers of Preschoolers meeting on Tuesday nights, elementary school church education on Wednesday afternoons, and a senior knitting group on Thursday mornings. Any way to encourage multiple genders and generations to enjoy the facilities will meet this goal.

Moreover, you don't need to focus on gender or age-specific groups/ meetings daily. Look for ways to involve men and women, young and old on the same day, during the same event. It fosters a wider sense of community and a stronger sense of ownership where the church and its grounds are concerned.

> *Build community. Get people involved. Help them come to feel ownership and love for the church.*

Target Hardening

Target hardening is the principle most people associate with security. Target hardening is "making it physically difficult for offenders by the use of locks, bolts, bars, doors, or gates: the medieval fortress approach" (van Soomeren, n.d., p. 8). The process includes making sure doors are not easily broken or removed from their frames and that windows only open from the inside (ACPI, 2012, p. 516). Additional examples include improving locks, using alarms, and having dual access safes.

Malene A. Little pointed out that although the Bible did not refer to CPTED principles by that name, they were used by God's people in ancient times. Nehemiah described how each ruler carried out repairs of Jerusalem's walls in his district (Nehemiah 3:15-32). Thus, Nehemiah encouraged territoriality by having people rebuild areas near their residences. The people provided surveillance of the areas near their homes. Rebuilding the wall was also an act of target hardening by making it more difficult to penetrate the area.

Using CPTED is effective. Houston's Berean Baptist Church had numerous car thefts and burglaries occurring more than monthly. The church built a fence around its 11-acre property (target hardening), installed an electronic access gate to the parking lot (surveillance), started a check-in system for the nursery and Sunday schools, and hired off-duty police officers for big events (surveillance). For the next six years, there were no car thefts, only one burglary, and a kidnapping was thwarted (Sullivan, 2009).

Build smart. Design strategically. Remodel for security, protection and prevention.

In the end, assessing your church grounds, the building itself, and everything contained therein is the key to creating a strategic security and safety plan. Remember – it's not all about protecting against threats of violence from the world outside your doors. It's about ensuring that everyone who enters the church grounds is safe, whether they're a kid playing on the playground equipment, an adult working on the AV equipment, a senior walking down the aisle to find their pew, a child in children's church, or someone else.

Security and safety go hand in hand, but you cannot ensure either if you don't know the vulnerabilities that apply to your church.

- How old is the playground equipment and what state is it in?
- Do you have an existing security system?
- What threats are common in the neighborhood?
- How trustworthy are the individuals you have in charge of the youth ministry?
- How much vetting has been done with ministry leaders, deacons and others with authority in the church?

These are just the tip of the proverbial iceberg when it comes to questions that you must answer to assess your church's security and the safety of those on your property. Use the preceding sections to guide your assessment. Write down your findings. Then, work with your committee and other church leaders to create policies, procedures and training plans to counter the threats you are most likely to face.

Unit 4 Overview: Attacks and Threats – Understanding the Perils Facing Your Church

Once you've completed your security and safety assessment, you will need to determine where your church stands in terms of preparedness for the myriad of threats out there. Of course, that requires you to know more about what threats your church might face. They are legion, but with the right preparedness and understanding, they can be met successfully. In the following chapters, you will learn about:

- **Emergency and Hazard Training Basics:** In this chapter, we'll cover the basics of emergency and hazard training that your Church Security Team needs to know. These apply to all situations that your team might face, from fires to threats of violence, and everything in between. Think of this as "emergency training 101".
- **Financial Threats:** Financial threats can wreak havoc in your church, from theft to embezzlement. We'll walk you through how to identify potential financial threats and attacks, and how to deal with them. We'll also touch on practices that help to prevent these threats from occurring in the first place.
- **Biological Hazards:** Biological hazards range from illnesses and disease to foodborne sicknesses. In this chapter, we'll discuss how to safeguard your congregation from illnesses, how to prevent food contaminated sickness, and more.

- **Child and Vulnerable Adult Protection:** Children and the elderly are at high risk for abuse (sexual, physical, mental and emotional). In this chapter, we'll discuss warning signs and symptoms, as well as how to address these threats within your church.
- **Arson and Fire Threats:** Fire is one of the most common threats churches face, whether accidental or intentionally set. In this chapter, we will discuss fire safety, evacuation procedures and essential planning to help safeguard your congregation, as well as the church building.
- **Acts of Violence and Physical Threats:** From active killers to confrontations with upset congregation members, violence in many forms will threaten your church. In this chapter, we discuss how to identify potential threats, how to deal with potentially violent situations, how to diffuse tensions, what to do in the case of an active shooter/killer, and a great deal more.
- **Natural Disasters:** From hurricanes and tornadoes to floods and periods of intense heat or cold, natural disasters can cause immense harm to your congregation. In this chapter, we'll discuss what you need to know about the many natural disasters that could occur, how to plan for them effectively, and more.

Chapter 8:
Emergency and Hazard Training Basics

In this chapter, we will focus on medical emergencies and hazards. Hazards include natural hazards, human-caused hazards, and technological hazards. We'll go over most of the material at a rather high level, and most will be broken down to a more granular level in later chapters to help you better understand those particular threats and your responses. Think of this chapter as emergency/hazard training 101 and the other chapters as 102 material.

Hazard Types

First, let's take a look at some of the hazard types that you and your teams might be required to respond to – that's the initial step needed to really start wrapping your mind around the situation.

- **Natural hazards** include meteorological disasters such as severe thunderstorms, flooding, tornadoes, hurricanes, and winter storms; geological hazards such as earthquakes, tsunamis, landslides, and volcanoes; and more.
- **Human-caused hazards** include accidents such as workplace accidents, transportation accidents, and mechanical breakdowns, as well as intentional acts such as riots, bomb threats, robbery, violence, terrorism, and attacks on information technology (DHS, n.d., "Risk Assessment").
- **Technological hazards** include problems with information technology such as hardware failure; utility outages such as an electrical power outage; hazardous materials problems such as transportation accidents, toxic waste spills, chemical incidents, and natural gas leaks; chain interruption such as supplier failure or transportation interruption; and fire/explosion (DHS, n.d.,

"Risk Assessment"; Maryland Emergency Management Agency, n.d.; United Nations Office for Disaster Risk Reduction, 2007).

Power outages have increased significantly between 2000 and 2014 due to aging infrastructure, growing demands, and more extreme weather (Wirfs-Brock, 2014). The five-year annual average doubled every five years (Wirfs-Brock, 2014).

Each type of hazard will be discussed thoroughly in this book. In responding to emergencies and disasters, your church will have to use one of four responses (DHS, n.d., "Emergency response plan"):

- Go on lockdown
- Shelter in place
- Be a shelter
- Evacuate the facility

We'll discuss each of these in more detail.

Lockdowns

Lockdowns are self-explanatory. It's really nothing more than having people hide and find shields (such as tables or desks) to keep them safe during a potential act of violence (DHS, n.d., "Emergency response plan"). Just as with the other responses to dangerous situations, lockdowns should be practiced so that everyone is familiar with what is expected of them, and to reduce the time required to respond during an actual emergency.

Sheltering in Place

Sheltering in place is a short period of sheltering in order to avoid hazards outside such as traffic accidents, chemical spills, or outages affecting a small area (DHS, n.d., "Emergency response plan").

During sheltering in place, people should (DHS, n.d., "Emergency response plan"):

- Get inside and away from windows.
- Close all exterior doors.
- Shut down the ventilation system if there is an airborne risk.
- Being in the middle of the building and on the highest floor is safest.
- The DHS recommends staying out of the basement.

An example of when to shelter in place is in the instance of a nearby traffic accident. The National Center for Statistics and Analysis (2017) reported that each year between 2006 and 2015, an average of 35,527 people died and 2,354,100 people were injured in traffic accidents (p. 3).

Bad weather is a factor in about 22% of crashes because it causes visibility issues and decreased pavement traction, as well as creating obstructions such as wind-blown snow and debris (Federal Highway Administration, 2017). If an accident such as a traffic accident occurs near the church, the congregation should shelter in place until the area is cleared. It is important to give professionals time to respond to the accident without complicating the issue by adding more traffic to the scene.

Church members should listen to a local radio station, or monitor emergency personnel/first responder/police communications to determine when the accident has been cleared. During instances of severe weather, including thunderstorms, tornado threats, snow storms, periods of high wind, and more, church members should monitor National Oceanic and Atmospheric Administration Weather Radio to determine the affected area(s), so they know when it is safe to go home.

Sheltering

Churches often serve as shelters during emergencies such as hurricanes or act as receiving facilities for other institutions' evacuations (e.g., during a nursing home fire). Therefore, your planning committee should decide if it will shelter people and, if so, establish plans for how to house them safely.

Defending the Flock

When acting as an emergency shelter, there are special issues to address. The following questions will help you plan for how to shelter people (Brotherhood Mutual Insurance Company, 2016, "Guidelines"):

- According to our fire codes, how many people can the church's sheltering area hold?
- How will we provide security, food, and janitorial services?
- How will we provide sanitation (abilities to use toilets and showers) and supplies such as toiletries?
- Do we have a generator in case the power goes out?
- How will we store people's possessions including weapons, valuables, and medications?
- Is the area childproofed?
- Is there a smoking area?
- What type of ventilation system is required?
- How will we ensure the children are safe from sex offenders?
- How will we report any crimes that occur?

Use Sheepdog Church Security's intake form to track people sheltering at the facility.

If the church functions as a refuge in severe weather, it is important to have emergency supplies stocked. Include at least three days' worth of the following supplies (American National Red Cross, 2009; American National Red Cross, 2016, "Hurricane"; Brotherhood Mutual Insurance Company, 2016; Federal Emergency Management Agency, 2014):

- A whistle to signal for help
- A NOAA Weather Radio
- First aid supplies
- Clean water: at least a gallon per person per day
- Nonperishable, ready-to-eat food (such as granola bars)
- Nonperishable, easy-to-prepare food
- A manual can opener

- Hygiene items such as toilet paper, feminine supplies, and moist towelettes
- Infant supplies such as bottles, formula, and diapers
- Flashlights
- Extra batteries

Do not use candles because they are likely to start fires (Centers for Disease Control and Prevention [CDC], 2015, "Winter weather").

Evacuations

Emergency evacuation plans are an important part of church safety. If civil authorities require evacuation, you should already have a plan in place to safely evacuate your staff, volunteers, and attendees. In many instances, you will be required by law to have a codified evacuation plan and to have that plan posted visibly throughout your church. Fire evacuation plans are perfect examples and are generally required by the fire marshal in order for your property to legally operate.

Special care should be taken in evacuating children, people in poor health, and the elderly. All evacuation types require detailed planning and practice. Hold practice drills for each type of evacuation.

Christensen, Blair, and Holt (2007) explained there are four types of evacuation procedures:

- **Protective**: Relocating people prior to danger before an impending event, such as a hurricane.
- **Preventative**: Relocating people quickly and in less distance due to danger, such as a bomb threat.
- **Rescue**: Removing people from an environment following an emergency, such as a fire.
- **Reconstructive**: Moving people from one environment to another for continued care, such as "moving evacuees to camps or temporary housing programs" (pp. 249-250).

In creating evacuation plans, it is important to determine which type of evacuation each plan is meant to include.

Christensen, Blair, and Holt (2007) listed three overlying factors in all evacuations (Christensen, Blair, and Holt, 2007, p. 250):

- **Individual behavior**: Behavior includes how people respond to the emergency evacuation based on their "previous experience, perception of the hazard, and social attachments".
- **Planned systems**: Planned systems include evacuation routes, practice drills, and evacuation equipment.
- **Built environment**: Built environment refers to the physical building such as the presence of stairs or blocked exits.

These three factors should be considered when planning all evacuation procedures. People can be expected to behave similarly to how others behaved in similar crises. People's thinking is impaired when they are in emergency situations (Prati et al., 2013, p. 770).

Prati et al. (2013) found that people do not consistently correctly identify gestures made by first responders. Specifically, gestures indicating "Move back" or "Stop" were not understood (Prati et al., 2013, p. 768). Therefore, it would be helpful to familiarize church attendees with common first responder gestures during practice evaluations.

Creating Evacuation Procedures

There are general steps that Church Safety Team leaders should perform when planning evacuation procedures (Pandolfo, 2015, pp. 36-37):

- Plan
- Purchase equipment
- Train staff
- Conduct drills

The first step is to plan. Know who is responsible for what functions during the evacuation. After Hurricane Katrina in 2005, the Office of the Inspector General (OIG) evaluated the Centers for Medicare and Medicaid Services' oversight of nursing homes (Brown, Hyer, and Polivka-West, 2007, p. 656).

Brown, Hyer, and Polivka-West (2007) analyzed OIG's report and its 25 elements of disaster planning. One of the most important provisions OIG found was the importance of direction and control because so many facilities did not have clear guidelines about who handled what aspects of the emergency (Brown, Hyer, & Polivka-West, 2007, p. 668).

If possible, have a building inspection done during the planning process. Since 2009, building codes have made provisions for fire safe elevators that function during fires (Bukowski, 2012, p. 128). Know if the elevator(s) in the church is/are safe for evacuations.

Throughout the church, post maps that easily identify all exits and areas to avoid (e.g., rooms containing hazardous materials or high-voltage electrical systems) (Christensen, Blair, and Holt, 2007, p. 251; Wilson, 2015, p. 25).

When planning the evacuations, understand that people do not behave rationally during crises. Kugliowski (2013) explained that people often do not immediately leave when there is a crisis. Instead, they go through a decision-making process that includes denial and behaviors to find more information such as "milling" when people gather to discuss what has happened and what should be done, and "keynoting" when leaders emerge to propose actions (Kugliowski, 2013, p. 105, 108).

Even though people should understand that emergency evacuations require quick reactions, they often delay evacuation. Kugliowski (2013) found:

> *Over two-thirds of the injured and over half of the dead in building fires could have evacuated but instead were performing activities that delayed their safety, including fighting the fire, attempting to rescue others, and moving to [unsafe locations] inside the build-*

ing. (pp. 101-102).

Although rescuing others and fighting the fire might seem to be the right thing to do, those activities are best left to the professionals. It is thus important to plan how the Church Safety Team will respond to people who are not following professionals' directions to evacuate.

It's important to know how to inform people about crises. Kugliowski (2013) noted that information during crises "can be incomplete, ambiguous, or contradictory" (p. 111). In one incident, an employee went on stage and announced a fire, but the patrons thought it was part of the evening's entertainment (Kugliowski, 2013, p. 107). Obviously, that caused serious challenges with the evacuation. Therefore, it is important to be clear and concise about the reality of the situation and how to evacuate.

Pandolfo (2015) emphasized that people should plan for a worst-case scenario (p. 36), and you should do the same when planning for evacuations. Consider what will occur if emergency responders are unable to assist in evacuations or how the building will be evacuated during a power outage (Pandolfo, 2015, p. 37).

Plan wide passages for evacuation (Wilson, 2015, p. 25). Make sure that there are passages designed for incoming emergency responders and people evacuating the building. Farlow (2014) reported that a July 2012 evacuation of a 16-story building was complicated by bottlenecks created by people going up and down all stairwells rather than having designated ascending and descending stairwells (pp. 89, 90).

Plan at least two areas that can serve as assembly points where evacuees will reconvene and be counted. In one case, a nursing home did not track its patients well; some patients self-evacuated and left with family (Farlow, 2014, p. 92). It is essential that there is no question if anyone is left in the building.

The second step is to purchase equipment. There are three types of evacuation equipment (Pandolfo, 2015, p. 37):

- Carry devices
- Wheeled devices
- Evacuation sled devices

Make sure that evacuation equipment is available on every floor and near exits (Pandolfo, 2016, p. 60). Consider the church's needs by evaluating the building and the church membership.

The third step is to train staff, and the fourth step is to conduct drills. Train all Church Safety Team members, so they understand how to evaluate possible risks, inspect equipment, and communicate with others during evacuations. Conduct drills regularly. Bukowski (2012) reported that experts recommend drills at least once or twice a year (p. 131).

Give people notice that a drill will be conducted. When conducting drills, create environments that are likely to occur in real emergencies such as shutting off lights and not using elevators (Pandolfo, 2015, p. 37). Drills can expose inefficiencies in the evacuation procedures (Wilson, 2015, p. 26), as well. For instance, running an evacuation drill with the lights off could highlight the need for battery-powered emergency lighting in stairwells.

In addition to writing good evacuation procedures, it is important to review them at least annually and revise them as needed. Brown, Hyer, and Polivka-West (2007) found that nursing home employees often did not follow emergency evacuation procedures during Hurricane Katrina because "the plans were not updated with current information or did not include instructions for a particular circumstance" (p. 664). Therefore, it is important to revise the procedures anytime changes occur (e.g., new construction to the facility).

Evacuating People with Special Needs

Although most church members are able to attend church with minimal support (such as having a caretaker pushing a wheelchair or helping the person walk), the lessons nursing home administrators have learned in previous emergencies can be beneficial to the planning team while creating emergency plans for their congregations.

When planning evacuations, it is not enough to consider the needs of individuals with permanent disabilities because people with temporary disabilities or injuries (including injuries received during evacuation) will also need assistance (Pandolfo, 2016, p. 59).

Blanchard and Dosa (2009) found that nursing home administrators were more likely to evacuate residents during Hurricane Gustav in 2008 than during Hurricane Katrina in 2005 due to criticisms about residents' deaths and injuries. Brown, Hyer, and Polivka-West (2007) reported that 70 nursing home residents died in Hurricanes Katrina and Rita in 2005 (p. 655), and 70% of the people who died in New Orleans during Hurricane Katrina were over 60 (p. 664).

It is also immensely beneficial to install evacuation elevators that are "'hardened' to function during conditions reasonably expected during a rescue evacuation" or build horizontal exits so that people with mobility issues can evacuate to an area on the same level (Christensen, Blair, and Holt, 2007, pp. 251-252).

Only use elevators if they are emergency elevators, or firefighters assure you they are safe. It's important to know if the elevators in the building are usable during fires. For the past two decades, signs have conditioned people to believe that elevators are out of service during fires because the elevators automatically go to the main floor and are controlled by a firefighters' special key (Bukowski, 2012, p. 128). However, elevators can be useful in evacuations. Since 2009, the US model building code included provisions for elevators as emergency egress (Bukowski, 2012, p. 128).

Elevators are especially beneficial for evacuating high-rise buildings and super high-rise buildings where people are likely to become fatigued or have delays in evacuation (Liao, Lo, Ma, Liu, and Liao, 2014, pp. 363-365). The authors also found that people are open to using elevators in emergency evacuations (p. 367). Although there was fear that elevators could not work safely in fires, most people would follow firefighters' instruction to use elevators (Liao, Lo, Ma, Liu, and Liao, 2014, pp. 368).

Elevators are also a good choice for evacuating people with disabilities because they would not have to leave behind assistive equipment or service animals (Bukowski, 2012, p. 131). Likewise, people who are blind are likely to have used elevators in everyday access and would not be forced to walk an unfamiliar route during the evacuation (Bukowski, 2012, p. 131). If the elevators in the building for which you are designing evacuation plans do not have fire safe elevators, you can consider discussing the installation with a contractor.

Another consideration is evacuating children. Oftentimes, the adult to child ratio makes it difficult for the workers to evacuate all children. When developing the evacuation plan, address nursery evacuations and consider adult to child ratio and the availability of fire crib strollers and wagons. Nursery workers should ensure all doors are closed and that children remain calm. Church Safety Team members should assist in the evacuation.

Medical Emergencies

Cardiac arrest is an electrical problem in which an irregular rhythm disrupts the blood flow to organs (The American Heart Association [AHA], 2013). The American Heart Association (AHA, 2013) reported, "Nearly 360,000 out-of-hospital cardiac arrests occur annually in the United States."

Nearly 90% of those people die (AHA, 2017). Therefore, all Church Safety Team members should have current certifications in cardiopulmonary resuscitation (CPR), first aid, and using an automated external defibrillator (AED) (DHS, n.d., "Training"). It is also important to understand the proper role of CPR and how to achieve the ideal rate of compressions. To reach the rate of 100-120 compressions per minute for CPR, use the beat of "Stayin' Alive" (AHA, 2017).

If a Church Safety Team member is a medical professional, he/she should be encouraged to share additional first responder training. Church Safety Team members should immediately call 911 regarding medical emergencies even if someone is administering CPR or other procedures. There is no exception for professional medical attention – provide all aid possible immediately, but make sure you call 911/emergency responders, too.

Implementation

After the planning committee has decided how to address each response (lockdown, sheltering in place, sheltering, and evacuations), you must conduct drills. After drills for sheltering in place and sheltering, ask participants what they wish they had access to so they could be more comfortable if they could not leave that area for three hours, six hours, two days, etc. (FEMA, 2011, "Storm safe"). This information can provide you with data necessary not only for comfort but ultimately, for safety and security for longer sheltering periods.

In addition to other planning, different alarms should be assigned to signal whether people should lockdown, shelter in place, shelter, or evacuate (DHS, n.d., "Training"). Alarms should be both visible and audible, so people with hearing or seeing difficulties are alerted to the danger (Christensen, Blair, and Holt, 2007, p. 251).

Teaching the Content

To teach this section about the different methods of protecting the congregation (lockdowns, sheltering in place, sheltering, and evacuations), a jigsaw activity would be beneficial.

- Break the students into four groups.
- Each group should be given a floor plan of the church and the set of questions below for that group/activity.
- Encourage each group to think up additional questions to also answer.

- After the groups have completed the assignment, each group reports its findings to the class as a whole.

It would be beneficial to have the presentations throughout the church so everyone can see the places discussed. Once the entire class has heard each jigsaw piece of information, the "puzzle" is complete.

Lockdowns Group Questions

- Are there rooms or closets that can be locked from the inside?
- What rooms are best for hiding? Why? (Plants, desks, closets, etc. can help conceal people but will not stop bullets if found.)
- What areas should be avoided for hiding? Why?
- Where are areas of cover that will prevent bullets from penetrating (e.g., cinder blocks, layers of metal)?

Sheltering in Place Group Questions

- Where are the safest areas to shelter in place? Why are these areas safest?
- Can bathrooms be accessed from these points?
- If the sheltering lasts hours, is there access to food and water?
- How will those sheltering communicate with family and emergency personnel outside the church?
- Is there access to a National Oceanic and Atmospheric Administration Weather Radio from these areas?

Sheltering Group Questions

- How many people can be sheltered according to the fire code?
- Where are some areas that can serve as temporary shelters (up to a week)?
- Can bathrooms and shower facilities be accessed from these points?
- Is there a backup generator should the power go out?

- Do we have the ability to provide food and water?

Evacuations Group Questions

- Where are potential areas that will be difficult to evacuate (such as the nursery or narrow stairwells)?
- Are there any places to avoid?
- How will every place be checked to ensure people have evacuated?
- If the power is out and elevators are not working, how will people with mobility issues or people who are hurt during evacuation get out?
- Where are areas outside the church that can be used as assembly points?
- If there is more than one assembly point, how will staff communicate to ensure complete evacuation?

Chapter 9:
Addressing Financial Attacks and Threats to Your Church

Churches are just as likely as any other institution or organization to be victimized by criminals, including burglars, thieves and other perpetrators of financial crimes. Eckstrom (2008) explained that megachurches are particularly vulnerable to criminals who are looking to inflict maximum damage or are motivated by greed because they can have 20,000 worshippers each weekend and make $115,000 a week in income (p. 17).

General Information

There are many types of financial attack, including theft, burglary, robbery, and embezzlement:

- **Theft** is defined as the "unauthorized taking of property from another with the intent to permanently deprive that person of the property" and includes taking property left unwittingly by the owner (such as setting down a purse and walking off) (Findlaw, 2017).
- **Burglary** is "unlawful entry" with the intention of committing a crime (such as a locked sanctuary or church office), and is a crime whether or not another crime occurs (Findlaw, 2017; Law Office of Peter Blair, 2015).
- **Robbery** is stealing by using force, intimidation, or threats (such as grabbing the bank deposit or showing a gun).
- **Embezzlement** is using resources in a way that was not authorized by someone entrusted with access to the resources (Law Office of Peter Blair, 2015) and includes people who make bank deposits or manage the bookkeeping.

There are several methods that can be used to prevent all types of theft. They are discussed below.

One way to prevent financial attacks through burglary or robbery is using Crime Prevention Through Environmental Design (CPTED), as we discussed in chapter 7. As a refresher, CPTED (pronounced sep-ted) is the use of "physical design, citizen participation and law enforcement strategies in a comprehensive way to protect facilities or neighborhoods" (ACPI, 2012, p. 23). Van Soomeren (n.d.) explained there are six principles of CPTED:

- Access control
- Surveillance
- Territoriality
- Image and maintenance
- Activity support
- Target hardening

These principles should be used together to achieve the best results. For a full discussion of these six principles, please see the relevant section in chapter 7.

How to Implement Preventing Financial Attacks

In addition to using CPTED to reduce the likelihood of criminal activity, churches also need to have good policies about handling money. The following policies are examples of ways to prevent embezzlement and to "harden" the church as a target by outside criminals:

- Increased numbers of Church Safety Team members
- Use of safes and combination locks
- Safe access log
- Surveillance by other administration workers

Assisting with and monitoring donations is one of the most important duties of the Church Safety Team—Security because of the significance of people offering their money to the church. That action represents the trust between the members and their church. Members would be deeply upset to learn their money was stolen. The following suggested policies will help you prevent financial attacks regardless if they are theft, burglary, robbery, embezzlement, or stealing computer data.

Cash/Offering Security Policies and Procedures

Use surveillance and target hardening to prevent theft of cash and offerings. For unsecured cash venues (think bookstores, coffee bars, or breakfast fundraisers), always schedule at least two people for all shifts.

Having more workers on duty lessens the chance of someone attempting to steal the money when one worker is busy by ensuring the possibility of surveillance. Having more people working also decreases the potential for false accusations and temptation.

Use surveillance, image and maintenance, and target hardening when transporting money to prevent robbery. When moving money from cash venues or donation plates, one Church Safety Team—Security member should hold the money bag but refrain from handling the money if possible. A second member should put the money into the bag.

Other Church Safety Team—Security members will survey the area for threats (surveillance). The Church Safety Team—Security members should monitor people for suspicious behavior until the money bag has been locked in the safe (surveillance and target hardening). During some special events, the offering may be picked up twice (image and maintenance). If multiple pick-ups will occur, the Church Safety Team—Security members will be notified at the start of their shifts.

Safes Policies and Procedures

Using safes applies the principles of access control, surveillance, and target hardening. All donations must be kept in safes in a main office.

Keeping the safe in the office ensures access control, as no one would be able to enter without notice. Surveillance is done by people who work in the office or regularly visit the office.

Invest in locks with a changeable combination. Target hardening happens by using the safes themselves, and combination spelling keys will further be useful because they allow department heads to give combinations to whoever needs them. Change the combination at least annually and anytime someone who had safe access stops working/volunteering at the church.

For further surveillance, two or more people should be present each time the safe is opened. Explain that the person opening the safe needs to be protected from attempted robberies or false accusations.

If someone accesses the safe alone, determine who the person is, and why he or she 1) had access to the area without another person being present, and 2) opened the safe in the first place. Remember to educate, not reprimand. It is very possible the person honestly did not know the policy or its purpose.

For additional monitoring, the safe access log should be completed by at least two of the people present every time the safe is opened. The following should be recorded in the areas indicated on the form:

- The date/time of opening
- The purpose of opening the safe (adding cash/valuables, counting donations, preparing for bank deposit, etc.)
- The names and signatures of at least two people who opened the safe

Requiring this information on the safe access log ensures that no one adds/removes church resources without authorization.

When money leaves the safe to be counted prior to deposit, at least two people should be present. One should count the money, and the second should recount it to confirm the amount. This can be done simultaneously with one person putting the money aside and each person counting silently in his/her head.

Counting can also be done with one person counting and the other watching. The counter writes down the number he/she counted and then the two switch positions. The two numbers should match. Both people should sign the deposit slip.

For target hardening, money should be put in a locked bag when it is leaving the safe to be deposited into the bank. After the bag is locked, the person depositing the money should not have a key to the locked bag. Locked bags protect the money, and they also protect people from facing false accusations.

The bank teller can open the bag with the bank's key and count the money. That count will alert the church if there has been any tampering because the church bookkeeper can compare the church's account with the bank's record. It should be easy to determine if a theft has occurred.

If a robbery occurs at any point, the Church Safety Team—Security members should not use physical means to detain a thief, even if they do not appear armed. A robber may be armed and yet choose not to brandish their weapon. It is impossible to determine whether or not they're armed, so don't take chances.

Do not place any church member or visitors at risk to stop a robbery. Instead, Church Safety Team—Security members should try to see the robber well enough to provide a thorough description when they immediately contact local police. If possible, run drills using actors to help the Church Safety Team – Security members build their memory and ability to recall facial features and other details.

Preventing Embezzlement

If the policies for transferring money to and from the safe are followed, the chances for embezzlement are lowered. In addition to these policies, churches should also have multiple people working as bookkeepers to ensure that no one person is tempted to transfer money to private accounts.

Having only a single person responsible for all bookkeeping greatly increases the temptation to embezzle funds, and provides ample opportunities. Finally, every expenditure over a certain amount (which your church chooses, such as $2000) should be approved in writing by at least two people in the administration.

Computer Data

Churches also should be aware that their computer data may be vulnerable to theft or corruption. In fact, data theft has become more common than the theft of money – identities can be sold on the black market, or used for personal gain. Financial records, Social Security numbers, bank account information, and other data can be sold to the highest bidder.

For example, if your members provide information for automatic withdrawals, then those bank numbers potentially could be stolen. This unauthorized access is as much (or even more so) a cause for members to lose trust as if their cash had been stolen from the donation plates. The following guidelines will help keep your information secure:

- Require passwords for access to computers (ACPI, 2012, p. 410).
- Backup information on a regular schedule (ACPI, 2012, p. 411).
- Keep an off-site backup in case the church is destroyed by a tornado or other disaster.
- Encrypt confidential information (ACPI, 2012, p. 411).

These steps should lessen the vulnerability of your data, but you are encouraged to ask your local police if they have suggestions for further protections.

How to Teach Preventing Financial Attacks

Struggling with the idea of teaching your Church Safety Team members how to prevent financial attacks? Don't worry – it's not difficult, and we've broken the process down into a handful of simple steps for you.

Icebreaker

Almost anything can work as an icebreaker. Tell a joke. Share an anecdote. Share a personal experience. The point is to alleviate the tension in the class. By diffusing tension, you help your team come together as one, and also focus on the lessons about to be learned.

Lecture

You can lecture on the material presented in this chapter in nearly any way you might want, up to and including reading the material verbatim to your team members. While lecturing, make sure to hit all the salient points we've covered in the preceding chapter. You may also find it necessary (and even beneficial) to pause for questions from your team members so that you can provide on-the-spot guidance for them.

Conversation

Don't let your lecture be the limits of the conversation surrounding financial threats. They're quite prevalent, and only becoming more so. In the future, financial threats, particularly those targeting financial data (both church-owned and member-specific) will constitute a larger and larger percentage of the total threats your church must face.

Ask the trainees, "What (if any) experiences have you had in preventing theft of resources (including cash, resources, church property, or data)?" Listen to trainees' insight because they may have ideas on how to improve church policies or procedures.

Group Activity

For each group, you need to make 14 slips of paper: three Church Safety Team—Security members, 10 bystanders, and one thief. Divide trainees into groups of 10-12 people.

Using the slips you previously marked, have each person draw a slip which will show one of the three titles. No one should reveal which title he/she drew. Have everyone close his/her eyes. Ask the Church Safety Team—Security members to raise their hands. If there are at least two people, you can proceed. If not, people need to redraw the slips.

Choose two of the Church Safety Team—Security members to transfer cash (using fake money or precut slips of paper) from a fake donation plate into a fake money bag. They should simultaneously be watching the bystanders. If there is a third Church Safety Team—Security member, he/she should try to blend in with the bystanders but be watching them all for suspicious behaviors that might alert him/her to the thief's identity. Some of those potential behaviors include the following:

- Fumbling with the "cash" in the donation plate.
- Making "change" from cash in the donation plate.
- Touching multiple bills on the plate.
- Engaging others in conversation in an attempt to distract them from the person's actions.
- "Accidentally" knocking bills out of the plate to the floor so they must be picked up

Bystanders are free to chat with everyone and generally be happy and oblivious to the cash transfer. If anyone drew the slip for thief, that person should try to blend in with the bystanders but be watching the cash transfer. The thief should try to take the money at some point.

The Church Safety Team—Security members should try to prevent the attempt before the person tries by noticing suspicious behaviors and intercepting him/her. If an attempt is made, the Church Safety Team—Security members should try to stop the person through verbal de-escalation or by following your church's predetermined protocol/ policy for dealing with thieves.

Discussion

After the group activity, it is important to ask the following questions and let the trainees debate the answers:

- Why may there not have been a thief in every group?
- What behaviors did the Church Safety Team—Security members notice that alerted them to the thief's intentions?
- What other behaviors should be considered suspicious?
- Are there reasons people might act in a suspicious manner when they have no criminal intentions?

Close

Close the class by reviewing the most important lessons learned today, thanking trainees for their hard work, and praying that God will guide us all in making the church a safer place.

Chapter 10:
Child and Vulnerable Adult Protection

Jesus said, "If anyone causes one of these little ones—those who believe in me—to stumble, it would be better for them to have a large millstone hung around their neck and to be drowned in the depths of the sea." (Matthew 18:6)

The Realities of Abuse within the Church

There are few issues that cause children to "stumble" so completely as being abused. Abuse affects every area of the victim's life. Survivors of abuse often have issues with substance use, eating disorders, intimate relationships, obesity, smoking, and mental health problems including suicide attempts (Chartier, Walker, & Naimark, 2009; Felitti et al., 1998).

Felitti et al. (1998) found that the more trauma a person suffered in childhood, the more likely he or she was to suffer from the issues above as well as diseases such as "ischemic heart disease, cancer, chronic lung disease, skeletal fractures, and liver disease" (p. 245).

To those in church leadership, the most painful reactions of these abused children can be their loss of religion and even hostility toward the church (Vieth, Tchividjian, Walker, & Knodel, 2012, p. 327). Some victims refer to this loss of spiritual life as "soul murder" (Doyle, 2006, p. 208). When children are abused, the effects are lifelong.

Soul Murder – The loss of religion, and hostility toward it on the part of those who have been abused.

Abuse in the church can take many forms. Children and vulnerable adults (such as the elderly and disabled) can be victims of sexual, physical, psychological, or financial abuse or neglect. Victims can be any age and either sex. Journalists covering Catholic Church scandal at the end of the 20th century mainly focused on male child victims, but Marcel (2013) pointed out that there were numerous cases of female victims, as well.

In 2007, **794,000** children in the United States were victims of child abuse and neglect (O'Neill, Gabel, Huckins, & Harder, 2010, p. 383). Looking at lifetime totals, Perry-Burney, Thomas, and McDonald (2014) reported that *"one in three girls and one in seven boys will be sexually abused during childhood"* (p. 987).

Additionally, **10% of all elderly adults** suffer some form of abuse, although financial abuse is more common with the elderly than other forms. With that being said, elder abuse is reported less frequently than child abuse (Lachs, M., & Pillemer, K. (2015). Elder abuse. *New England Journal of Medicine*, 373, 1947–56. doi: 10.1056/NEJMra1404688)

Protecting the most vulnerable members of the church is of the utmost importance. If people are abused, church leaders must act quickly to respond to their abuse by reporting the crimes to proper civil authorities and making sure the perpetrators are removed from duty while investigations are conducted.

Definitions of Abuse and Neglect

The Centers for Disease Control and Prevention published uniform definitions to "promote consistent terminology and data collection related to child maltreatment" (Leeb, Paulozzi, Melanson, Simon, and Arias, 2008, p. iv). Your local authorities may have slightly different definitions, but the following are good guidelines for this discussion.

The CDC's definitions include acts of commission (abuse) and acts of omission (neglect). All forms of abuse can also be inflicted upon older victims.

- **Sexual abuse** is "any completed or attempted (non-completed) sexual act, sexual contact with, or exploitation (i.e. noncontact sexual interaction) of a child by a caregiver" (Leeb et al., 2008, p. 14).
- **Physical abuse** is "the intentional use of physical force against

a child that results in, or has the potential to result in, physical injury" (Leeb et al., 2008, p. 14).

- **Psychological abuse** is "intentional caregiver behavior (i.e., act of commission) that conveys to a child that he/she is worthless, flawed, unloved, unwanted, endangered, or valued only in meeting another's needs" (Leeb et al., 2008, p. 16).
- **Financial abuse** is stealing from the victim or committing "fraud, exploitation, pressure in connection with wills, property or inheritance or financial transactions, or the misuse or misappropriation of property, possessions or benefits" (SCIE as cited in Redmond, 2016, p. 87).
- **Neglect** is "failure to provide for a child's basic physical, emotional, or educational needs or to protect a child from harm or potential harm. Like acts of commission, harm to a child may or may not be the intended consequence" (Leeb et al., p. 11). Neglect includes failure to provide for the child and failure to supervise the child (Leeb et al., 2008, p. 11).

Costs of Child Abuse to Churches

Since 1950, churches have paid nearly **$4 billion** to victims (Ruhl & Ruhl, 2015, p. 1). Money paid to victims who had to sign nondisclosure agreements is not included in this total (Rotondaro, 2015, p. 15). Chan and Scott-Ladd (2014) explained that churches see decreases in membership donations (tithes) after financial or sexual scandals come to light (p. 327). Rotondaro (2015) gave the further details that churches lose an average of **$2.36 billion per year** in decreased giving (p. 15).

Areas where churches had sexual abuse scandals also had decreased giving in social programs such as soup kitchens and homeless shelters (Rotondaro, 2015, p. 15). Other costs such as evaluating and treating abusers, operating safe environment programs, paying for public relations firms to handle damage, and paying for victims' therapy cannot accurately be calculated (Cozzens, 2003, p. 47; Ruhl & Ruhl, 2015, p. 16).

The Costs in a Nutshell

- *$4 billion paid to victims (not including money paid to "settle" allegations.*
- *$2.36 billion per year in decreased giving.*
- *Decreased giving through social outreach programs (shelters, soup kitchens, etc.)*
- *Untold amounts lost through:*
  - *Abuser evaluation and treatment*
  - *Safe environment program development and implementation*
  - *Public relations assistance*
  - *Paying for victim therapy*

Laws about Child Abuse

Several important laws were created to protect children from abuse, particularly sexual abuse. The following were all named after high-profile cases:

- The Jacob Wetterling Crimes against Children and Sexually Violent Offender Registration Act of 1994
- The Pam Lychner Sexual Offender Tracking and Identification Act of 1996
- Megan's Law of 1996

All of the above laws required people convicted of sexual offenses to register as sex offenders (sometimes for life) on the National Sex Offender Registry and to require authorities make information about registered sex offenders publicly available (Office of the Attorney General, 1998).

Of course, abuse and neglect are illegal. The definitions may vary throughout the nation, but general definitions are provided above. Most churches are mandatory reporters. This means that if church staff members have knowledge of abuse or neglect, they are required by law to report it to civil authorities, which include police and social services agencies such as Child Protective Services.

The US Department of Health and Human Services, the Administration for Children & Families, and the Children's Bureau, along with the Child Welfare Information Gateway, have compiled important information about the varying US state and territory statutes that apply to mandatory reporters. This report can be downloaded as a PDF, or accessed online here (https://www.childwelfare.gov/topics/systemwide/laws-policies/statutes/manda/).

How to Prevent Abuse

We as a collective have had years during which to figure out ways to prevent both child and elder abuse. There is no reason any child or vulnerable adult should suffer any form of abuse or neglect while a part of your congregation. The following information will guide you in crafting your own policies.

Develop a "Zero Tolerance" Policy on Sexual Conduct

Moore, Robinson, Dailey, and Thompson (2015) reported that only 43% of U.S. churches have policies related to abuse. They argued that having a policy is the first step in preventing abuse. Vieth, Tchividjian, Walker, and Knodel (2012) recommended contacting insurance companies in creating policies.

Insurance companies can help guide you by providing information pertinent to your area's demographics, as well as other information, such as:

- The most important policies for your church
- How to safeguard both at-risk congregation members and the church as a whole
- Understanding civil and criminal penalties that could apply both to perpetrators and churches not instituting policies

However, they noted that child abuse experts (e.g. law enforcement, prosecutors, sex offender treatment providers) should also be consulted because insurance companies may be more concerned with limiting liability (p. 324). Wurtele (2012) reported that it is not enough to have a "zero tolerance" policy on abuse. The organizations must "eliminate all inappropriate sexual conduct (including jokes, inappropriate dress, and sexual innuendos)" (p. 2445).

This can be a particularly difficult task – the "inappropriate joke mindset" is particularly ingrained in blue-collar individuals. It can also be difficult for individuals who have been steeped in a culture of indifference and inappropriateness to even realize their actions can be seen as sexual in any "real" way.

At Least Two Adults Present

Several experts recommended requiring at least two adults for all activities that involve children (Moore et al., 2015, p. 153; Vieth, Tchividjian, Walker, & Knodel, 2012, p. 324; Wurtele, 2012, p. 2447). Moore et al. (2015) further specified that the adults should not be spouses (p. 153).

Spouses are welcome to work within church projects and initiatives, but in any environment where they are in contact with children, they cannot be the only two adults present, as this makes it more likely one will alibi the other's bad behavior or fail to report out of fear of reprisal, a sense of obligation to protect the other spouse, and for other reasons.

If a child needs to be removed from the group, both the child and the adult should remain within eyesight of another worker (Vieth et al., 2012, p. 324). If an adult shares sleeping accommodations with children, at least two adults should be present (Vieth et al., 2012, pp. 324-325). Events should take place in public, not an adult's home (Vieth et al., 2012, p. 325).

Never Leave Them Alone

Children should not be alone with adults, even those whom the parents trust. Abuse has begun after the offender tries to make himself seem like a mentor to the child, offering to teach him/her an instrument or take the child to a sporting event (Parkinson, Oates, & Jayakody, 2010, p. 189).

Often, the abusers made themselves father figures to those whom they abused (Parkinson, Oates, & Jayakody, 2010, p. 190). Parkinson, Oates, & Jayakody (2012) noted that the abusers even targeted boys from dysfunctional families (p. 561) where the need for such a father figure is great, in order to create an emotional connection with their targets.

Other Essential Steps to Safeguard Youth in Church Protection

- **Gateway Substances:** Prohibit substance use (drugs, alcohol, tobacco) at youth events. Sometimes victims are first violated through these "sexual boundary violations" such as being offered a substance (Wurtele, 2012, p. 2449).
- **Technology Issues:** Create clear technology policies. For example, do not allow adults to become "friends" with children under 18 on social media (e.g. Facebook) (Wurtele, 2012, p. 2447). Church leaders can also ask parents to sign authorization forms before staff members give children their cell phone numbers (Wurtele, 2012, p. 2447).
- **Protect Their Privacy:** Ensure privacy is protected by prohibiting camera use in bathrooms, bedrooms, locker rooms, etc. (Wurtele, 2012, p. 2447). Give children as much privacy as possible while helping them with toileting or bathing activities.
- **Vet Adults:** Evaluate adult personnel prior to their working with children. Moore et al. (2015) reported that many of the church abuses that have occurred happened because the personnel were not evaluated prior to their interactions with children (p. 151). Evaluating personnel include (Moore et al., 2015, p. 153):
  - Checking their references
  - Interviewing them
  - Running criminal background checks

- Requiring six months of active church membership prior to working with children

Wurtele (2012) pointed out that "only the FBI's Criminal Justice Information Services Division searches fingerprint records in all states" (p. 2446). The Diana Screen (http://dianascreen.com/) is a computer-based option to assess people's risk to children (Wurtele, 2012, p. 2446).

- **Invest in Training:** Provide ongoing training to adult personnel about church policies. Moore et al. (2015) argued that when adults are inexperienced about their settings, there is more risk of abuse (p. 151). Wurtele (2012) advised the creation of a code of ethics that adults sign.

  She also recommended that "all staff members receive adequate monitoring, supervision, and evaluation through documented performance reviews" (p. 2447). Most churches probably would not think about taking these steps for volunteers, but the practices are important.
- **Create the Right Environment:** Create safe environments for care. Moore et al. (2015) argued that an "isolated environment" can lead to abuse (p. 151). Specifically, the classroom doors and windows should be open and a monitor should routinely check the classroom (Moore et al., 2015, p. 153).

  Posthuma (2012) detailed rules for secure check in/check out procedures. Depending on the size of the church, some of these guidelines (such as computerizing the registration process) can be onerous. However, the overall attention to documentation and ensuring children go home with approved adults is essential.

  This process can be as simple as having a notebook in which parents record drop off and pick up times and write who is allowed to pick up the children. Check driver's licenses before allowing the children to leave with the adults. A child may happily leave with someone he/she knows but who wasn't approved for pick up. Employees and volunteers should also check in and out so there is a record of who was working at which times.

Posthuma (2012) provided further recommendations (which we've provided below) to help churches with their documentation:

- Know the specific time and date the parent checked the child into and out of your ministry.
- Maintain on hand all parental care instructions for each child.
- All medical or special needs concerns for each child should be kept on hand.
- All communications to the parent regarding the care of a child under 18 months old must be kept on hand.
- Always know who was responsible for and had access to each child.
- Maintain scheduling records that show multiple adults in each room.
- Always know and abide by court-appointed custody restrictions.
- Maintain a copy of all incident reports regarding accidents, injuries, fights, discipline, and abuse (Posthuma, 2012). It is important to record even minor incidents such as a child biting another child.

   Often, you can create forms and have them printed on carbon paper, or simply copied in bulk. If your church has the resources, these forms can be electronically created and made available via worker smartphones, tablets or computers. This practice would allow temporary caregivers a quick way to record pertinent information.

   One copy of the report can be given to parents and a second copy can be filed in the church's main office. This practice would allow for accurate and detailed documentation should any allegations arise later.

- Develop safe environments for reporting abuse. Moore et al. (2015) argued that children who are abused are less likely to report the abuse if they feel they will face accusations or that their abusers will not be punished (p. 151).
- Create an accountability structure. Make sure there are checks and balances so that people are held accountable for their actions (Moore et al., 2015, p. 151).
- Encourage people to take care of themselves so they do not become overwhelmed. Wurtele (2012) noted that priests who sexually abused youth had recently experienced increased stressors from work (p. 2450).
- Make sure everyone in the organization understands whistle blower responsibilities and ramifications (Wurtele, 2012, pp. 2450-2451).
- Collaborate with social service providers. O'Neill, Gabel, Huckins, and Harder (2010) reported that churches are often hesitant to inform social services agencies about suspected abuse or neglect because they fear that the children will be removed from the families and the church would lose its ability to intervene (p. 394).

O'Neill et al. (2010) recommended that churches build collaborative relationships before abuse is suspected so that staff understand what the social service providers do. They also advised churches to collaborate for purposes of developing educational groups and committees and sharing resources (p. 404). Wurtele (2012) recommended partnering with schools or local universities to defray costs of training (p. 2451).

<u>What to Do If You Suspect Abuse by a Caregiver</u>

It can be difficult to detect abuse based on observations that occur for an hour a week. There are signs that indicate abuse. Smith and Segal (2016) recommended watching for inappropriate behaviors such as the following:

- Being fearful or excessively watchful
- Acting like an adult and taking care of other children or acting inappropriately infantile
- Having frequent bruises or injuries
- Wearing ill-fitting clothes or that inappropriate to weather
- Having bad hygiene
- Having trouble walking or sitting
- Avoiding certain people

Straughair (2011) noted that financial abuse may be indicated by the vulnerable adult looking as if he or she is "neglected or malnourished, despite the fact that [he or she has] adequate financial means to support" him/herself (pp. 52-53). Smith and Segal (2016) explain the steps one should take if a child reports abuse (Smith & Segal, 2016, "Tips for talking to an abused child"):

- First, stay calm. A child may shut down if he/she senses a reaction of denial, shock, or disgust.
- Let the child tell you what is going on in his or her own words without interrogating or asking questions.
- Tell the child he/she did the right thing.
- Contact authorities.

It may be best not to ask any questions but to instead immediately notify Child Protective Services so the child can be questioned by someone trained in forensic interviewing. Even if a child or vulnerable adult does not confide in you, if you suspect abuse, remember your role as a mandatory reporter and inform the police, social services, and your church leader.

Make sure to follow up and know who is going to report the problem to the authorities. It is better to have two people report the same incident than to have no one report it.

What to Do If You Suspect Abuse by a Church Staff Member

Transparency and accountability are of vital importance to prevent abuse and to repair relationships should abuse occur (Cozzens, 2003). Much of the outrage people have felt about the abuse by church leaders is that abusers' supervisors did not punish the perpetrators and often hid the assaults and even destroyed evidence (Brown, 2016, p. 9; Doyle, 2006).

Maher (2016) explained that priests were routinely transferred to different locations. Doyle (2006) reported that offenders' supervisors "regularly withheld essential information from psychiatrist or psychologists and had either intentionally misinterpreted medical reports or totally ignored psychiatrists' recommendations" (p. 202).

Church leaders further victimized the abused by (Doyle, 2006, pp. 203-207):

- Trying to reverse the victim-victimizer role (for example telling the accuser that he/she will ruin the offender's reputation)
- Devaluing critics (for example by saying that people just want to destroy the church and are spreading lies)
- Ignoring reports of abuse by not investigating the claims or reporting to civil authorities

These issues were complicated by the complicity of civil authorities. Indeed, not only did church leaders cover up abusers' actions (sometimes by transferring offenders to different churches) but government officials, police officers, and district attorneys also chose not to pursue investigations or charges because they did not want to tarnish the reputation of the church or its leaders (Brown, 2016).

Vieth et al. (2012) recommend that if a staff member is accused of abuse, the church should request investigators to broaden the investigation because other children may have been abused and may not disclose unless asked (p. 324). If a church staff member is accused of abuse, keep the following information in mind:

- Remember that he/she is innocent until proven guilty.
- Remove the accused from service during the investigation.
- Work with civil authorities.
- Report the allegations to law enforcement and the appropriate social services agency.
- Report the allegations to church leadership.
- Do not release information about the allegations to the public.
- Work with legal counsel to understand criminal proceedings and civil liabilities.

Prevention is the best outcome. If a crime is committed, reporting it and working to heal the victim is the next best outcome.

Teaching the Content

It can feel quite difficult to teach this particular material. Abuse, whether related to children or vulnerable adults, is never an easy topic to tackle. However, it's absolutely vital that you do so, and that you and your team take everything explained in this section as seriously as possible.

Rather than opening with an icebreaker, my recommendation is that you open with statistics about child abuse and/or elder abuse in the United States. You can find that information at the following sources:

- The American Society for the Positive Care of Children: You'll find a host of important information and statistics here, along with supplemental information about neglect, abuse, domestic

violence, and more. (https://americanspcc.org/child-abuse-statistics/)
- The National Children's Alliance, National Statistics on Child Abuse: This webpage includes pertinent, eye-opening statistics about abuse and neglect, as well as links to other facts, experts, and tools to help protect children in your care. (http://www.nationalchildrensalliance.org/media-room/media-kit/national-statistics-child-abuse)
- The Centers for Disease Control and Prevention: We've cited the CDC many times throughout this book, and the organization has a wealth of information pertaining to child abuse and neglect, including a facts at a glance cheat sheet that would be ideal for use in starting your team's education in this area. (https://www.cdc.gov/violenceprevention/childmaltreatment/datasources.html)

Icebreaker

This is an icebreaker activity and gives learners permission to talk and share their knowledge. You want learners to understand that you are not an "expert" and they bring ideas and experiences, which can make the training more effective.

- Hand out pieces of paper and pencils/pens. Provide all instructions regarding the activity before learners begin to work in groups.
- Complete the activity yourself in advance and be prepared to share your responses in class.
- After groups are done sharing, introduce yourself and your responses to the class using the same format.

Activity

- Divide the students into groups of not more than four people.

If feasible, have them rearrange the room to facilitate group discussions.

- Have them draw a horizontal and vertical line to create four boxes on the paper.
- In the top-left box, have them draw a picture of what they do for a living. Remind them that they don't have to be good artists. Stick pictures are OK.
- In the top-right box, have them draw what they most value in this world. Suggest a person(s) but avoid Jesus Christ. We know that's true for all Christians.
- In the bottom-left box, have them draw their spiritual gift or God-given talent.
- In the bottom-right box, what role in church or safety team they could fill. (i.e., Child Protection, Equipment Manager, Trainer, Shift Lead, etc.)
- Give every group two to three minutes to draw, and then stop them.
- Then give each group two to three minutes to share amongst themselves.
- Afterwards, share your own drawings and responses with the learners.

Explain to your team members that the purpose of this activity is to understand and recognize that everyone has unique qualities that they can contribute to the church.

What Is Child Abuse?

Now that the ice has been broken, you can move on to the meat of the material. Explain to your team members that we have a duty and an obligation to protect our youngest and most vulnerable members. Read the passage from Matthew 18:6.

Ask learners to read the passage silently. Give them a moment to do it. Once they are done, ask the following:

- What do you understand this passage to mean? What does it say about the care of children?
- If you suspected a child had been abused by someone connected with this church, what would you do?

The Subject of Child Abuse...

Is Difficult and Complex: This is not an easy topic to address, partly because it's so complex. As you will see, there are many kinds of abuse and great care must be taken to protect our children from would-be perpetrators and abusers.

Makes Us Feel Uncomfortable: This is also a topic that makes us uncomfortable. No one likes to think of children being victimized or preyed upon.

Could Scare Away Church Volunteers: There will be people who say the rules are too burdensome, too difficult to follow. They'll say things like, "But you know me. I've been a member of this church for years. Why do I have to jump through all of these hoops?" Or they'll say, "What? Don't you trust me?" Some of the discussions on this topic will cause some of our youth volunteers to walk away, or change their minds about working with your children.

Explain to your volunteers that:

- This training is intended to prepare all of them to fulfill the biblical mandate discussed previously.
- Child abuse is painful and difficult for its victims. Often, people spend years overcoming the psychological scars or the shame associated with abuse they suffered as children. You can't allow anything like that to happen to your children.

- Despite the difficulty of this topic, it is important that you talk about it because it's important for the church to be prepared.

The Definition of Child Abuse

Explain to your team members that the Center for Disease Control (CDC) defines child abuse as: An "intentional act committed by a person in a position of trust (parent, caregiver, or other) which harms or threatens to harm a child's welfare or physical/mental health. It includes both acts of commission (abuse) and omission (neglect)."

Types of Abuse

Experts have identified four categories of child abuse:

- Physical Abuse
- Emotional Abuse
- Neglect
- Sexual Abuse

Let's look at each category in more detail.

Physical Abuse

Physical abuse is the "intentional use of physical force against a child that results in, or has the potential to result in, physical injury." It can include:

- Assault
- Shaking or slapping
- Burning or scalding
- Kicking or strangling

Emotional Abuse

Emotional abuse is "intentional caregiver behavior…that conveys to a child that he/she is worthless, flawed, unloved, unwanted, endangered, or valued only in meeting another's needs." Emotional abuse is an act of commission—something someone actually does to the child, and can include:

- Closed confinement
- Excessive/extreme punishment
- Permitting drug/alcohol abuse
- Verbal humiliation

Neglect

By neglect, we mean the "failure to provide for a child's basic physical, emotional, or educational needs, or the failure to protect a child from harm or potential harm." Neglect is an act of omission; that is, it's not something actively done to the child. Instead, it is something withheld from the child. Harm to the child may or may not have been the intended consequence. Neglect includes any of the following instances of negligence or maltreatment:

- Failure to provide adequate food, shelter, clothing or medical care
- Inadequate supervision, abandonment
- Exposing child to hazardous conditions
- Ignoring needs for nurture/contact

Sexual Abuse

Sexual abuse is "any completed or attempted…sexual act, or sexual contact with…a child by a caregiver." It includes any exploitative behavior such as:

- Inappropriate verbal stimulation
- Fondling, incest, or rape
- Exposing a child to pornography or adult sexual activity

the Problem

ve you an idea of how serious the problem of child abuse is, consider these facts:

- **3 million incidents** of child abuse are reported each year.
- **More than 80% of incidents** are perpetuated by a familiar person. That is, the overwhelming majority of those incidents are carried out by someone the child knows—a family member or trusted caregiver.
- **1 in 3 girls and 1 in 7 boys** are sexually abused by age 18.
- It is the **#1 lawsuit** brought against churches.

This last fact should be particularly troubling. We tend to think of churches as one of the last places where something like this might occur. Yet, this statistic reminds us that we need to always be vigilant.

Signs and Symptoms of Abuse

You just learned the definitions of various kinds of abuse. Now we will discuss how to identify the signs and symptoms of abuse in children, so we can help them. Keep in mind that every child is different and that different children will behave in different ways. Also note that a child suffering from abuse may exhibit behaviors other than those listed here.

Warning Signs

- Fearful of particular people
- Destructive behavior by child towards self, others, property
- Repeated inexplicable injuries
- Severe depression or withdrawal
- Failure to thrive
- Suicide threats
- Eating/speech disorders
- Ill-fitting or inappropriate clothing

- Untreated medical conditions
- Poor hygiene
- Unusually advanced sexual knowledge
- Promiscuous behavior
- Runs away and refuses to return
- Bruising or trauma to vaginal or anal areas
- Frequent ailments and severe fatigue
- Flashbacks
- Difficulty walking or sitting
- Sexually transmitted diseases
- Nightmares with a particular leader as scary character
- Unusual nervousness in being left in settings that were not a problem before
- Unexplained hostility towards worker or another youth
- Disruptions in memory or consciousness
- Unexplained mood swings and distrust
- Fear of the dark, in the case of ritual abuse
- Agitation and despair that occurs in cycles
- Fear of ministers, people in robes, or uniforms

Please note that some of these symptoms will be obvious cases of child abuse (e.g., a child with repeated unexplained physical injuries or with injuries to the genital or anal area). Other symptoms may have other explanations. A youth may have an eating disorder or depression, for example, that has nothing to do with abuse.

For the symptoms that reflect obvious abuse, you should take immediate steps to report the abuse. We'll talk about what to do in the next sections, but for symptoms that could be caused by other factors, be observant and be vigilant. Observe the young person when he/she is around parents, youth leaders, and other adults.

Share your concerns with the Safety Team Leader. Decide on a plan of action. It would be bad to falsely accuse an adult, but it would be worse to fail a young person who needed help. Now, ask if your team members have any questions about the topics covered thus far.

Child Protection Policies

In this section of the course, we're going to look at the some of the policies and procedures churches should have in place to protect children and minimize the possibility of abuse.

Why We Need a Protection Policy

By creating and implementing a Child Protection Policy, we are making a commitment to maintaining our church as it should be—a sanctuary where children and youth are confirmed and strengthened. Creating a plan to prioritize child safety will ensure that the message is continually reinforced to all responsible parties.

Ask your team members: What kinds of things do you think should be included in a Child Protection Policy? After they have answered, explain that there are four essential elements of a Child Protection Policy:

1. Screening Procedures
2. Supervision
3. Reporting
4. Response

Screening Procedures:

Only people who are "authorized" or "certified" should be allowed to work with youth in the church and there should be a screening process to select and vet those people. To become an authorized youth/childcare worker in the church, a person should:

- Complete an application
- Have references thoroughly checked
- Submit to an interview
- Submit to a criminal background check

- Have at least six months of active church membership prior to working with children

Note that the background check should be done using a reliable, trustworthy vendor. The FBI Justice Information Services Division is a good example.

Supervision:

Policies about how authorized workers are to do their jobs can be set up to make it less likely that abuse can occur. For example, you can have policies that prevent adults from being alone in private areas with children, that require more than one adult to be present in most situations, that forbid adults from "friending" youth on social media, etc.

Policies also protect staff and volunteers from unwarranted accusations. These policies protect the children, but also protect adults who work with the children. When the policies are followed, there will be fewer opportunities for adults to take advantage of children. This should result in fewer reasons for anyone to accuse staff and volunteers of inappropriate behavior toward a child.

Anyone in the church responsible for working with children in any way should be fully trained so they know the policies. They should also be required to take refresher courses regularly. We will cover policies that lay the bare minimum in terms of groundwork. You may need to create more stringent policies.

A Note on Training and Accountability

Training and accountability should be part of the supervision process for anyone working with youth or in any childcare capacity. Training and accountability should include the following:

Have a Code of Conduct: The church should have a written code of conduct for working with young people, for the training and supervision of those who work with young people, and for the reporting and handling of suspected cases of abuse. All authorized workers should sign and be familiar with the code of conduct. Having adults sign a paper serves as a strong commitment mechanism.

Provide Ongoing Training for Adults: Regular, refresher training will be important.

Conduct Performance Reviews: No one working with children in the church should consider their job permanent. Instead, they should expect to have regular performance reviews to make sure they are following established procedures. Performance reviews allow the church to be able to reinforce proper behavior and/or remove someone who repeatedly puts the church at risk by violating procedures.

Create an Accountability Structure: Everyone who works with children in the church should have a supervisor or manager – someone who is responsible for keeping tabs on their performance and on what is going on inside all of the youth activities.

Suggested Policies for Activities

Below, we've provided some suggested policies that can easily be implemented to increase the safety and security of youth within the church.

- Youth activities should ALWAYS take place in public locations. For example: No youth activities held at someone's home without other non-related adults present.
- Two or more authorized youth workers should ALWAYS be present. At least two authorized workers must always be on hand. The two should not be related. If the group involves children of both genders, there should be adults of both genders as well.
- Adults should NEVER meet with youth one-on-one in a private location. No conferences with youth held behind closed doors—unless the room has windows so all activities are visible. Disciplinary or counseling sessions should be held in a private area of

a public, open space. For instance, talk with the youth quietly in the hallway or in an office with the door open. Two adults should be present in the conference, if at all possible.

- When there are not enough adults to have two in every activity, an acceptable alternative is to have a "roamer" – an authorized adult or Church Safety Team member who is designated to float between all youth activities and show up at will, unannounced.
- The Child Protection Policy should include rules for what to do if a child needs to leave the activity area. Here are some suggested policies:
  - Children under nine should always be accompanied by an adult. If a child under nine years of age must temporarily leave the classroom or activity, they must be escorted by an authorized youth/childcare worker or official helper. The adult escorting the child should always inform another adult before leaving with the child.
  - Children ages 10 to 15 years old should be monitored. If a child in this age range must temporarily leave the classroom or activity, they must advise where they are going and when they will return. The authorized youth/childcare worker should note when the student leaves and look for them if they do not return on time/in a timely manner.
  - Children ages 16 to 17 may come and go with parental permission. These children may have the freedom to come and go as they like, so long as they have parental permission and their comings and goings are not distractive to the other children.
  - Any child 15 years old or younger permanently leaving the class or activity should be escorted by an authorized youth/childcare worker.

Variations of these rules should extend to adults having a youth in a vehicle (e.g., giving a youth a ride home from a church activity) or being with a youth on an activity off-campus. There should be very clear rules about

113

hotel rooms and sleeping arrangements for overnight trips with youth.

Rules for Documentation

We've mentioned rules for documenting children coming and going and for other needs. In this section, we'll detail a few of the most important ones to implement. Written records help keep the children safe, and they also protect the adults supervising them. At a minimum, documentation should include the following:

- Date & Time of Check-in/Check-out: Documentation should include when each child checked in to the activity area and when each child left.
- Special instructions & Medication: This includes any special care instructions from the parent and all medical concerns for each child.
- Communication with Parents: Any conversations or discussions with the parent about care of the child should be documented.
- Who Has Access to the Child: Persons who were responsible for and have access to each child should be documented. Also, court-appointed custody restrictions should be in church records, and should be known to the authorized child care workers.
- Incident Reports: All incidents, including accidents, injuries, fights, discipline, and abuse, should be documented.
- Records of Which Adults Were on Duty: Scheduling records— showing who was on duty in which areas, and that multiple adults where in each room—should also be kept.

In addition to everything we've talked about, the church may also want to develop additional policies, including:

- Substance Use Policy: Substance use should be prohibited at all youth events.
- Social Media Policy: Establish clear technology policies regard-

ing child-adult interactions. For example, do not allow adults to become Facebook "friends" with children.

- Cell Phone/Communication Policy: Similarly, under what circumstances is an adult allowed to contact a youth directly on the child's cell phone. It may make sense to allow this to facilitate young people being picked up or dropped off for activities, but this should be up to the church. In all cases, parental permission should be required.
- Privacy Policy: Prohibit camera use in bathrooms or locker rooms. Preserve a child's privacy as much as possible.

Reporting:

To recap where we are: We are discussing the four elements of a Child Protection Policy. We've looked at screening and supervision. The third element is reporting. This has to do with who must be alerted, how, and when, if there is a known or suspected case of child abuse. The general rules are as follows:

- Accusations must be dealt with speedily and according to policy. Once an incident of child abuse occurs or allegation of an incident is made, it is crucial that it be dealt with quickly and in a clearly outlined manner.
- Adults are REQUIRED to report any known or alleged cases of abuse. If you, or another staff member, ministry team leader or authorized youth/childcare worker observes abuse or is informed about abuse, you are required to report it.

If a child comes forward with a claim of abuse:

- Stay calm.
- Let the child tell what happened. Encourage the child to tell what happened in his or her own words, without adults in the room being aggressive or overbearing.

- Reassure the child. Let the child know they did the right thing.
- Follow procedure for reporting abuse.

Now, let's review what to do when you must report an incident of child abuse. There's a five-step process:

- Inform
- Contact authorities
- Report
- Document
- Respond

The important part to remember is this: If you learn of abuse, you must report it.

Step 1 – Inform

- Appropriate people inside the church should be informed immediately.
- Report the incident right away to the Lead Pastor, the appropriate Ministry Director and the Church Safety Director.
- They will attempt to obtain necessary information such as the name of the alleged victim, his/her address and family information.

As you can see, the first step when you learn about abuse is to inform those in charge. The church's Child Safety Policy should identify those who would be contacted in the event of such an incident. Now, ask your team member, if you learned about abuse in our church, what people inside the church would you contact?

Step 2 – Contact Authorities

Once you have alerted those who will take charge of the situation, they will contact the authorities and begin an investigation.

- If there is a fresh crime scene where evidence may be collected or it is reasonable to believe further abuse could be imminent, immediately notify local law enforcement.

- If not, call the county's Health and Human Services Department to make a report.
- In either event, take the necessary steps required to complete this task as quickly as possible.

Step 3 – Report

Next, an official written report of the suspected abuse must be filed with the county's Health and Human Services Department. This line of reporting should be followed in all cases, even if the events, activities, or persons involved are not connected with the church. (Example: If we suspect a child is being abused at home, or we become aware of possible abuse involving a child whose family does not belong to our church.)

Step 4 – Document

Once a report is submitted externally to the relevant authorities, the incident must be documented internally as well.

- Written incident reports should be filed by any staff member, ministry team leader, authorized youth/childcare worker, or Church Safety Team member who has knowledge or information about the alleged incident.
- These reports should be filed within 24 hours.

Step 5 – Respond

- Take all allegations seriously.
- Demonstrate a quick, compassionate and unified response.
- All church personnel should assist investigating agencies. All staff, interns, authorized youth/childcare workers and adults present at the church activity where the alleged abuse took place

or where it was reported should assist the agencies that conduct the official investigation.

The church's response to such allegations is crucial. Anyone who can be of assistance to the investigating authorities is expected to do so. Ask your team members, what does a bad response look like? What does a compassionate church response look like?

Response Plan

The response plan for handling alleged incidents of abuse should include the following elements:

Responding to the Media: Only one person should speak on behalf of the church. The Lead Pastor or his designee should be the only person authorized to make statements to representatives of the media. All requests for statements should be directed to the Lead Pastor. Everyone else should demonstrate a spirit of cooperation in helping the media get in touch with the "official spokesperson."

Alerting Caregivers: If the allegation is against a member of the staff, a ministry team leader, an authorized youth/childcare worker, helper or other person, the custodial parent should be notified immediately. A face-to-face meeting with the parent should be scheduled. Pastoral support should be available to all persons involved with the incident as indicated.

Handling the Accused: Any person who is the subject of the report should be required to refrain from all church youth activities until the incident is resolved. Care should be taken in the removal of a person from church youth activities. It should be done in a discreet manner, recognizing that an investigation is still being conducted.

Assisting with the Investigation: If the alleged offender is a staff member, intern or authorized youth/childcare worker, that person should initiate contact with the county's Health and Human Services Department to resolve the allegation in as soon as possible. We highly encourage seeking legal counsel.

Once finished with this section, ask your team members what questions they have about the Abuse Reporting Plan.

Review and Discussion

We covered a great deal of material, and it's very important that we understand it. It's important to review the five steps involved in the reporting of abuse. A group activity will work well for this.

Assemble the learners into five groups. Each group should consist of at least one person. If the class has fewer than five learners, do this activity as a large group rather than as five smaller groups.

Assign one of the steps in the Abuse Response Plan to each group. Ask them to review their notes and be prepared to explain what should happen in their assigned step. Give the groups one to two minutes to work on this.

Call on one group at a time, in number order and ask them to explain what should happen in their assigned step. For example, call on Group 1. Ask them to explain what happens in the "Inform" step of the Abuse Response Plan. Write their responses on a flip chart or chalk board. Allow others outside the group to add anything Group 1 has left out.

Continue in this manner with Groups 2 through 5 until the entire Abuse Response Plan has been reviewed.

If there are fewer than five learners in the class, do this activity as one big group. That is, simply ask all learners to review their notes and tell you what happens in the "Inform" step of the Abuse Response Plan. Write their answers on a flipchart or chalkboard. Make sure everything is covered, then continue with the next step of the plan, until all five steps have been covered.

Explain to your team members that it is crucial that they be able to recognize warning signs and know what to do in the event of an incident. Remember, preparation is key. Ask them, what questions do you have about the Abuse Reporting Plan, or anything else we've talked about today?

Discussion

Facilitate a brief discussion on how the topic of child abuse might be raised in your church. Ask your team members:

As we start setting up policies and procedures to protect our children, there will likely be people in the church who will object. What are some of the objections our church members are likely to raise?

Possible answers you will receive include:

- This kind of thing would never happen in our church.
- This kind of thing doesn't happen in our community.
- Our congregation is so close knit. Everyone knows everyone else.
- I've been working with the children in this church for years. Why do I have to start doing all of this checking and documenting?
- It sounds like you don't trust us.

Next, ask your team, what should we say when people raise these objections? What's a good way to answer some of these objections? Listen to their answers and clarify or guide as necessary.

Use this discussion to help learners develop helpful ways of talking with church members about this issue and about the need for child safety policies. If necessary, take the objections one by one and come up with some good responses to each of them. Bring the class to a close by answering any final questions they have. Thank the learners for participating, and close with a prayer of thanks.

Chapter 11:
Arson and Fire Threats

Churches face a great many threats. Many of those are natural – earthquakes and the like, for instance. However, just as many are perpetrated at the hands of human beings. Two of the most frustrating and frightening threats are vandalism and arson. While these are very different from one another, they both rob the body of believers of their confidence and strength.

What Is Arson?

To truly understand these threats, we need to first define them.

Arson: Turning to the same two sources once more, we find that Merriam-Webster defines arson as, "The willful or malicious burning of property (such as a building) especially with criminal or fraudulent intent." The Cambridge English Dictionary defines it similarly as, "The crime of intentionally starting a fire in order to damage or destroy something, especially a building."

So, arson involves intentional damage or destruction. In addition, it carries with it the potential for loss of life if the structure is occupied when the arsonist strikes, as well as the potential for massive loss of value (a fire consuming everything within the church, as well as the church building itself).

In this chapter, we will walk you through planning and preparedness for handling both arson and fire threats. We will also touch on how to evacuate in case of a fire, whether it starts accidentally, or is intentionally set.

Fire Evacuations in the Church

Emergency evacuation plans are an important part of church safety. There are many important differences to understand in terms of evacuating due to a violent intruder, bomb threat, or fire.

Types of Evacuations

We discussed the four types of evacuation in a previous chapter, but we'll review them again below:

- Protective: Relocating people prior to a danger before an impending event such as a hurricane.
- Preventative: Relocating people quickly and in less distance due to a danger such as a bomb threat.
- Rescue: Removing people from an environment following an emergency such as a fire.
- Reconstructive: Moving people from one environment to another for continued care such as "moving evacuees to camps or temporary housing programs".

All evacuation types require detailed planning and practice. Hold practice drills for each type of evacuation. Everyone needs to understand whether to seek shelter or to leave the building immediately.

Christensen, Blair, and Holt (2007) listed three overlying factors in all evacuations. They are provided below verbatim from the source (Christensen, Blair, and Holt, 2007, p. 250):

1. The behavior(s) of the individual
2. The planned systems active in the event
3. The environment in which the event occurs

These factors should be considered when planning evacuation procedures. As previously discussed, people can be expected to behave similarly to how others behaved in similar crises. As a refresher, remember that people's thinking is impaired when they are in emergency situations (Prati et al., 2013, p. 770). Prati et al. (2013) found that people do not consistently correctly identify gestures made by first responders.

Specifically, gestures indicating "Move back" or "Stop" were not understood (Prati et al., 2013, p. 768). Therefore, it would be helpful to familiarize church attendees with common first responder gestures during practice evaluations. This familiarization could take place in any number of ways – as part of Sunday School, or after a Wednesday night potluck dinner, for instance.

Creating Evacuation Procedures

There are general steps that church safety team leaders should perform when planning evacuation procedures (Pandolfo, 2015, pp. 36-37):

- Plan
- Purchase equipment
- Train staff
- Conduct drills

We thoroughly explored those areas in Chapter 8, so please see that section if you feel that a further refresher is needed on general evacuation planning.

Fire Evacuations

Fire evacuations require additional planning as compared to general evacuations. Fires need three elements to be present in order to grow and consume:

- Oxygen
- Heat
- Fuel

If one of those elements is missing, there cannot be a fire. This fact is important to Church Safety Team members because understanding the basics of fire science will help explain why it is important to look for specific conditions that may cause a fire. This section explains general fire hazards but can't cover them all. It is up to the Church Safety Team members to use their knowledge and discretion to identify fire risks.

Fire produces light, heat, flame, and smoke. In fire deaths, smoke is the primary killer (Bush, 2015). Depending on what is burning, deadly chemicals can also be released into the air. It is important to conduct consistent fire safety inspections of the following to reduce the risk of fire and to reduce the risk of injury should a fire occur:

- Fire hazards
- Doorways
- Hallways
- Stairways
- Fire exit signs
- Emergency lights
- Alarm pulls
- Fire extinguishers

Fire Hazards

Below, we've compiled a list of some of the most common fire hazards. However, remember that this list is not exhaustive. It merely includes common examples. During your safety assessment, checking for fire hazards specific to your property is vital. Some threats include:

- Overflowing dumpsters and piles of debris are invitations to arsonists.
- Overloaded wall sockets or extension cords underneath rugs can create electrical fires.
- Unattended stoves can cause fires.

- Storage lockers, sheds, and garages can become areas where people dump garbage and other items with little care.
- Flammable liquids that are improperly stored are a fire risk.
- Every church has a smoking area, even if it is not officially designated as such. Watch the building to find where people smoke. Oftentimes, they will be around garbage dumpsters because they tend to be out of the way and hidden from general view. Wherever people gather to smoke, the area should have a proper disposal for cigarettes.

Doorways

Check for locked or blocked exits. Fire doors should have a breaker bar and open outward, not inward. They should never be locked; people should always be able to exit from inside.

Doors should also be checked to ensure there is nothing blocking them from opening. Doors should never be propped open. Many fire doors have magnetic holders that release when a fire alarm is activated. These doors close to choke off the fire from oxygen and slow the spread of the fire.

If the doors fail to close because they were propped open, then smoke and fire could spread quickly and reduce the time to evacuate. If doors do not have magnetic holders, they should be left closed at all times.

Hallways

Hallways should be cleared of items that would impede people evacuating the building. Fire exits, including doors and hallways, are rated based on how many people can effectively evacuate through the area. Chairs, ladders, tables, and other items stored in the area reduce that number.

Stairways

Items such as plants, bookshelves, and tables should not be placed in stairwells. Stairs should also be clear from other items that may become tripping hazards.

Fire Exit Signs, Emergency Lights, and Alarm Pulls

Fire exit signs and emergency lights must be in working order at all times. Check them regularly for operation. They run on battery backup which ensures they will work even during a power outage.

Check the signs and lights by pressing the test buttons. Check that lights are pointed correctly and operable. Finally, make sure that all fire alarm pulls are functional and not obstructed.

Fire Extinguishers

Fire extinguishers should be easily seen, and access to them should be unobstructed. The labels with operating directions should be pointed outwards so they can be easily read. Understand the fire extinguishers' specific purposes, and inspect them regularly to ensure operability.

Purposes

Fire extinguishers come in various sizes and types, so it is important to read the labels of the fire extinguishers your church owns. The fire extinguishers were put there based on fire code so they are the correct fire extinguishers for the most common fires in your building.

However, it is still very important to read the labels. The letters on a fire extinguisher indicate the class of fuel against which the fire extinguisher could be effectively used (South Brazos County Fire Department, 2013; "Fire Extinguisher Types," 2016):

- Class A — An ordinary combustible including wood, paper, rubber, or plastic

- Class B — Flammable liquids such as oil, alcohol, and gasoline
- Class C — Electrical equipment
- Class D — Reactive metals
- Class K — Mostly for kitchen fires, especially cooking oils and fats

The numbers on the extinguisher label indicate the relative effectiveness of the fire extinguisher based on size of fire. For Class A fires, the number indicates how many gallons of water the extinguisher is comparable to. Each number is 1.25 gallons, so a Class 1-A is equivalent to 1.25 gallons of water and Class 2-A is equivalent to 2.5 gallons (South Brazos County Fire Department, 2013).

For Class B fires, the number indicates the approximate square foot area that the extinguisher can treat, so Class 1-B extinguisher could put out one square foot of flammable liquid and a Class 540-B extinguisher could put out 540 square feet of flammable liquid (South Brazos County Fire Department, 2013).

Placement

The National Fire Protection Association has given several guidelines about the placement of fire extinguishers. The "maximum travel distance" should not exceed the following (Great American Insurance Group, 2016):

- 75 feet for Class A or Class D hazards
- 50 feet for Class B hazards
- 30 feet for Class K hazards

Additionally, fire extinguishers weighing 40 pounds or less should be hung no higher than five feet from the ground, and fire extinguishers weighing more than 40 pounds should be hung no higher than three feet from the ground (Great American Insurance Group, 2016).

Inspections

Inspect fire extinguishers on a regular basis. The first type of inspection is a quick check, which can be conducted by anyone in the church and should be done monthly. The second type of inspection is a thorough check and must be completed by a certified inspector annually.

Quick Check: A quick check ensures that the fire extinguishers are available and will function. The following information from the University of California San Diego (2014) is provided verbatim from the source ("Fire extinguisher inspection checklist," 2014):

- Confirm the extinguisher is visible, unobstructed, and in its designated location.
- Verify the locking pin is intact and the tamper seal is unbroken. Examine the extinguisher for obvious physical damage, corrosion, leakage, or clogged nozzle.
- Confirm the pressure gauge or indicator is in the operable range or position, and lift the extinguisher to ensure it is still full.
- Make sure the operating instructions on the nameplate are legible and facing outward.
- Check the last professional service date on the tag. (A licensed fire extinguisher maintenance contractor must have inspected the extinguisher within the past 12 months.)
- Initial and date the back of the tag.

Thorough Check: A thorough check should be completed by a certified inspector annually. The tag will be attached indicating the month and year the maintenance was performed and the identification of the person performing the work.

RACE: What to Do During Fire Evacuations

If there is a fire in the church, respond by using the acronym RACE: Rescue, Alert Others, Confine the Fire, Evacuate and/or Extinguish (Kiurski, 2008).

Rescue

The first step is rescue. Evacuate people from the immediate area surrounding the fire. This could include a person on fire. The key is to not panic or run.

Wrap the person in a blanket if one is available. Have the person roll side to side, assisting him/her if necessary. Once the fire is out, keep the injured person calm and notify emergency medical personnel.

Alert

Next, alert the proper authorities. Know where alarm pulls are located and how to operate them. Call 911 and make sure to press send. In a crisis, some people can forget how to operate their cell phones.

Advise the 911 dispatcher of the nature of the emergency, your name, and your location. Stay on the phone until the dispatcher hangs up. While the dispatcher is talking, he or she is entering the information into a computer and alerting first responders about the call.

In most situations, first responders are dispatched before you even hang up the phone. Your church may also want to consider using two-way radios. This is a good way to alert other team members, staff, and volunteers.

Confine

Confine the fire by closing all doors and windows around the affected area to choke the fire of any air and to slow the spread of flames and smoke.

Defending the Flock

Evacuate

Evacuate the church if the fire cannot be controlled or if the congregation is in any danger. There are two types of fire evacuation: preventative, which is a partial evacuation of the immediate area and rescue, which is removing everyone from the church.

Check doors and routes prior to evacuation. When evacuating, go past the smoke and fire doors. Look for smoke, feel for heat, and be careful of hot metal. Brace a foot and a shoulder against the door and open it slowly.

If there is smoke and/or fire, have everyone keep low and cover their faces. Do not run. Close all doors as you pass through them. Move 100 feet away from the building to the assembly area. Do not allow anyone to return to the building.

A Note on Elevators

Do not use elevators unless they are emergency elevators or fire fighters assure you they are safe. It's important to know if the elevators in the building are usable during fires. See Chapter 8 for more information about emergency elevators, and related information.

Trapped in the Building

If people are trapped in the building, have them move away from the fire, close doors between them and the fire, and seal vents to reduce smoke. They should stay low to avoid smoke and heat. Have them call 911 and stay on the line.

If you are with a disabled person, remain with them as long as it is safe. However, it is conceivable that you may have to evacuate to save yourself with the knowledge there is nothing at all you can do to help the other person.

Consider alternate means of escape, such as windows. A broken leg is better than no escape. If it is possible to lower the other person out the window, then lower him/her as far as possible before dropping him/her.

Evacuating Children

Evacuating the nursery can be a real challenge. Oftentimes, the adult to child ratio makes it difficult for the workers to evacuate all children. Nursery workers should ensure all doors are closed and they should remain calm because help is on the way.

Churches need to develop a plan to address nursery evacuations and consider adult to child ratio and the availability of fire crib strollers and wagons. Ushers and Church Safety Team members should assist in the evacuation.

Extinguish

If the fire is small, use fire extinguishers to fight the flames. When there is a fire, the closest Church Safety Team member should grab the nearest fire extinguisher. Other responding Church Safety Team members should grab fire extinguishers closest to them and respond to the fire.

Using a fire extinguisher is not complex if you can remember the acronym PASS (National Fire Protection Association, 2012):

- (P)ull the pin—pointing the nozzle away from yourself—and release the locking mechanism.
- (A)im low at the base of the fire.
- (S)queeze the handle.
- (S)weep the hose from side to side.

When fighting Class A fires, aim the extinguisher at the base of the fire and move it up and out. For Class B fires, aim at the base of the fire and "spread along the surface of the liquid, not into it" (South Brazos County Fire Department). Do not use fire extinguishers for fires over your head. If the room fills with smoke, leave immediately (National Fire

Protection Association, 2012). Fires have a way of growing and restarting, so do not leave an extinguished fire unattended even if you believe it is completely out (unless it is unsafe to stay there).

After the fire, never rehang a partially discharge fire extinguisher. Report missing and discharged fire extinguishers to building maintenance.

Planning for Evacuations of the Disabled and Elderly

Although most church members are able to attend church with minimal support (such as having a caretaker pushing a wheelchair or helping the person walk), the lessons nursing home administrators have learned in previous emergencies can be beneficial to church safety team members who create emergency plans for their congregations. Refer to Chapter 8 for more information about evacuating the elderly and/or disabled.

Teaching the Content

We estimate it should take about two hours to teach the content covered in this section. We've included a general outline to follow for teaching your team members below. Remember that this outline can and should be customized to your unique needs, situation, church body and building, and other considerations.

Ice Breaker Activity

The purpose of this activity is to "break the ice" and give learners permission to talk and share their knowledge.

Step 1. Create a list of common fire safety equipment and activities people use in their homes.
Step 2. Ask learners to list on a piece of paper the fire safety equipment and activities they use in their own home. Note: They are welcome to list things that are not shown on the list.

Step 3. Ask each learner to get a partner—preferably someone they don't know well.

Step 4. Have the partners exchange information and discuss what they do at home to keep themselves and their families safe from fire. Give them one to two minutes to do this.

Step 5. Call the group back to order and ask some of the partners to share the fire safety activities they came up with.

Step 6. Ask some questions of the group to get them thinking and talking. For example:

- Why is it important to pay attention to fire safety in the home?
- How often do you check your smoke detector batteries?
- Has anyone here ever conducted a family fire drill? [If yes, ask them to describe how they did it and how it went. If no one has ever done it, ask why not.]
- Is there anyone here who doesn't do any of these things? [If yes, gently ask them to explain why. They're likely to say they're too busy, never thought about it, been meaning to, didn't think it was important, etc. Whatever they say, thank them for being honest with their answer.]

Explain to your team members that, sometimes we do take fire safety for granted. We think a fire is something that can never happen to us. In fact, the reason for training is that many churches take fire safety for granted. However, the fact is, fires do happen and they can happen anywhere.

With a little effort, we can lower the risk of fire in any church and ensure that if there is a fire, people will not panic because they will know what to do. Ask your learners, what questions do you have before we get into the lesson?

The Basics of Fire Science

Explain to your learners that they will begin this course by giving a basic introduction to fire science and the different kinds of fire.

The Components of Fire

For a fire to develop, three components must be present:

- Oxygen
- Heat
- Fuel

Oxygen, of course, is present all the time in normal situations; it's in the air. By fuel, we mean, there must be something to burn. In everyday, common household fires, that's often paper, trash, wood, cloth, etc. Fuel for fire is also available almost everywhere. The classroom, for example, is full of things that could be fuel in a fire.

The third component that fire needs is heat. When oxygen and fuel are present and enough heat is added, a fire can erupt. That heat can come from a match, a lit cigarette, lightning or other electricity, a stove, a space heater, a faulty furnace, etc.

If any one of these components—oxygen, fuel, heat—is not present, or is taken away, the fire cannot survive. Fire prevention involves controlling or mitigating the interaction of these three components. Much of what you will do on the Church Safety Team involves fire prevention—making sure the components necessary for fire are absent or removed.

Firefighting requires the removal of one of these three components. For the most part, that is the role of fire department, although we will be talking today about fire extinguishers and how they can be used to fight a small, contained fire.

The By-Products of Fire

Explain to your learners that fire produces:

- Light
- Heat
- Flames
- Smoke

Most fire deaths are caused by smoke inhalation—not by burns. Depending on what's burning and how close people are to the fire, the inhalation of smoke can incapacitate people quickly—so quickly that they are unable to get to nearby exits.
Toxic aspects of smoke include:

- **Carbon Monoxide** – An otherwise odorless, colorless gas which can be deadly even in small amounts
- **Hydrogen Cyanide** – A by-product of burning certain types of plastics, which can interfere with breathing
- **Particles** – Tiny, partially burned substances which can damage the lungs if inhaled
- **Vapor** – Fog-like moisture that is poisonous to inhale and toxic if absorbed through the skin

In other words, the smoke produced by fire is toxic and can kill or severely injure people in the area of a fire.

Effects of Reduced Oxygen

Explain to your learners that fire can also kill because it reduces the amount of oxygen in the air. Normally, the air we breathe is about 21% oxygen. However, a fire can consume the oxygen in the air, lowering that percentage. Also, the air can fill up with the toxic gases we just discussed, lowering the percentage of oxygen that way.
As the bullet points below illustrate, a small reduction in the percentage of oxygen in the air can have deadly consequences.

- When the percentage of oxygen in the air drops below 17%, people become confused with diminished capacity to make good decisions. They may have trouble finding the exits even when they are familiar with the building.

- As the percentage of oxygen decreases, victims begin to get sick and may lose consciousness.
- Death occurs when the percentage of oxygen drops below 9%.

It's important to remember these facts if you are ever in a fire emergency. To minimize smoke inhalation during a fire, cover your nose and mouth (with a damp cloth if possible) and keep low to the ground. There will be more oxygen closer to the floor.

If necessary, crawl to the exit. We'll come back to this in a few minutes when we talk about fire evacuation. Ask your learners, what questions they have so far about fires and the dangers of smoke inhalation.

Types of Fires

Explain to your students that fire can be categorized based on the kind of fuel that is burning. Let's take a look at each type of fire.

Class "A"

Class A fires are fires that are fueled by everyday combustibles like wood, cloth, paper, or trash. A small fire in a trash receptacle is likely to be a Class A fire.

Class "B"

Class B fires involve flammable liquids, gases, solvents, and petroleum products. This might include gasoline, cleaning solvents, propane, oil, or paint thinner. This type of fire might be "runny" or "liquidy" if the fuel is a liquid.

Class "C"

Class C fires involve live electrical equipment. This might include computers or fires started by overloaded electrical outlets.

Class "D"

Class D fires involve burning metals and alloys like sodium, potassium, magnesium, lithium, titanium, or zirconium. This type of fire is not very common in homes or churches, although you might see it in factories and industrial situations, or in schools and colleges with science labs.

Class "K"

Class K fires Involve vegetable oil or animal fat at very high temperatures. Typically, only commercial deep fat fryers can heat fats enough to start a Class K fire. If your church has a commercial deep fat fryer in the kitchen, there should be a fire extinguisher that is rated for Class K fires.

Extinguishers: Read the Label

You may never have noticed this before, but fire extinguishers are always marked with the letters, colors, symbols or pictograms of the types of fires they can extinguish.

Ask someone in the class to explain what kinds of burning fuel this extinguisher can put out.

Answer: This extinguisher works on A, B, and C type fires. That includes common everyday paper, trash, wood and cloth. It also includes solvents, cleaning fluids, oils, and propane. It can also put out electrical fires.

In all likelihood, the fire extinguishers around the church will also be rated A-B-C. Ask your learners why the church probably does not have any D-rated fire extinguishers?

Answer: D-rated extinguishers put out combustible metals like magnesium, lithium, and titanium. It's not so likely we would have a fire like that around the church.

Review: Types of Fires

Study these classes of fires and their colors and symbols. Commit them to memory. Having this information in your head could help save a life in a fire emergency. Ask your learners what questions they have before leaving this section of the course.

Conducting Safety Inspections

Three-Pronged Approach to Fire Safety

Fire inspections will help you minimize the possibility of a fire happening in the first place. The Fire Response Plan describes what you will do in the event of a fire to minimize loss of life and damage.

Earlier we talked about the difference between fire prevention and firefighting. We said that firefighting involves putting out fires, but that fire prevention is about making sure fires don't happen in the first place. That's the job of the Church Safety Team: taking steps to minimize the likelihood of a fire breaking out in the first place and taking steps to minimize loss of life and damage if a fire should happen.

There are three ways you will do this:

1. Fire Inspections
2. Fire Response Plan
3. Education & Drills

Education and drills allow the Church Safety Team to learn and practice what to do in case of fire. Education and drills also allow the Church Safety Team to instruct church leaders and members how to prevent fires and what to do if a fire breaks out. For the remainder of this section, we'll be looking at these three ways you will carry out your fire prevention role—starting with Fire Inspections.

Fire Safety Inspections

The Church Safety Team should conduct regular fire inspections. Most public buildings and workplaces are required to have inspections conducted by the fire marshal or by OSHA (the Occupational Safety and

Health Administration) on a regular basis. The Church Safety Team should do inspections in between the ones mandated by the authorities.

How often you do them probably depends on the size of your physical facilities and the number of people on your safety team. During inspections, make sure to do the following:

- Check fire safety equipment: One purpose of these inspections is to check that fire safety equipment is where it should be and is operational.
- Identify and correct fire hazards: Another purpose is to watch for fire hazards. Many churches are busy places where members come and go throughout the week. Members may, without thinking, pile boxes in front of a fire extinguisher or move a piece of furniture so that it blocks an emergency exit.

Regular inspections allow you to spot these mistakes and fix them. You may also have the opportunity to gently correct or educate church members when you see them doing things like this.

Fire Inspection Checklist

A fire inspection should include an examination of:

- Buildings and Grounds
- Hallways and Exits
- Electrical
- Kitchen
- Extinguishers and Protective Equipment

Let's talk about what to look for in each of these categories.

Building and Grounds: Trash receptacles inside and outside the building should be emptied on a regular basis. There should never be trash overflowing or piled outside of trash containers. For church events (e.g., a picnic on church grounds) thought should be given in advance to how the extra trash will be collected and stored until pick up.

Defending the Flock

Most churches don't encourage or allow smoking on church grounds. However, if your church does, be certain there are proper fire-proof receptacles for cigarette butts near each entrance. As we've discussed, fire needs fuel in order to burn. Boxes of paper, piles of discarded files or classroom materials make excellent fuel for fire. If you spot anything like this in offices, classrooms, or outside, take steps to have it removed.

Combustible materials like cleaning fluids, solvents, paint thinner, etc. are also a fire hazard and must be properly stored. Be certain that the lighting near the main exits and near emergency exits is adequate.

Here's what to look for during a fire safety inspection of the buildings and grounds:

- No overflowing trash containers or dumpsters
- Proper disposal containers for cigarette butts
- Grounds free of combustible and hazardous materials
- Exit areas well lit
- Exit areas free of ice and snow

The custodial staff usually clears ice and snow from the main entrance. But also be sure that ice and snow are being cleared from around emergency exits. You want to be sure that nothing prevents people from leaving the building safely and quickly through a fire exit.

Hallways and Exits: Are all exits clearly marked? Pay particular attention to emergency exits. People are not likely to know where they are. In an emergency, would they be able to find them?

Here's what to look for during a fire safety inspection of the buildings and grounds:

- Exit signs visible and lit
- Adequate lighting in stairwells and corridors
- Emergency lighting works when tested
- Exit doors easy to open, self-closing, and well lit
- Corridors and stairwells free of clutter and combustible material

Verify that lighting is adequate. Work with the custodial staff to correct any deficiencies. Test emergency lighting to make certain that lights come on when power is shut off to the main lighting.

Arrange for the immediate servicing of any defective emergency lighting equipment. Emergency exit doors should open outward, should be easy to open, and should close on their own. Arrange for immediate repair or servicing of exit doors if they don't work as they should.

Sometimes church members use hallways or stairways to store extra furniture, file cabinets, papers or boxes. In addition to being a fire hazard, these items can also be in the way if people need to leave the building quickly. Take immediate steps to remove any clutter or combustible materials in hallways or stairwells.

Electrical: There should be no frayed electrical cords, and no equipment that is overloaded. No equipment that is blowing fuses or if otherwise being used inappropriately. Watch for the overuse of power strips or extension cords. Look for outlets where someone has added an adaptor so they can plug in several appliances.

Similarly, make sure that appliance cords and extension cords never run under rugs or anywhere where they cannot be monitored or could set fire to building materials. In older buildings, members often use space heaters to warm up cold areas. If your church is in this situation, develop a procedure for monitoring the use of space heaters (e.g., Church Safety Team member assigned to check on the area or stay nearby).

Here's what to look for during a fire safety inspection for electrical issues:

- All electrical equipment appears in good condition
- Minimal use of extension cords and multi-plug adapters
- No electrical cords running under rugs, through walls or ceilings
- Control use of space heaters
- No broken or faulty switches or outlets

Make certain that all light switches and electrical outlets work. Arrange for an electrician to inspect and repair any that do not. Many older buildings lack the electrical capacity for the number of electronic gadgets we use today. There may not be enough places to plug in appliances or the wiring may not support what church members want to plug in.

If you frequently find electrical issues—too many extension cords, too many items plugged into one outlet, over-reliance on space heaters, etc.—make church leaders aware of the potential fire hazards. Do whatever you can to get funds allotted for needed upgrades.

Kitchen: Here's what to look for during a fire safety inspection of the kitchen:

- Stove clean and in good repair
- Hood and deep fat fryer, if applicable, clean and in good repair
- Commercial range has easily accessible emergency fuel shut off
- Type "K" fire extinguisher within 30' of deep fat fryer, if applicable

Fire Extinguishers: 6-Step Inspection

Your fire safety inspection should include an inspection of the fire extinguishers. Fire extinguishers should be inspected and serviced by a professional every 12 months. The Church Safety Team should do regular inspections of the extinguishers in between the professional visits. Here's a summary of the six steps involved in an extinguisher inspection:

1. Verify placement of extinguisher
2. Check readability of nameplate and instructions
3. Check the locking pin and tamper seal
4. Check reading on the pressure gauge
5. Visually examine the body for signs of damage
6. Verify last professional service date

Let's look at each of these steps in detail.

Step 1 - Placement

To prevent the extinguisher from being moved, the Occupational Safety and Health Administration (OSHA) recommends that it be mounted on the wall with brackets or placed inside of a cabinet. Make sure each extinguisher is where it's supposed to be. (Make sure, for example, that some church member is not using it somewhere as a doorstop!)

The extinguisher should be easy for the average person to reach. The handle should be 3.5 to 5 feet above the floor. Larger extinguishers should be mounted lower. Make sure that the extinguisher is unobstructed by anything.

Step 2 - Nameplate and Instructions

Verify that the nameplate and instructions are readable. Notice the letters and symbols on the label. In a fire emergency, someone who has never used a fire extinguisher might try to use one. If there are no instructions, or the instructions are not readable, the extinguisher should be replaced.

Earlier, we talked about the different classes of fires and the letters, colors, and symbols that correspond to each type of fire. Ensure that the extinguisher is rated for the proper type of fire. Your local fire marshal should be able to help you determine the right extinguishers for your needs.

Step 3 - Locking Pin and Tamper Seal

Check the locking pin and tamper seal. If the locking pin has been pulled or the tamper seal has been broken, someone has used the extinguisher or has been playing around with it. It should be serviced or replaced.

Step 4 - Pressure Gauge

Verify that the extinguisher is properly charged. The gauge should be in the green zone. If the extinguisher does not have a gauge, do a "heft" test. Depending on how the extinguisher works, it may not have a gauge. If that's the case, lift it to determine that it's still full. If in doubt, have it serviced or replaced.

Step 5 - Examine for Damage

Visually examine the extinguisher for obvious physical damage. Look for corrosion, leakage, a clogged nozzle, or other signs of deterioration or wear and tear.

Step 6 - Check the Tag

Verify the last professional service date. The extinguisher should have been examined and serviced by a professional within the last 12 months, and this information should be recorded on the tag attached to the extinguisher.

Complete Your Inspection

Complete your inspection by signing and dating the back of the tag. Ask your learners the following questions:

What questions do you have about inspecting the fire extinguisher? What questions do you have about conducting the fire safety inspection?

Fire Safety Inspections - Discussion

Note that it is likely that as you were describing what to look for during a fire safety inspection, learners could think of possible fire safety issues that currently exist in your church. Facilitate a brief discussion [5-10 minutes] on some of the fire safety issues your church currently has. To get the discussion going, ask some or all of the following questions:

- What potential fire safety hazards have you noticed around this church? That is, what issues do you suspect we'll have to address when we do our first fire safety inspection?

- How many fire extinguishers do we have? Where are they located? When were they last examined by anyone in this church?
- What kind of fire safety equipment do we have in the kitchen?
- Does this building need any electrical upgrades?
- How often would it be feasible for us to do fire safety inspections? Once a month? Every three months? Every six months? When should we plan to do the first fire safety inspection?

Be sure to have someone take notes during the discussion so the Church Safety Team can take action on any issues that are raised.

Preparing Your Church's Fire Response Plan

What Is a Fire Response Plan?

Your Fire Response Plan is an important reference document that describes in detail how a fire emergency at your church would be handled. All new Church Safety Team members should have training on what's in the Fire Response Plan. It should also be reviewed at least once a year as part of Church Safety Team member refresher training. In addition, the pastor and all church staff should also be familiar with the Fire Response Plan.

Elements of a Fire Response Plan

At a minimum, the Fire Response Plan should explain:

- The alert system (i.e., how people will be notified of a fire)
- The evacuation procedures (i.e., how people will get out of the building)
- The Church Safety Team roles (i.e., what the Church Safety Team will do in a fire emergency)

Below, we'll expand on each of these to help ensure that you and your team fully understand.

Defending the Flock

Alert System

Review the protocol for alerting the Church Safety Team. The Fire Response Plan should describe fire notification procedures. For example, if a Church Safety Team member discovers a fire while on patrol, what is the notification procedure? What is the radio protocol? Who is notified? What radio codes (if any) are used? Who is responsible for contacting the authorities?

Or, what if a church member reports a fire. What happens? Who is in command of the situation? How are Church Safety Team members alerted? Who has the authority to institute a building evacuation?

Determine how people in the building will be alerted. Newer church buildings will likely have fire alarm systems or public address systems. In older buildings, the Fire Response Plan should indicate how people throughout the building will be notified that there is a fire and they must evacuate.

Remember to notify the pastor. In addition, if the pastor is not on the premises, he/she should be notified as soon as it is safe to do so. The plan should indicate who is responsible for doing that.

Evacuation Procedures

The Fire Response Plan should describe the procedure for evacuating the building. For example:

Evacuation during worship service: Determine how the pastor should be alerted of the need to evacuate if worship is in progress. Also determine in advance what exits should be used and how evacuation should proceed if most of the members are in the sanctuary. Determine who would be responsible for evacuating members who were not in the sanctuary during worship service (e.g., church members in the kitchen, people in the children's area or classrooms, people in the lavatories, custodial staff perhaps in the basement, etc.)

Evacuation when worship is not in session: Also, consider how evacuation would take place if worship was not in session and there were people scattered throughout the building. Who would find and alert people throughout the building?

Evacuation routes: The Fire Response Plan should include maps or floorplans showing the evacuation route for each room in the building. There should also be an alternative evacuation route for each room, in the event that the first exit is blocked.

Assembly and reunification areas: The fire response plan should indicate where people are to assemble when they evacuate the building. They should, for example, be directed to stand a good distance away from the building and to keep streets and roadways clear so emergency response vehicles can approach the church. A reunification area should also be designated so that people can reunite with family members.

Verifying that everyone is out: It will be ideal to be able to report that everyone is out of the building and accounted for when the fire department arrives. The Fire Response Plan should indicate how the building will be swept to be certain it is empty.

Church Safety Team Roles

There are certain things the Church Safety Team would have to do during a fire emergency. The Fire Response Plan should describe the role of the Church Safety Team and how Church Safety Team members would be assigned their tasks. Here are the tasks that they would be responsible for:

- Contact the fire department
- Find/notify people in remote parts of the building
- Assist adults with mobility issues
- Assist with evacuation of children
- Conduct a sweep of the building

Evacuation of Disabled Adults

Disabled adults, elderly adults, and adults with mobility issues may pose a special challenge during an evacuation. The Fire Response Plan should consider how these adults with special needs will be evacuated.

Know the mobility-challenged adults in your congregation. In most small and medium sized churches, you can probably name the adults who have mobility issues. You probably know where they sit in the sanctuary and whether they typically have family members with them who can help them. In a few minutes, we'll take some time to figure out who our mobility-challenged members are and how we can assist them.

Always know when they're in the building and where they are. Set up a procedure for making note of when any of your mobility-challenged members are in the building during non-worship times, and where in the building they are. This will make it easier for the Church Safety Team to find them if there's an emergency.

Instruct wheelchair-bound members to navigate to designated rescue areas. When you have church fire drills and member safety training, teach wheelchair-bound members who are not on the ground floor to navigate to designated recue areas where they are to wait for a Church Safety Team members.

In newer buildings, the stairwells are often built to protect from fire and smoke. If you have such a building, designate a rescue area inside of the stairwell. In older buildings, create rescue areas near the stairs. Be sure to instruct wheelchair-bound members not to block the stairs. Also during church fire drills, make all members aware of the need to help older and mobility challenged members.

Evacuation of Children

The evacuation of young children poses a similar challenge to evacuating seniors. Here are some things you can do to help minimize the possibility of fire injury to children in the church.

- Plan youth activities for fire safety: Because young children move slowly, whenever possible, arrange for activities involving young children to be on the ground floor and near exits. The nursery should also be on the main floor and near an exit to facilitate getting infants and toddlers out.

- Train youth workers on fire emergencies: All youth workers should have training on fire safety procedures and should be required to know the evacuation routes for their activity area. They should be required to have regular refresher training on these issues.
- Conduct regular fire drills with children: Fire drills help children understand what to do in case of fire and should be conducted with children in Sunday School and youth activities one to two times per year.
- Assign a Church Safety Team member to assist with evacuation of children: If possible, assign one or more team members to be responsible for assisting with the children during a fire emergency.

Fire Safety Plan – Discussion

As a note, you as the instructor will need to facilitate a discussion [10-15 minutes] on some of the issues your Fire Response Plan would have to address. Remind learners that they don't have to figure out all the answers today. Your purpose is just to get them thinking about possible solutions. To get the discussion going, ask some or all of the following questions:

- Which of our members would need assistance during an evacuation? What kind of plan can we put in place to make sure they get out safely? (Hint: if there are not enough Church Safety Team members, the plan might include training a number of able-bodied members to assist them)
- Do we need designated rescue areas for wheelchair bound members in this building?
- Do we need to make changes to where any of our youth activities are held to make it easier to evacuate the children?

• Where might the assembly and unification areas be?

Be sure to have someone take notes during the discussion so the Church Safety Team can take action later on any issues that are raised.

Education and Drills

In this section of the course, we will give you some resources for training the congregation and church staff.

Keyword: RACE

Use the acronym RACE to remember the steps to take in a fire emergency.

- Rescue: The first step is to rescue people from the immediate area of the fire.
- Alert: Next, alert the proper authorities. Know where alarm pulls are located, if your building has them. Know how to operate them. Call 911 and make sure to press send. Advise the 911 dispatcher of the nature of the emergency, your name, and your location. Stay on the phone until the dispatcher hangs up. While the dispatcher is talking, he or she is entering the information into a computer and alerting first responders about the call.
- Also alert the other Church Safety Team members, church staff, and volunteers. If your Church Safety Team uses two-way radios, use the radio for this purpose. A public address system or other announcement from a centralized location can be effective for communicating an emergency situation. If your church does not have this, figure out a "runner" system that will send Church Safety Team members throughout the building to alert church members.
- Confine: Confine the fire by closing all doors and windows as you leave an area. Doing so cuts off the flow of oxygen, which helps

choke the fire. It also slows the spread of smoke. (Take time to close windows only if it's safe to do so.)

- Extinguish or Evacuate: If the fire is small, extinguish it with a fire extinguisher. If the fire cannot be put out quickly or if church members are in any danger, evacuate the building. Be sure to evacuate the people closest to the fire first.

Rescuing Someone on Fire

The thing to understand here is stop, drop, and roll. Someone on fire should not run. That only causes the fire to grow. Instead, they should stop, drop, and roll. Use a coat or blanket to smother the flames. Have the person drop to the ground and roll from side to side to extinguish the flames.

If you have a coat or blanket, wrap the person in that before assisting them with rolling on the ground. If available, put cold wet cloth on burned skin. Once the fire is out, put cold, wet cloths on any burned skin, if you have them. Wrap the person in a coat or blanket and keep them warm until help arrives.

Evacuation Reminders

Refresh your team members on the following topics:

Do not use elevators. Elevators should not be used during a fire emergency. Elevator shafts create updrafts that pull in smoke. This could cause elevator occupants to be overcome by smoke. Additionally, an elevator could open on a floor where there is fire, exposing the occupants to immediate smoke and fire danger. Be sure to stress all of this during any fire safety training you offer to church members and staff.

If there's smoke, keep low and cover your face. Earlier we discussed the dangers of smoke inhalation. In a fire emergency where smoke is present, cover your nose and mouth with a cloth—preferably a damp cloth—to minimize the amount of smoke you are inhaling. There will be more oxygen near the floor and smoke closer to the ceiling. Therefore, if smoke is present, stay as low to the ground as possible, as you move toward the exit. Crawl if necessary.

Close all doors behind you. Closed doors inhibit the spread of fire. So, when you leave an area, close the doors behind you.

Do not allow anyone to return to the building If someone is missing or didn't get out, alert fire fighters when they arrive. If possible, tell fire fighters where in the building the missing person might be.

Keyword: PASS

Be sure that all Church Safety Team members have had training in how to use a fire extinguisher. Your local fire department may be able to assist you with this. Use the acronym PASS (pull, aim, squeeze, sweep) to remember how to use an extinguisher.

- Pull – Pull out the locking pin that keeps the two handles from engaging.
- Aim – Stand 10-15 feet away. Be careful not to aim at the fire itself as pressure from the extinguisher could spread the fire. Instead, aim at the base of the fire. In Class B fires, the flame might be moving if a liquid is on fire. In runny, liquid fires, aim at the leading edge of the fire.
- Squeeze – Squeeze the two handles together.
- Sweep – Sweep from side to side. Try to use the contents of the extinguisher to completely coat the object that is burning and the area around it.

Fire Extinguisher Reminders

Remind your trainees of the following:

- Use good judgment about whether to attempt to put out a fire. The decision should be based on how large the fire is, where it's located, and what's burning. You may be more help to the church and its members by alerting and rescuing people than trying to put out a fire that can no longer be easily controlled.

- Extinguishers are for small fires only! The spray from a fire extinguisher only lasts about 8-10 seconds before the canister is empty. You can't put out an entire burning room with that! Extinguishers are ideal for very small fires, especially those in containers, like a trash can. Also remember, if it's a small enough fire, you can sometimes smother it by covering the container It's in, or by putting something over it like a coat or blanket.
- Make sure you have a way out. Keep your back to the exit when you use an extinguisher so you have a way to get out if you are not successful in putting out the fire.
- Extinguishers should only be used by people who have been trained You may want to train church members outside the Church Safety Team to use them.

Educating Church Members

Explain to your learners that safety and prevention depends on everyone. As you can hopefully see by now, everyone in the church plays a part in keeping the church safe from fires. In addition, lives are saved if everyone knows what to do in the event of a fire.

Church leaders and staff need to know what to do. If a fire were to break out during worship service or while the pastor was on the premises, people would look to him/her for guidance. For this reason, the pastor and church leaders need to know the basics of the fire evacuation plan.

Furthermore, church leaders and staff may be in the building during the day on weekdays, or at other times when the Church Safety Team is not on duty. They will need to know what to do even if no one from the Church Safety Team is around.

Key ministries need to know what to do. Adults who work with youth need to know how to get to the nearest exit and how to evacuate the children from classrooms and activity areas. Ministries like the ushers or greeters may be on duty during a fire emergency and may be called upon to help get church members out. For this reason, people in these key assignments and ministries should be educated in the basics of the fire safety and evacuation procedures.

Practice and drills can save lives. People are more likely to survive a fire emergency if they know what to do. That's why many schools, hospitals, and workplaces have fire drills. This church should have them too. The Church Safety Team should conduct regular drills so team members know what to do. In addition, there should also be occasional evacuation drills for the entire church so everyone learns how to get out safely.

Why Fire Drills Are Important

Explain to your team members that a church fire drill allows you to accomplish the following:

- Familiarize church members with evacuation procedures: As we just said, fire drills help people learn what they need to know to get out safely in the event of a fire.
- Identify weaknesses in your strategy for notifying church members: A fire drill lets you assess how well you are able to find and notify people throughout the building.
- Identify problems/challenges with getting people out: How long did it take to evacuate everyone? Did people have trouble finding their exits? Did people understand to move away from the building and toward the reunification area once they were out? How did you know for sure that everyone was out? A fire drill lets you assess so you can figure out what you need to do differently.
- Evaluate and improve procedures for assisting mobility-challenged members: A fire drill lets you determine whether your system for evacuating children and special needs adults works. You can identify what doesn't work and make changes to the procedure.

Prepare for the Fire Drill

Explain to your learners how to prepare for a fire drill using the following pointers:

- Alert the local fire department in advance. Let the local fire department know when you are planning to have a drill so that they are not summoned accidentally. Better yet, seek guidance from your local fire department as you plan your drill. Their help will be invaluable.
- Work with church leadership to set a date and time. Immediately after worship service works well. Many people will be in attendance and the pastor can even remind members of the importance of the drill before it begins.
- Coordinate it with another family activity to ensure participation. Work with other ministries to make it a fun event. For example, plan the drill so that a dinner, a picnic, or some other church get-together takes place immediately afterward. This ensures participation, but also makes it something members look forward to.
- Ensure that the Church Safety Team has practiced in advance. The team should have its own training and practice in advance of the all-church drill so that each Church Safety Team member knows his/her role.

Observe and Debrief

Observation during the drill is important, as is debriefing everyone afterward. Have people designated as "observers" during the drill. Assign several people to observe as the drill is being carried out. Have them make note of what worked well and where there were glitches.

After the drill, debrief observers and Church Safety Team members. Have a general session as soon after the drill as possible where Church Safety Team members and observers can candidly discuss how it went.

Make changes to procedures based on what you learn. Use what you learn to improve your procedures. Ask your learners the following questions: What questions do you have about education and drills, or about anything else we have discussed today?

Review & Discussion

What's Our Next Step?

As the instructor, you need to facilitate a discussion with your team members on what fire safety and training issues the Church Safety Team should tackle first.

Activity

- Step 1. Ask each learner to write down what he/she thinks are the top three fire safety or training issues the Church Safety Team needs to tackle. Give them one to two minutes to do this.
- Step 2. Ask one learner to share their list with the class. Ask them to explain why they chose each item. Write their answers on the chalkboard or on a flipchart.
- Step 3. Ask other learners for their items and add them to the list.
- Step 4. Once you have a generous list of issues on the chalkboard, see if the group can agree on the top five that need to be taken care of in the next three to six months.
- Step 5. Try to see if they can also agree on the next five – the items that will perhaps be handled over the next six months to a year.
- Step 6. End the discussion by verifying that everyone is more or less comfortable with the items on the list. If feasible, set a date and time for Church Safety Team members to reconvene to begin working on the top priority items.

When you're finished, ask if there any additional questions, and then close the class with prayer.

Chapter 12:
Acts of Violence and Physical Threats

While fires and natural disasters might be the most common threats your team and your church congregation will face, we do live in dangerous times. There is always the possibility that you will be faced with human threats – the headlines today are filled with stories of violence against churches.

Often, the attacker is a member of the congregation itself, but sometimes they are members of the immediate community, and in others, they're complete strangers. It is absolutely essential that your Church Safety Team understand how to handle these types of threats and the possibility of human-borne violence. In this chapter, we'll discuss active shooter neutralization and lockdown drills.

Active Shooter Statistics

The FBI conducted extensive research in 2014, and identified active shooter trends and information that should be eye-opening for virtually anyone. That data was collated into several important statistics, as follows:

- **160** active shooting incidents occurred between 2000 and 2013.
- **1,043** casualties resulted from those incidents, including deaths and injuries, but not including the deaths of the shooters.
- An average of **11.4** incidents occurred per year, but the trend was upward, with attacks increasing in frequency year over year. Note that the actual breakdown is **6.4** incidents for the first half of the study, and **16.4** incidents per year for the second half of the study.
- In those 160 incidents, **486** people were killed.
- **557** people were wounded in those incidents.
- Shootings occurred in **40** states, plus Washington D.C.

- In **60%** of instances, the police **did not arrive** until the incident was over.
- In the vast majority of instances, the shooter is a white male. Of the incidents covered in the FBI study, **only six attackers** were female.
- **70%** of incidents occurred in a commercial or educational space. Only **3.8%** occurred in churches or other houses of worship.
- All but two of these incidents involved **only a single shooter**.
- In many incidents, the shooter killed a family member elsewhere, and then moved to the incident area.
- **Less than 50%** of shooters ultimately kill themselves (most of those who do, do so at the incident scene).

Intruder Response: Active Killer

Some organizations call an "active killer" an "active shooter," but Lieutenant Colonel Dave Grossman emphasizes that the distinction is important. The police or victims may also be shooting when the incident is occurring, but it is only the intruder who is an "active killer" (McKay, 2014).

Only the intruder is an active killer – active shooter can describe anyone else in the conflict who is armed and firing, including law enforcement.

Active killers have been prevalent in Christian churches for years, but the number of incidents is increasing. Since 1999, Carl Chinn, a leader in church security, has been tracking deadly force deaths and other related incidents in Christian churches throughout the United States. Chinn (2016) recorded 626 people killed (including intruder suicide) and 694 people injured between January 1, 1999 and December 31, 2015.

More than half of those deaths occurred in the five years between 2011 and 2015 (Chinn, 2016). One of the worst church shootings in recent history occurred on June 17, 2015 at the Emanuel African Methodist Episcopal Church in Charleston, South Carolina. Around 9 pm, 21-year-old

Dylann Roof joined 12 churchgoers in a Bible study. Initially, he participated very little in the meeting; however, as the church members started to share scripture, he began to argue with them (CNN, 2015).

Then during the closing prayer he pulled a Glock .45-caliber model 41 and started shooting (CNN, 2015; Sanchez & Payne, 2015). During the shooting, church members pleaded with him to stop. He swore at them and used racially charged language (CNN, 2015). By the time he was done, nine people were dead and one was injured (Costa, Bever, Freedom du Lac, and Horwitz, 2015).

He was arrested the next morning during a traffic stop in Shelby, North Carolina approximately 250 miles from the church (Costa, Bever, Freedom du Lac, and Horwitz, 2015).

Another well-known church shooting occurred on December 9, 2007 at the New Life Church in Colorado Springs, Colorado. In this shooting, 24-year-old Matthew Murray killed four people in two locations (Nicholson, 2008; "U.S. Church Gunman," 2007). The fatality rate would have been much higher if it weren't for Jeanne Assam, a former police officer who volunteered as a security guard ("U.S. Church Gunman," 2007).

Assam shot Murray multiple times, "which put him down. He then fired a single round killing himself" ("U.S. Church Gunman," 2007).

Another horrifying attack occurred in late 2017, when Devin Patrick Kelley entered the First Baptist Church in Sutherland Springs. He shot and killed 26 people before fleeing and ultimately being shot himself by an armed private citizen. Kelley entered the church in search of family members of his ex-wife, although they were not present at the time (NBC News, 2017).

When you examine all deadly force incidents, you'll see there are numerous circumstances surrounding these deaths. Churches need to be alert to the possibility of dangerous incidents occurring. Most active killer incidents are unpredictable and evolve quickly. Safety ministries need to plan and train so they will be prepared to deal with the situation until law enforcement arrives. Sheepdog Church Security can help you plan for violent intruders.

Important Terms to Remember

There are many important terms that you will need to remember when dealing with an active killer situation within your church. These apply to virtually all aspects of the experience, from the attacker to the congregation, and the building itself. Let's cover some of the most important.

Active Killer

An active killer is a subject who uses a firearm and possibly explosives to kill as many people as they can in a building or populated area. These killers are unpredictable and generally have no pattern to their selection of victims (United States Department of Homeland Security [DHS], 2008, p. 2). Their activity evolves quickly. They often do not stop until police or another armed person confronts them (DHS, 2008, p. 2).

Cover

Cover is a term used to describe anything that will stop bullets. Examples of cover include a cinderblock wall or many layers of metal and wood.

Concealment

Concealment is a term used to describe anything that will hide a person from view. Examples of concealment include large plants, interior walls (sheetrock does not stop bullets), and office furniture.

Soft Target

A soft target is a person or location that is relatively unprotected or vulnerable, especially to terrorist attack.

- Churches are soft targets for a number of reasons.
- Churches stand for a religious truth many find narrow minded and offensive.
- Churches are open to the public with open access to anybody during services.
- Church service times are publically known or easy to find online and elsewhere.
- A number of churches in the United States are gun-free zones. They may not recognize their own vulnerability.
- Most churches have no Safety/Security Ministry.

Soft Lockdown/Lockout

A soft lockdown/lockout is when the active killer is outside the building, so only the exterior doors are locked to keep the killer from entering.

Lockdown

A lockdown is when the active killer is in the building and/or the interior rooms are secured with people sheltering inside them.

Fatal Funnels

Fatal funnels are areas such as a hallway or doorway which prevent the active killer from moving side to side. In this way, the containment team is able to limit the active killer's movements and more easily take him down.

Unification Point

A unification point is an area where people evacuate to that is removed from the setting of the active killer. The church should have several unification points arranged before an attack ever occurs.

Mindset

Mindset is the thought or attitude that enhances survivability. With a strong mindset, you have a foundation upon which to base decisions and actions. Your mindset enables you to act quickly and effectively. It is a state of being mindful, but not fearful. It allows you to take appropriate survival action and use all senses. With the proper mindset, you trust your intuition, which is that gut feeling of knowing the right thing to do in a situation.

Before an Attack

There are steps you can take to prevent an attack or at least to mitigate the damage done by an attacker:

- Conduct a facility assessment.
- Develop lockout and lockdown plans.
- Teach skills for emergency situations.
- Create engagement and containment teams.
- Conduct trainings and drills.

Conduct a Facility Assessment

When preparing your facility assessment, you will need to identify access points and communication systems. Identify all potential security vulnerabilities. Identify building access routes of travel, as well as areas in your church that can serve as a shelter or safe area.

Access

Assess all access points including doors, windows, roof latches, etc. Assess existing controls for primary and secondary access control. (This is essentially how doors are locked and secured.) Identify problems by asking questions such as:

- Does your church have doors that are easily forced open?
- Do the doors have windows without security mesh or glazing?
- Do you have exterior windows without glazing?

There are several secondary access control items that can assist in securing doors. You'll need to assess existing controls for primary and secondary security barriers. Several items can be used to delay an active killer from accomplishing his goal. Even something as simple as placing a large planter in front of the church prevents automobiles from crashing into the building.

Security

Assess facility security components for functionality, such as closed-circuit televisions, intrusion alarm systems, and perimeter lighting.

Communication

Identify existing communication devices. Information is key to making good decisions. It should flow in all directions. Provide as much information as possible to as many people as possible. Plan to use any and all available means of communication, including:

- Two-way radios
- Text messaging
- PA system
- Digital signage
- Social media, like Twitter, Facebook, etc.

Find out what forms of communication your church has. Communication systems must be put in place to notify all personnel in the church.

Develop Lockout and Lockdown Plans

Based on your facility assessment, you will need to develop lockout and lockdown plans.

Lockout

In a soft lockdown/lockout, the killer is outside the building, so only exterior access points need to be secured. This can happen when an event in or around the church triggers a need to fully secure access to the church. For example, when an active killer hits a school, all of the other schools may go into a lockout and continue with classes. If a bank gets robbed and the person flees into an area, police may advise businesses and churches to lock all exterior doors so the robber can't hide in the building.

It is also wise to keep employees and children inside to prevent a hostage being taken. When initiating a lockout, secure all perimeter access doors and vehicle gates. Consider moving all personnel not directly involved with critical job functions to secure areas in order to optimize safety.

Monitor all available security cameras. During a lockout, do not open perimeter doors or gates to anyone not authorized to enter the property. Depending on the purpose of a self-initiated lockout, consider contacting law enforcement. If you have moved to a safe location and/or the building is secure, do not leave until you are sure it is safe.

Lockdown

In order to develop a facility lockdown plan, you will need to review a detailed site map or floorplan of your church. Familiarize yourself with communication methods and emergency lockdown procedures. Use what you learned in the assessment phase to decide how to secure doors and how to use communication devices. In your plan, include information that answers questions like these:

- Are secondary locking devices needed?
- How are you going to communicate with each classroom and other sections of the church?

- Can you watch the intruder on cameras so you can tell police dispatch where the intruder is?
- Where are good areas to set up a containment team person using cover, concealment, and fatal funnels?
- What are good avenues of approach for the engagement team?
- Can they circle around him to shoot from behind?
- Where are places for good cover and concealment while on approach?

Create battle plans with details such as, "If he's in the lobby, team member #1 approaches down hallway #1. Member #2 approaches from sanctuary." In addition, create ways for people to be successful in a lockdown by placing **bug-out kits** strategically around the church.

Of course, your staff and volunteers should be trained in the proper use of medical equipment and first aid. You should also create a plan to resume normal operations once the lockout or lockdown is over. Know the answers to such questions as:

A bug-out kit should include emergency water and food supplies, medical supplies including large bandages for severe bleeds and tourniquets for life-threatening bleeding, extra ammunition, and anything else you might need in an emergency situation.

- How will you notify people the lockout/lockdown is over?
- Will you resume operations that day or wait until the next day to start the scheduled activities?

Teach Skills for Emergency Situations

If an active killer situation occurs, people need to:

- Evacuate
- Hide
- Call for help

- Engage the active killer

Let's touch on each of those.

Evacuate

People are often surprised when they hear evacuation is now considered one of the most important elements to an active killer response plan. They often think of those rare situations when a second person is waiting near the assembly area to ambush people.

The truth of the matter is that very few violent intruder events involve more than one person. Remember, the Federal Bureau of Investigation (2013) reported that in the 160 incidents identified, only two involved more than one killer (p. 7).

Teach your staff and volunteers how to evade detection and escape the building. Show them routes that they might have not thought of before. Many times, people do not know about back doors, nor do they think of windows as an escape possibility.

If the killer is inside, get outside. When evacuating, do not use your car. Automobiles will bottleneck at exit points and with the increased stress, accidents and injuries are likely. Pick unification points that are far enough away from the church to provide a level of safety.

Hide

Teach your staff and volunteers how to barricade doors and use cover and concealment. Find places where the violent intruder is less likely to find you. Hide behind something that will stop bullets should guns be fired in your direction. For example, you should hide in a room that is closable with a lockable door and little to no glass.

If there is an interior window, ensure it is closed and covered, and move as far away from it as possible. Avoid the fishbowl effect, which is when the active killer can shoot through large glass windows into a large crowd of people.

Try to maintain your freedom of movement. Rooms with a second door leading to another area of the church or a window out of the church give you evacuation options. If the active killer is
breaking down one door, you can evacuate through the other exit. When hiding out, do the following:

- Lock and blockade doors and other entryways.
- Remain quiet and silence phones.
- Do not huddle together in a large group. Instead, spread out throughout the room and hide behind large items that may provide cover.

Call for Help

Make sure people know how to contact law enforcement. The United States Department of Homeland Security (DHS) (2008) explains what information callers should provide to law enforcement or dispatchers. This information is taken verbatim from the source (p. 5):

- Location of the active killer
- Number of killer, if more than one
- Physical description of killer(s)
- Number and type of weapons held by the killer(s)
- Number of potential victims at the location

Engage the Active Killer

Teach your staff and volunteers how to swarm an active killer with one or two people grabbing each of the killer's arms and legs. Teach them how to remove and secure the person's weapon when they gain the upper hand.

Create Engagement and Containment Teams

There are two types of response plans: engagement and containment.

Any person who responds to an active killer situation is putting his/her life in great danger. This response has to be an individual decision and not dictated by policy or training.

- The engagement team tries to de-escalate the situation and/or prepare to use force.
- The containment team moves people from the area and initiates the lockdown.

Note that the location of your team members in relation to the active killer may dictate how each member must react during the incident (i.e. a containment team member may have to work as an engagement team member or vice versa).

Conduct Trainings and Drills

Conduct mock violent intruder training exercises. Local law enforcement is an excellent resource for designing training exercises. They can teach you how to:

- Recognize the sound of gunshots
- React quickly when gunshots are heard and/or when a shooting is witnessed
- Evacuate the area

Train your staff, volunteers, and your congregation how to respond during a lockdown. Training should include information on:

- Evacuation
- Hiding
- Calling 911
- Acting against the killer
- Helping treat injured
- Reacting when law enforcement arrives
- Adopting the survival mindset

The Truth about Active Killers

The truth is that if a bad guy is really determined, then he will get into your church. If a bad guy is able to hurt you, he will. Passive or stationary targets are easy victims. Compliance is dangerous. Submission to terrorists or active killers rarely pays off.

During the 2007 Virginia Tech shooting, students were advised by the university to "Please stay put" (CNN, 2016). Students sat in their chairs as the killer shot one at a time (Grossman, 2012). He even reloaded and the kids just sat there waiting to be killed (Grossman, 2012).

The victims the Charleston Church begged for their lives but Roof coldly shot them (CNN, 2015). Waiting for police is not a sufficient defense strategy for an active killer. Active killer situations are often over before law enforcement arrives (DHS, 2008, p. 2). The Federal Bureau of Investigation (2013) found that 70% of the incidents it reviewed were finished in five minutes or less (p. 8).

During an Attack

When an active killer starts shooting, everyone will be caught unaware. It will take time to realize what is happening so people can take action to survive. Shortly, we will get to what actions should be taken by safety and security team members. For now, we are going to address the staff, guests, and children of the church.

Staff, Guests, and Children

When in lockdown, staff, guests, and children should follow these steps in this order based on the detailed information they learned from the lockdown plan and drills:

- Evacuate
- Hide
- Call for help when it is safe to do so

- Engage the active killer only if you are in imminent danger

Evacuate

The first course of action you should take is to get out. Leave your things behind and evacuate. Help others to evacuate if you can, but go without them if they will not leave with you. Leave the seriously wounded behind. On your way out of the building, try to prevent others from going into the dangerous area.

Hide

Remember to use cover and concealment to your advantage. Rooms with more than one exit are best so that you can escape through one exit if the intruder comes from a different one.

Call for Help

When it is safe to do so, call 911. In a panic, it is common for people to forget to hit send after dialing 911 on a cell phone. If you can't speak, leave the line open to 911 so the dispatcher can hear what's going on. When it's possible, provide as much information as possible to the dispatchers.

Take Action

Escape and evasion should always be your first actions, but you may have to engage the killer. If you are confronted by the active killer, you should take action. If your life is in imminent danger, you should do everything to disrupt or incapacitate the active killer. You will need to be as aggressive as possible and follow these steps to interrupt his decision cycle:

- Turn chaos and mayhem into an advantage and try to escape the area.
- Cause sensory overload and distractions by yelling.

- Throw whatever is available at the intruder's face.
- Find anything you have that can be used as a weapon.
- Swarm the intruder. Use large numbers of people to gain control. Keep your plan simple. Swarm the intruder and control his limbs.

Never comply with an active killer's demands. Do whatever it takes to survive. Recent events show that active killers are not interested in making deals or negotiating. They just want to murder as many people as they can.

Safety and Security Team Response

Any person who responds to an active killer situation is putting his/her life in great danger. As mentioned, this response has to be an individual decision and not dictated by policy or training. Before starting this section, we must make it clear that Sheepdog Church Security strongly encourages that the following requirements are met:

- All armed people have met the minimum legal requirements to carry a firearm.
- All armed people are familiar with the use of force laws and policy.
- All armed people are sufficiently trained to use their firearms in a tactical situation.

If You Have Warning/A Potentially Violent Person Has Been Identified

When dealing with a potentially violent person, you should immediately call 911 for police response. Do not be afraid to call the police. It is far better to have police respond to the church before the person acts out in violence.

If you use the Sheepdog Church Security radio procedures, this is a Code Orange 911. "Code Orange" means "a violent person or potentially violent person" has been identified. 911 is an enhancement code meaning "call police." An example transmission would be, "Code Orange 911 in lobby. I say again, Code Orange 911 in lobby."

Don't use codes for an active killer. Instead, send this transmission (but change the location as appropriate): "Active killer in the lobby. Active killer in the lobby. Lockdown. Lockdown. Lockdown."

Second, the lockdown procedure should be initiated. This should be done quietly without arousing suspicion. If the intruder is already in the church, only the interior rooms of the building should be locked. Leave the exterior doors unlocked so responding police can get in.

When possible and safe, use verbal de-escalation. If it's working, keep at it. If verbal de-escalation is not working and it is relatively safe to do so, use self-defense techniques. Swarm the subject if feasible. Consider the use of non-lethal weapons, such as defensive spray.

As a last resort, use the force reasonably necessary and in accordance with the law to neutralize the threat. Position armed persons where they have clear lines of sight to the subject. You should consider what's behind the subject. You don't want to shoot towards a crowd. Armed persons should consider cover, concealment, and maneuverability. They should ask themselves, "If I am taking heavy fire, how can I escape?"

Presenting or pointing a firearm at the subject has legal implications, and it may trigger a violent response. It also slows your ability to respond with self-defense techniques because transitioning to self-defense techniques requires you to spend several seconds holstering the weapon. Additionally, if you can attack someone physically, it may be an opportunity to swarm him.

If you're too close to the killer, the gun can turn the situation into a deadly force altercation. Many police officers are shot with their own guns because they took it out when in close proximity to the subject (Federal Bureau of Investigation, n.d.).

If You Don't Have Warning/Active Killer Incident Happens

Suddenly

The engagement team should move toward the target to neutralize the threat. Along the way, they advise others to go into lockdown or evacuate the area. People should be moved as far away from the sound of gunshots as possible.

The engagement team should continue to move toward the sound of gunshots using cover and concealment. They should be careful while going around corners. The engagement team's task is to neutralize the threat using whatever force is necessary.

The containment team takes up a position that prevents the threat from entering a populated area of the church. People providing containment should find a good position of cover and take advantage of fatal funnels.

During an active killer incident, people will be looking to leaders, staff, and safety team members for guidance. Remain calm and direct people to evacuation routes and secured areas. Nobody knows the church like you do. In fact, they may be completely lost and panicked. You need to remain calm and in control.

Finally, containment personnel need to hold their position, pray, and keep calm.

After Intruder Is Neutralized

Engagement Team Actions

After the active killer has been neutralized, the engagement team should holster their firearms. The police might not be able to distinguish between the active killer and the engagement team and may accidentally shoot the engagement team members. Follow these other steps:

- Notify the containment team and 911 dispatch that the subject has been neutralized. Keep in mind that even if you advise 911, police may not know that the threat has been neutralized when they arrive.

- Notify church staff that the threat has been neutralized.
- Maintain lockdown until police advise you to lift it.
- Provide medical aid to injured people. Treat the most severe injuries first. Treat the intruder as well only if it is safe to do so. He may have other weapons or explosives.
- When medical personnel respond, provide assistance if requested.
- Evacuate to unification area.

Containment Team Actions

After the active killer has been neutralized, the containment team should holster their firearms. Follow these other steps:

- Notify 911 that the threat has been neutralized.
- Notify church staff that the threat has been neutralized.
- Maintain lockdown until police advise you to lift it.
- Provide medical assistance.
- Cooperate with first responders.
- Evacuate to unification area.

When Law Enforcement Arrives

DHS (2008) has a lot of information about what happens when law enforcement arrives, and that information is provided verbatim here (p. 5):

- Officers usually arrive in teams of four (4).
- Officers may wear regular patrol uniforms or external bulletproof vests, Kevlar helmets, and other tactical equipment.
- Officers may be armed with rifles, shotguns, handguns.
- Officers may use pepper spray or tear gas to control the situation.

- Officers may shout commands, and may push individuals to the ground for their safety.

DHS (2008) also explains how victims should respond when law enforcement arrives. This information is taken verbatim from the source (p. 5):

- Remain calm, and follow officers' instructions.
- Put down any items in your hands (i.e., bags, jackets).
- Immediately raise hands and spread fingers.
- Keep hands visible at all times.
- Avoid making quick movements toward officers such as holding on to them for safety.
- Avoid pointing, screaming and/or yelling.
- Do not stop to ask officers for help or direction when evacuating, just proceed in the direction from which officers are entering the premises.

DHS (2008) also notes that the first officers to arrive on the scene will not stop to help injured persons. Expect rescue teams comprised of additional officers and emergency medical personnel to follow the initial officers.

These rescue teams will treat and remove any injured persons. They may also call upon able-bodied individuals to assist in removing the wounded from the premises. Once you have reached a safe location or an assembly point, you will likely be held in that area by law enforcement until the situation is under control, and all witnesses have been identified and questioned. Do not leave until law enforcement authorities have instructed you to do so (DHS, 2008, p. 5).

Planning for the Future

We pray that you never have to go through a violent intruder attack. If you do experience this issue, we encourage you to contact us at Sheepdog Church Security to help you assess how your team was effective and what could be done differently should another attack occur.

Teaching the Content

Teaching the content within this section should take about 2.5 hours. We've provided a framework in the content that follows, but don't forget that it should all be customized to meet your church and team's specific needs.

Within the following framework, you will learn how to understand the nature of an active shooter event, how to instruct and lead civilians during an active shooter event, and how to develop a response plan for handling an active shooter event.

Ice Breaker Activity

Explain that in the course of the training today, we're going to be talking about how the Church Safety Team would respond if someone came in to purposely kill some of the members. We will be talking about some of things you might have to do to protect church members and how you might have to put your own life at risk.

Your work on the Church Safety Team demonstrates a willingness to make sacrifices for the church. So, before we start, let's do something to help encourage one another. Each team member should share at least one reason you have chosen to be part the Church Safety Team.

Follow these simple steps to kick off the activity:

Step 1. To stimulate their thinking, ask everyone to read to themselves this passage of scripture: "I will encamp at my temple to guard it against marauding forces. Never again will an oppressor overrun my people, for now I am keeping watch." (Zechariah 9:8)

Step 2. Ask the learners to write down up to three reasons they are willing to give of their time and their talent to "guard the temple against marauding forces." Give them a minute or two to do this. If someone has only one or two reasons, that's OK.

Step 3. Ask them to choose a partner. If the partners don't know each other, they should introduce themselves. Ask the partners to share with each other what they wrote down. Give them one to two minutes to do this.

Step 4. Invite one or two people to share their reasons with the class. Give encouragement and/or applause to those who share their reasons.

Step 5. Conclude the activity by thanking everyone in the room for their willingness to serve God's people as a Church Safety Team member. It's not always an easy job, but it is a very important one.

Why Churches Need to Prepare for Active Shooters

Explain to your learners that in this section of the course, they will be given some background information on active shooter events and some information on why churches need to think about how they might handle such an event.

What Is an Active Shooter?
The Department of Homeland Security defines an active shooter event as a situation in which:

- One or more individuals is actively engaged in killing or attempting to kill people, often in a confined space. Some active shooter events do take place outdoors in open spaces.
- Firearms are used.
- There is no pattern to the selection of victims. The shooter seems to want to kill as many people as possible. Victims are selected at random.

Number of Shooter Events
In 2014, the FBI released a comprehensive research study on active

shooter events in the U.S. based on data collected by law enforcement jurisdictions throughout the country. Between 2000-2013, the FBI identified 160 active shooter events. The image below highlights key findings from that report, including the fact that active shooter incidents are increasing year over year.

- Between 2000-2006, the average number of events per year was 6.4
- But between 2007-2013, the average number of events per year was 16.4

Location of Shooter Events
Almost half of them (73 of them—45.6%) occurred in businesses. The next highest number (39 of them – 24.4%) occurred in educational facilities, including schools and colleges. Note that six of them occurred in churches and houses of worship.

Active Shooters in Churches
The FBI report lists 21 people killed and 27 wounded in active shooter events at houses of worship. That number does not include the nine people killed at Emanuel African Methodist Episcopal Church in South Carolina. It also does not include the 26 individuals killed at the First Baptist Church in Sutherland Springs, Texas. These events were particularly troubling because the victims were doing what Christians are called to do.

Other Deadly Force Events
The numbers on the previous slide reflect only the events characterized by the FBI as active shooter events. One researcher, Carl Chinn, has done a more comprehensive count, recording all deadly force events in houses of worship, and counting deaths resulting from:

- Robbery
- Domestic violence that spilled over into church
- Personal conflict

- Mental illness
- Gang or drug-related activity
- Religious bias or bigotry
- Suicide
- Unsolved or suspicious homicide
- Aggressors killed in the act

According to Chinn, there have been:

- 1,264 deadly force incidents in U.S. houses of worship between 1999 and mid-2016.
- These incidents resulted in 639 deaths.

In other words, active shooters do not present the only threat to churches. Churches are subject to the same kind of violence that plagues society in general.

Churches are "Soft" Targets

Churches by their very nature are "easy" targets for someone who wants to create mayhem.

- They are open to the public with free access to all. No ID is generally required to enter a church. The doors are often unlocked and strangers are not questioned or challenged. On the contrary, strangers are often welcomed and invited in.
- Service times are publicly posted. Most churches post a sign out front that tells a stranger what time the doors will be open and, therefore, what time he can expect to just walk on in. If there's no sign out front, it's often easy to find this information on the Internet.
- They are often advertised as "gun-free zones." Many churches proudly post information that tells the world they do not allow weapons inside. Again, that tells a would-be shooter that he can expect to go unchallenged.

- May represent a theology or an ideology others oppose. Sometimes shooters want to harm people of a particular faith or ideology. A house of worship is an obvious place to find such people.
- Most churches have little, if any, security.

Discussion

In the following section, the goal is to ask a question and generate a discussion. Keep in mind there is no one right or wrong answer. The question is designed to get learners thinking and talking about the challenges faced by Church Safety Teams.

Explain to your learners that the Bible is clear about how we should regard strangers and about how we should encourage "outsiders" to come to Christ. "For I was hungry and you gave me something to eat, I was thirsty and you gave me something to drink, I was a stranger and you invited me in." – Matthew 25:35 (NIV)

The question you should ask is as follows: How can churches continue to welcome strangers and yet remain safe?

Your goal as the instructor is to try to hear from as many learners as possible. Wrap up the discussion and answer any questions learners have before moving on to the next section.

How to Respond to an Active Shooter Event

In this section, we're going to look at what typically happens in an active shooter event. We're also going to discuss what most experts recommend civilians do if they find themselves caught in an active shooter event.

The Active Shooter

First, it's important to understand that there is no physical profile that describes the "typical" active shooter. Most have been male—but there have been some female shooters. Most work alone, but there have been some active shooter pairs. In this instance, we'll refer to the shooter as "he," but if you find yourself responding to an incident, never assume the shooter will be male, or white, or anything else. That's a mistake that could cost you or others their lives.

The are some aspects of active shooter behavior that we have seen over and over again. For example:

- The active shooter seeks to kill or injure as many people as possible. Occasionally, the shooter is looking for a specific person (e.g., an estranged spouse or a former boss), and will kill anyone he can find before or after he comes across his intended victim. But usually, he's not looking for anyone in particular. His goal is to kill and injure as many people as possible.
- He is generally not concerned for his own safety or with escape. The active shooter doesn't usually try to hide or escape. He's probably prepared to die and may be planning to kill himself.
- He will continue to kill until stopped by law enforcement, suicide, or other intervention.

Events Happen Quickly

Active shooter events are usually over within minutes. 70% of events studied by the FBI were over within 5 minutes. 23 of them were over within two minutes. Because they happen so quickly, active shooter events are often over before law enforcement can arrive.

The people caught in the situation must often make life or death decisions before law enforcement gets there. That's why it's crucial that Church Safety Team members (and church members) know what to do in the event of an active shooter. Knowing what to do and how to respond may save lives.

Civilian Survival Tactics

The Department of Homeland Security recommends three survival tactics to civilians who find themselves in an active shooter event:

Defending the Flock

1. Take Flight: Get out of the danger area as quickly as possible. If that's not possible, then…
2. Take Cover: Find a place to hide where the shooter can't see you or can't get to you. If that's not possible, then…
3. Take Action: Do what you can to restrain or incapacitate the shooter.

Let's look at these tactics one at a time.

Take Flight

The best survival tactic is to take flight. That is, get out of the area as quickly as possible. This is what experts all over the country are teaching college students, government workers, and business employees. This is the best survival tactic for our church members, as well. To use this tactic effectively, you must:

Have an escape route in mind. This means you must always be aware of your surroundings. When you enter a building, pay attention to where the exits are and always have an escape route planned. As a Church Safety Team member, hopefully you KNOW where all the exits are. However, many church members are probably not paying attention to this and may only know the entrance they use when coming for worship. To get out quickly and safely, you must know where you're going.

Leave your belongings. Don't take anything with you—except maybe your phone.

Help others if possible. The Department of Homeland Security guidelines say don't stick around if others refuse to leave and don't try to assist the wounded. That may make sense in a public place like a mall where others are strangers—or even at work. But at church, you may be with your family, including small children and older family members. There are certainly older people or people with limited mobility in the building at any given time. This is what we mean by life or death decisions.

Keep your hands visible and open with finger spread apart.

Prevent others from entering danger zone. Once you're outside of the danger area, find a safe place to wait for help to arrive. Make sure that others who are unaware of what's happening don't inadvertently wander into the danger area.

Call 911 once you are safe. Be prepared to tell the dispatcher as many details as possible:

- Location and number of shooters
- Physical description of shooter(s)
- Number and type of weapons
- Number of potential victims

If you're in a situation where you have to remain quiet or can't talk, leave the line open so the dispatcher can hear what's going on.

Take Cover

The next best survival tactic—if you can't get away from the danger zone—is to take cover. Find a place to hide. Find an area out of the shooter's view. Remember: the typical active shooter kills anyone he can find. So, seek out a place to hide where the shooter can't see you and (preferably) can't get to you. In a moment, we'll talk about the difference between concealment and cover.

Hide behind a locked door, if possible. The best such place is in a locked office, or classroom, or bathroom. If possible, find a room like that and lock yourself in. Don't open the door until you are 100% certain the event is over and law enforcement is on the scene.

Blockade the door if you can. If possible, push heavy furniture against the door to prevent it from being openable. Lacking heavy furniture, stack a bunch of chairs, books, anything that would tumble or fall onto the shooter if he were to enter the room.

Turn off lights and all sources of noise, including computers, and cell phones. Even silence the vibration feature of your phone. Stay away from windows, and keep quiet and still. Call 911 if you can. This is when you may not be able to talk. If that's the case, just leave the line open.

Concealment vs. Cover

Know the difference between concealment and cover. Concealment hides you but does not protect you from a shooter's bullet. For example, pews, podiums, and other structures in the church sanctuary could provide concealment, but probably not cover. If your church is a newer building, its walls are likely made of sheetrock, which does not offer protection. Similarly, columns in modern buildings are sometimes hollow, or partially hollow. Again, they could provide concealment, but not cover. Cover, on the other hand, protects you from being struck by a bullet. Steel and concrete offer the best cover indoors.

Take Action

If you can't get out and you can't hide, your only chance of survival may be to take action against the shooter. Civilians are usually warned to only try to take action against the shooter as a last resort, when they are in imminent danger. It's worth noting, however, that in the FBI study, 13% of the active shooting incidents were ended when unarmed citizens confronted or restrained the shooter. Here is what the Department of Homeland Security advises in this situation:

- Act aggressively toward the shooter. That is, act as if your life depends on it—because it does. Use anything you can find as a weapon. A fire extinguisher, a candleholder, a solid metal cross—any of these things could be used as a weapon in an emergency.
- Yell and throw things. Anything you can do that catches the shooter off guard, even for a moment, may allow you or someone else to grab him. Throw whatever you can find. If he's suddenly pelted from several directions with pencils, pens, coins,

hymnals, Bibles, shoes, etc., it will probably disorient him for a second or two—long enough for someone to tackle him.

- Work with others, if possible. For example, if you're hiding with others, start figuring out how you can all yell, throw things, and charge him if he enters your area.
- Be committed to disabling the shooter. Do what you have to do!

When the Police Arrive

When law enforcement arrives, they will not tend to the injured right away or answer your questions. They will be single-minded in finding and stopping the shooter. Here is what the Department of Homeland Security advises civilians:

- Keep hands visible with fingers spread apart. (Be sure to holster any weapons you are authorized to carry so you are not assumed to be the shooter.)
- Avoid sudden movements or yelling.
- Don't ask questions or grab hold of officers for safety.
- Exit in the direction officers are entering.
- Leave the building and wait in a safe place or follow officers' directives.

Review the Civilian Tactics

Ask your learners to tell you the three civilian survival tactics, in order. [Answer: take flight, take cover, take action] If the person who answers does not elaborate, ask someone to explain what's involved in each of the three tactics. Take flight means: Get out of the danger zone as quickly as possible. Take cover means: If you can't get out, you should hide, preferably in a locked room. Take action means: If you can't get out and you can't hide, and you are about to come face-to-face with the shooter, prepare to fight back. Use whatever you can find as a weapon. Work with others, if you can. Try to surprise the shooter, disorient him, and grab him.

Church Safety Team Response

So far, what we've been discussing is what "civilians" should do in case of an active shooter event. In other words, it's what church members should try to do. As Church Safety Team members, you would be called upon to take additional steps. If there was an active shooter in the church, you would have two important roles.

Your first role would be to help church members get out of the danger area or into hiding. The Church Safety Team members who carry out this role would be called the Containment Team.

Your second, equally important, role would be to try to engage the shooter in an effort to bring the event to an end. The Church Safety Team members who carry out this role would be called the Engagement Team.

Prepare in Advance

Just as important as knowing what to do during an active shooter event is planning and preparing in advance. There are at least four ways you can prepare yourselves and the church for the possibility of an active shooter event.

Do a Safety Audit: This involves identifying the weaknesses in the church facility and surrounding area, as well as identifying any operational weaknesses. You look for things about the building or about how things are done that would make the church easy prey or that would hamper your response—and you get those things fixed.

Create an Emergency Action Plan: This involves thinking through everything that must happen before, during, and after an active shooter event, and putting it all together into a written plan.

Develop Containment and Engagement Teams: This involves making sure all Church Safety Team members know how to carry out Containment Team and Engagement Team roles. You should identify who would be on which teams in an emergency, although you must understand that active shooter events are fluid; Church Safety Team members in a real situation might have to do either role.

Train People on What to Do: This involves making sure Church Safety Team members regularly drill and practice their roles. Even better would be to have church-wide safety and active shooter drills that involve all church members and all church leaders.

Tell your learners that you'll delve deeper into these topics, but first, you need to cover a few questions. As the instructor, it is your role to create a discussion regarding these important topics and ideas.

Explain to your learners that the take flight, take cover, take action approach taught by the Department of Homeland Security assumes that each person is responsible only for himself. By following their approach, you increase your own chances of survival, but you survive at the expense of others. Scripture tells us: "Let each of you look not only to his own interests, but also to the interests of others." –Philippians 2:3-4

Ask your learners how a Christian community can carry out the take flight, take cover, take action plan? How can church members run to safety and leave behind elderly or disabled church members who cannot escape? How can church members remain safely locked inside an office as their fellow church members are being killed on the other side of the door?

As the instructor, bring the discussion to an end by reminding learners that although none of this is pleasant to think about, by talking about it and planning in advance, they help the church prepare and possibly save lives. Answer any questions learners have before continuing to the next section.

Conducting a Safety Audit

As mentioned, one of the first steps to preparing in advance for an active shooter event is to conduct a safety audit. The safety audit allows you to identify any weaknesses in your building or in your operations that might make you an easy target for a would-be active shooter. In this section, we're going to look at how to conduct a safety audit.

Facility Assessment

The safety audit starts with an assessment of the buildings and grounds. We'll call this part of the audit the facility assessment. Some things to take a look at include access points, exit routes, and safe rooms, cameras and security systems, and communication strengths and weaknesses. Let's look at these aspects of the facility assessment in more detail.

Access Points

Where could someone enter the building? Examine all doors, windows, roof latches, gates, etc. to be sure they are working as expected and that they are secure. Consider possibilities other than the main entrance. Are there fire escape doors? Doors or windows from the basement? Unsecured windows on the ground floor? Does the kitchen have a door to the outside? How can each entrance be fortified?

Determine what measures can be taken to make these access points more secure. Additionally, is there a way these access points can be monitored (e.g., cameras or door alarms)? Do church members understand the importance of keeping doors locked? Your system for fortifying the access points will only be as good as the people who use them. If members are in the habit of, say, propping an exterior door open because it's bothersome to have to go down and let people in when they're trying to have a meeting, you will have to educate them.

Identify Exit Routes

Are all exits clearly marked and easy to find? Are they fortified from the outside but easy to get out of from the inside? Map out two exit routes from all main church areas. Identify at least two ways to get outside from any given spot in the building. Consider posting diagrams throughout the church that show the path to the two nearest exits, similar to the diagrams hotels post on the doors of guest rooms.

Evacuating Worshippers

While looking at exits and exit routes, figure out how the sanctuary could be evacuated in the event of an emergency during worship service. How many worshippers typically attend service each week? How would they all get out if a shooter event happened during worship? Chances are, worshippers do not know where all of the exits are. Develop a plan for how members of the Containment Team would quickly guide worshippers to the exits and away from the danger zone.

Identify Safe Rooms

If people couldn't get out, where could they hide? Determine which rooms could be used as safe rooms during an active shooter event. The best safe rooms are those that have more than one way out. Be certain those rooms have locking doors. Make sure all potential safe rooms—including all classrooms and offices—have locks. Map out routes from populated areas to safe rooms. Take some time to figure out how you could get people from the sanctuary or the social hall to a safe room. Again, map out some routes.

Assess Building Security

You'll also want to look at all the security mechanisms your church has in place. What kind of security does the main entrance have? That is, who monitors the people entering the church before and during worship? Who monitors people entering the church when the building is open at other times? Are cameras well placed and working, and who monitors them? Who is responsible for monitoring the video feed from security cameras? Is the building security system adequate?

Examine and test all alarm systems, perimeter lighting, and closed-circuit television systems. Do they work properly? Are they adequate for your security needs? If not, determine what upgrades need to be made. How quickly could the building be secured against a potential threat on the outside? If you became aware of a threat outside the building, how quickly could the building be locked to keep the people inside safe?

Assess Communication

How would you communicate a threat in the building to the pastor during worship service? What about to members inside the building? Assess your communication protocols within the Church Safety Team and with church members.

Within the Church Safety Team: Does your radio communication system work adequately and meet your needs? If not, determine what you need and get it changed as soon as possible.

With Church Members: This one is trickier. How will people in different parts of the church know that an active shooter event is taking part elsewhere in the building? For example, if an active shooter event were to begin in the sanctuary during service, how would adults in the children's area know so they could lock classroom doors?

What about the people in the kitchen preparing food for after service? And what if service is not in session? What if service let out a few minutes ago or it's a Saturday morning or a weeknight? People could possibly be anywhere in the building. How would you communicate the emergency to them? If your church has no intercom system, you will need runners to alert people. This would be part of the Containment Team's role.

Come up with a plan for how it would work. How do you know what members are in the building and where they are? This is related to the issue of communicating the emergency to members. How do you even know who's in the building and where they are during non-worship hours? You may want to consider a sign-in/sign-out system for evenings and non-worship hours.

Discussion

Many churches find security issues that need to be addressed when they do their security audit. Discuss the following question: How can you raise awareness among church leaders about issues that need to be addressed so action can be taken?

Preparing an Emergency Action Plan

The security audit is just one step in the process. Once you've identified and are fixing your security weaknesses, you should prepare a written emergency action plan. In this section, we'll take a look at what should be included in that plan.

Lockout

If an active shooter or known threat were outside the building, lockout procedures would go into effect. The emergency plan should describe lockout procedures, including:

- Secure all access doors & vehicle gates.
- Consider moving members to interior/safe rooms.
- Monitor cameras.
- Call 911 or wait for all clear signal from law enforcement.
- Members would shelter-in-place until law enforcement issued an all-clear.

Lockdown

In the event of an active shooter in the building, lockdown procedures would go into effect. The emergency plan should describe Lockdown procedures, including:

- Containment Team helps church members get out of the building.

- Safe rooms are secured and members who couldn't get out shelter inside.
- Engagement Team works to de-escalate or neutralize the shooter.

Note: In a lockdown, exterior doors should be left unlocked to facilitate entrance by law enforcement.

Other Emergencies

Although this section is about active shooter emergencies, the emergency plan should include procedures for handling all types of emergencies. Note that different kinds of emergencies require different kinds of responses. Your plan should include fire evacuation and bomb threat procedures, as well as whatever weather or environmental emergencies are most common in your area (e.g., tornado, earthquake, etc.).

Is Worship in Session?

Your emergency plan needs to consider when the emergency happens. You will need different procedures depending on what's going on in the church. If worship is in session, you may have a large number of members all in one place. You also have the largest number of Church Safety Team members on duty.

However, as we've already discussed, the event could happen during off hours, when worship is not in session, which means the pastor may not be on property, and you'll have both fewer church members and fewer Church Safety Team members on hand. The challenges would be different (e.g., fewer Church Safety Team members on the premises, members spread throughout the building). Also, who would have the authority to execute emergency procedures if the pastor was not in the building? The plan should spell that out.

People with Special Needs

Churches have members of all ages and all abilities. The emergency plan should consider who will assist and protect children, the elderly, wheelchair and scooter-bound members, and the hearing-impaired/visually impaired members.

Plan for the Aftermath

A good emergency action plan also outlines how to handle the aftermath of an active shooter event. Activities after an event might include:

- Account for all church members: This will be difficult as you will likely have no way of knowing exactly who was in the building at the time of the event. Having a designated unification area where family members can reunite will help. (Make sure the action plan designates a unification area.)
- Notify families of casualties in cooperation with law enforcement: Law enforcement will probably take the lead on this. However, your knowledge about how to reach family members will help.
- Hold a press conference and/or respond to media: The press will show up with questions. Someone (preferably someone with PR experience) should be designated as the official spokesperson. Church Safety Team members and others should not answer questions or agree to interviews with the media. Instead, refer all media representatives to the designated person.
- Tend to the emotional/spiritual well-being of survivors: People who survive an active shooter event typically need counseling and help. Consider in advance how this might be handled.
- Cleaning/rehabilitation of building: The building—or parts of the building—may be unusable. Consider how and where worship and other church activities would be held if the church could not be used.

Discussion

Start a brief discussion by posing the following question: In an emergency, how can you protect and assist the members of the congregation who have special needs?

Containment and Engagement Teams

In this section, we are going to look specifically at what you as Church Safety Team members will do during an active shooter event. We'll talk more in-depth about Containment and Engagement Teams, and we'll review what you (hopefully) already know about the use of force.

Your Decision

The first thing to make clear is that responding to an active shooting situation puts your life in danger. Therefore, this must be your decision. No one can or should order you to do this. Everyone must make this decision for themselves, and everyone must accept whatever choice their fellow Church Safety Team members make about this. All of you should be prayerful about the role God wants you to play in protecting the people of the church.

Weapons Policy

Review the Church Safety Team's weapons policy. All members must meet the minimum legal requirements to carry a firearm, be familiar with use of force laws and church policy regarding use of force, and be sufficiently trained to use firearms in a tactical situation. Ask your learners: Do use of force laws allow you to use force against an active shooter in the church?

Use of Force

A full discussion on use of force laws can be found in Chapter 14, but this is a good time to remind everyone of the legal requirements regarding the use of force:

Use only the force that is reasonable and necessary for the situation: The law allows you only to use the level of force that is reasonable and necessary for the situation. The force you use can only be proportional to the force used by the aggressor. And, if the subject surrenders or stops using force, you cannot continue to use force against him.

Note: Deadly force should not be used unless it is necessary to prevent the aggressor from causing serious bodily harm or death to another person.

Avoid shooting toward a crowd: If you use a firearm, be aware of innocent people behind or near the aggressor.

Know that pointing a gun has legal implications. Be certain about what you are doing. Taking someone's life, even when you are legally justified in using deadly force, can change your life forever.

Know that drawing a weapon can escalate the situation and the precious seconds it takes to holster your weapon could slow down your ability to engage in a self-defense response.

Ask your learners: So, would deadly force be justifiable if it was used to stop a shooter who was actively engaged in killing people in the church? [Answer: It could be, but keep in mind that the decision as to whether deadly force was justifiable in any situation would ultimately be up to a judge or jury in a court of law. You don't automatically get to walk away a hero. You will likely face criminal and/or civil liabilities. The church may be subject to liabilities as well.]

Safety Team Response

During an active shooter event, the Containment Team moves people from the danger area and either out of the building or into hiding. The Engagement Team tries to de-escalate the situation and/or prepares to use force against the shooter.

Containment Team

The Containment Team is responsible for protecting potential victims. This includes:

Getting the pastor to safety: There should be at least one Church Safety Team member designated at each worship service as the pastor's safety detail, responsible for getting him/her to safety in the event of an emergency.

Getting children to safety and/or securing children's area: Similarly, one or more Church Safety Team members should be responsible for protecting the children in the nursery, in Sunday School, in the children's area, etc.

Communicating the emergency to members in offices, classrooms, kitchen, etc.: If your building has no intercom system, Church Safety Team members may have to be assigned as runners to alert people throughout the building.

Evacuating members, getting them to safe rooms, or helping them hide: A major task would be to help members get to safety by guiding them to exits, safe rooms, or hiding places.

Preventing shooter from entering populated areas: The Containment Team would be responsible for guarding the areas where members were in hiding, to keep the shooter from being able to get to them.

Engagement Team

Meanwhile, the Engagement Team would be moving toward the shooter with the goal of bringing the event to an end by:

- De-escalating the situation
- Swarming the shooter
- Incapacitating the shooter
- Using non-deadly force
- Using deadly force

Notice that deadly force is the last item on the list and should only be used if the shooter is actively involved in killing people and no other option is available.

When the Event Is Over

When the event is over, notify 911. Make sure law enforcement dispatchers know the threat is over. Note that arriving officers may not have been notified and may arrive on the scene expecting the event to still be in progress. Maintain lockdown until police arrive.

Allow law enforcement officers to comb the area and verify there are no additional shooters and no additional threats. Law enforcement will issue the all-clear signal. Many Containment Team members may be with church members in safe rooms or outside the building. Be sure to notify them when an all-clear has been issued. Also, if the pastor and/or key church leaders are not on the premises, they should be notified of the event right away. (They shouldn't find out about it on the news.)

Provide medical aid to injured people. Once law enforcement has verified that the threat is over, EMTs will be allowed to tend to the injured. Church Safety Team members may assist in caring for the wounded. Treat the shooter if it is safe to do so. Finally, church members should evacuate to the unification area and wait there until law enforcement permits them to leave.

Discussion

Start a discussion on how the Church Safety Team would respond during an active shooter event in your church, by asking the following questions: Why is deadly force considered a last resort? What are some of the ways Church Safety Team members could "engage" a shooter and possibly bring an event to an end without using deadly force?

If learners have trouble with the second question, offer the following hints: "Remember that approximately 13% of active shooter events in the FBI study were ended by unarmed civilians. Also, recall some of the tactics described as part of take flight, take cover, take action. Finally, keep in mind that Church Safety Team members will have an advantage because they know the building better than the shooter."

Training and Drills

In this section, we are going to look at strategies for giving the Church Safety Team and church members a chance to practice what to do in an active shooter emergency.

Active Shooter Drills

Many workplaces and schools have begun to have active shooter drills, for much the same reason that they have fire drills—when people have practiced what to do, they are more likely to stay calm during an emergency and more likely to survive. At many colleges, active shooter training is a required part of freshman orientation. Increasingly, churches are also having active shooter drills. The question is: should this church have active shooter drills?

Lay the Groundwork for a Drill

Once you decide to have an active shooter drill, you will need to plan carefully. Begin your plans for an active shooter drill by getting the support of your church leadership. Your pastor must be behind this 100% or it will never get off the ground. If necessary, conduct several meetings with the pastor and church decision-makers where you carefully explain why it's important.

Help your pastor understand that many schools and workplaces already carry out such drills and that—like fire drills—active shooter drills raise awareness and minimize death and injury if there is ever a real emergency. Consider calling the drill a "lockdown drill" if that makes it easier to accept.

Once you get your pastor's approval, set a tentative date and begin the planning. Local law enforcement can assist as you prepare for your drill. Have them visit your building, review your emergency plan, and make suggestions as necessary. They can provide tips for improving your plan or making it even more comprehensive. Also get their assistance in carrying out your drill. They can likely make your drill more effective by helping you create realistic practice situations.

Train the Safety Team

Training for the Church Safety Team ahead of the all-church drill is a must. Separate training for the Safety Team training will allow you to evaluate your communication procedures, evacuation procedures, safe room and lockdown procedures. It will also help you make certain that everyone on the Church Safety Team knows exactly what to do.

Prepare Childcare Workers & Children

You'll need special training for the adults who serve as childcare workers. They'll need to know how to lock and barricade their classroom or nursery, silence devices, turn off lights, draw shades and help the children hide and stay quiet. They should be taught not to open the door for anyone except Church Safety Team personnel who say a pre-arranged code word. The children and the childcare workers should have an opportunity to practice in advance of the large all-church lockdown drill—so everyone knows exactly what to do.

Educate Church Members

The entire congregation will also have to be trained in advance. This includes instruction on how to get to the nearest exit quickly if it is safe to do so, or how to go into lockdown and hide from the shooter, if necessary. Church members need to be taught the three-step protocol –take flight, take cover, take action—along with how and when to use each part of the protocol. They should have ample opportunity to practice and ask questions before the all-church drill.

During the Drill: Rules for Evacuation

If at all possible, get out of the area. Church members should leave belongings behind, take one of the pre-determined escape routes, and get away from the shooter. Once outside, they should keep moving and get as far away from the site of the shooting as possible. This is different from, say, a fire drill, in which church members may be instructed to meet in a unification area at a far corner of the property. During an active shooter event, the goal is to get far away, help others escape whenever possible, and warn unsuspecting people who may be unknowingly moving toward the shooter.

Try to stay together. Keep track of others who have escaped with you and don't allow anyone to run off on their own. Contact 911 only when you are well away from the shooter. Be prepared to tell the emergency dispatcher where the shooter is located, to give a description of the shooter, to tell what kinds of weapon(s) the shooter has, etc.

The Church Safety Team, at its discretion, may choose to evacuate safe rooms that are in parts of the building well away from the shooter. For this purpose, a code word should be established in advance. People in lockdown should be instructed to only open the door for Church Safety Team members who use the code word.

During the Drill: Rules for Safe Rooms

For people who can't get to an exit, it's important to know how to hide. If possible, try to get into a designated safe room. Close and lock the door. Barricade it with a file cabinet or other heavy furniture. Lacking heavy furniture, stack chairs, wastebaskets, or whatever is available in such a way that they would fall onto someone bursting into the room. Turn out the lights. Close any blinds or shades. Silence all computers, phones, toys, and other devices that make noise.

Don't huddle together in one area of the room. Instead, spread out all over the room and stay low to the ground. Know the difference between concealment and cover. Concealment hides you from view but does not stop a bullet. Whenever possible, choose cover rather than concealment. When you take cover, you hide behind an object that can protect you from being struck by a bullet.

Do not open the door for anyone except the police or a Church Safety Team member who uses the code word. When an active shooter event begins, Church Safety Team members should ensure that all doors are closed and locked, and church members are safely in hiding. If possible, Church Safety Team members should fortify hallways near the safe rooms in an effort to prevent the shooter from getting near those rooms.

Discussion

Create a brief discussion on the need for active shooter drills at your church, by asking the following questions: Would an active shooter drill be helpful for this church? Why or why not? How can church leadership be convinced of the need for drills? What are your next steps?

If learners agree that a drill would be beneficial for their church, try to guide the discussion toward how this might be accomplished, who would need to be convinced, what the next step should be.

Review What You Have Learned

Use the following activity to review important concepts discussed in this chapter.

Step 1. There are six concepts to review. Divide the learners into six groups. (Groups can be as small as one person if the class is small.) Assign one of the following concepts to each group. Ask the group to review their notes and be prepared to explain the concept to the class.

- Take Flight, Take Cover, Take Action
- Concealment vs. Cover
- Safe Room
- Lockout vs. Lockdown
- Unification Area

- Containment Team vs. Engagement Team

Step 2. Give groups one to two minutes to prepare. Call on groups one at a time to explain their assigned concept. Encourage them to be brief. Their explanations should not take more than one to two minutes. Ask probing questions of each group to be sure they really understand. If someone needs help, or really didn't understand a concept, ask others in the class to help explain it.

Step 3. Congratulate everyone for doing a great job. Explain that they've only scratched the surface in discussing some of these topics. The Church Safety Team may want to have follow-up meetings to talk in more detail about some of the topics raised in class, and to get to work on a safety audit and an emergency action plan. Close with a prayer.

Chapter 13:
Natural Disasters

In this chapter, we will briefly cover some of the most common types of natural disasters that might affect your church and its congregation. These are threats like fires, floods, earthquakes, tornadoes and the like. We touched on some of these topics back in Chapter 7, but we will flesh out your understanding better in the sections that follow.

Understanding the Need for Severe Weather and Natural Disaster Preparedness

Churches need to be prepared to deal with severe weather. Use this information to educate your congregation on how to deal with each type of severe weather situation and to plan how to act as a receiving facility during a severe weather event. This chapter will cover the following:

- Earthquakes
- Floods
- Hurricanes
- Thunderstorms
- Tornadoes
- Winter storms

Because churches are often receiving facilities for other institutions' evacuations, Church Safety Team leaders should also know how to prepare to be a receiving facility.

Plan Ahead

Evacuation Procedures

If civil authorities require evacuation, you should already have a plan in place for how to safely evacuate your staff, volunteers, and attendees. Special care should be taken in evacuating children, people in poor health, and the elderly. Please see Chapter 7 and Chapter 11 for more information on general evacuations.

Emergency Supplies

If the church is functioning as a refuge in severe weather, it is important to have emergency supplies stocked. Include three days' worth of supplies. Please see Chapter 8 for a full discussion on the types of supplies your church should stockpile.

Backup Information

Because church records may be destroyed during a severe weather situation, it is important to have an offsite backup of information such as the following:

- Insurance agents' contact information and policy types and numbers
- Church inventory lists
- Bank's contact information, account types numbers
- Telephone numbers of the electric, gas, and water companies (CDC, 2014, "Earthquakes")

Earthquakes

The American National Red Cross (2016) defines an earthquake as "a sudden, rapid shaking of the earth caused by the breaking and shifting of rock beneath the earth's surface" ("Earthquake preparedness").

There were 32 earthquakes within the United States in 2012 alone, with 27 of those rated as a magnitude 5.9 or higher.

At this time, there is no warning system to alert people that an earthquake is imminent, but a system is being developed and tested for the west coast of the United States (U. S. Geological Survey, 2016). During earthquakes, people are most often hurt and injured by falling furniture, such as bookcases, and shattered glass from windows (American National Red Cross, 2016, "Earthquake preparedness"; CDC, 2014, "Earthquakes").

Worldwide, earthquakes killed 9,624 people in 2015 alone.

People often think that doors are the strongest part of a foundation, but this is not true. Instead of standing in a doorway, take cover under a sturdy piece of furniture (American National Red Cross, 2016, "Earthquake preparedness"). If people can feel an earthquake while they are sheltering in the church, advise them to drop to the floor, find cover under furniture (such as a desk or table), and hold on to that cover (American National Red Cross, 2016, "Earthquake preparedness").

If possible, have people go to an interior room because exterior rooms are more likely to have doors and windows that break during the shaking (Southern California Earthquake Center, 2017, "How to protect yourself during an earthquake"). Smoke alarms and sprinkler systems may go off even if there is no fire (American National Red Cross, 2017, "Earthquake safety").

Here are tips for specific situations during earthquakes:

- If people are outside, they should stay outside and get low on the ground to avoid falling to the ground. People should avoid dangerous areas such as buildings, sinkholes, power lines, fuel lines, gas lines, trees, and streetlights (American National Red Cross, 2009, "Earthquake safety checklist"; CDC, 2014, "During an earthquake: Outdoor safety").
- If people are driving, they should pull over and avoid buildings, bridges, overpasses, and other unsafe areas as detailed above; set the parking brake; and stay in the car until the shaking has finished (CDC, 2014, "During an earthquake: Outdoor safety"; Department of Homeland Security, n.d., "Earthquakes").

- People in wheelchairs should lock their wheels and remain seated, covering their heads and necks with their arms and hands (CDC, 2014, "During an earthquake: Some specific situations"; Department of Homeland Security, n.d., "Earthquakes").
- People who are trapped in buildings should try to get someone's attention by hitting metal or a hard object (CDC, 2014, "During an earthquake: Some specific situations").

The above tips can save lives.

After an earthquake, do not turn the gas back on; do not use matches, lighters, camp stoves, or barbeques; do not use telephones unless you have a medical emergency or fire; realize that emergency responders may have other people they have to help before they can help you (United States Geological Survey, 2017, "Things NOT to do"). There may be aftershocks even months after the earthquake. People should drop, cover, and hold on during these aftershocks (American National Red Cross, 2017, "Earthquake preparedness").

Earthquakes can also cause landslides and tsunamis (American National Red Cross, 2009, "Earthquake safety checklist"; American National Red Cross, 2017, "Earthquake preparedness"). Great ShakeOut Earthquake drills are held annually to help individuals and organizations prepare for earthquakes. Your church can register to be part of the next drill at https://www.shakeout.org/register/.

After an earthquake, there may be aftershocks. Advise people to drop, cover, and hold on during these aftershocks, which may come even months after the earthquake (American National Red Cross, 2016, "Earthquake preparedness"). Earthquakes can also cause landslides and tsunamis (American National Red Cross, 2016, "Earthquake preparedness").

Floods

Floods are caused by heavy or steady rain (American National Red Cross, 2016, "Flood safety"). Flash floods usually occur within six hours and in one of three ways (National Weather Service, n.d., p. 8):

- Heavy or excessive rainfall
- Failure of a dam or levee
- Sudden release of water impounded by an ice jam

Flash floods and floods cause more than 90 fatalities each year in the United States alone (National Weather Service, n.d., p. 1). Most deaths occur because people do not realize how hazardous the flood can be.

Only heat kills more people in the US than flooding in terms of weather-related fatalities per year.

Only six inches of fast-moving water is necessary to knock someone off his/her feet and only "two feet of rushing water can carry away most vehicles, including SUVs and pickups" (National Weather Service, n.d., p. 8).

316 people were killed nationwide in flooding events within the United States in less than two years (2015 and part of 2016).

It is important to know the different terms for emergency alerts so you can decide how to proceed. The American National Red Cross (2016) provided these definitions ("Flood safety"):

- Flood/Flash Flood Watch: flooding or flash flooding is possible.
- Flood/Flash Flood Warning: flooding is occurring or will occur soon.

Landslides

Landslides are "downhill earth movements that can move slowly and cause damage gradually, or move rapidly, destroying property and taking lives suddenly and unexpectedly" and usually consist of "rocky material, snow, and (or) ice" (American National Red Cross, 2009, "Landslide safety checklist"; United States Geological Survey, 2000, "Landslide hazards").

Defending the Flock

Landslides include debris flow, mudslides, mudflows, and debris avalanches (CDC, 2014, "Landslides and mudslides"; United States Geological Survey, 2000, "Landslide hazards"). Lahars are mudflows "composed mostly of volcanic materials" and are especially dangerous (United States Geological Survey, 2000, "Landslide hazards"). Debris and mudflows can travel rapidly and far; they can grow by picking up "trees, boulders, cars, and other materials" (DHS, n.d., "Landslides & debris flow").

Each year, between 25 and 50 people are killed by landslides in the US.

Landslides are caused by several factors (CDC, 2014, "Landslides and mudslides"; United States Geological Survey, n.d., "Landslides 101"):

- Gravity
- Erosion from water sources
- Snow or heavy rain
- Earthquakes
- Wildfires
- Volcanic eruptions
- Excess weight from rain, snow, rock piles, or man-made structures

Landslides occur in all states and U.S. territories, resulting in up to 50 deaths and over $1 billion in damage each year for the United States (United States Geological Survey, n.d., "Landslides 101"). Damage can include broken utility lines and blocked transportation (CDC, 2014, "Landslides and mudslides").

Prepare your congregation by encouraging them to do emergency planning and have supplies packed such as discussed in the previous chapter. Before a landslide occurs, contact local emergency planners to determine the likelihood your church will be affected by a landslide, and work with the local authorities to lessen damage (CDC, 2014, "Landslides and mudslides"; DHS, n.d., "Landslides & debris flow"). Talk to your insurance company about debris flow damage covered by flood insurance policies (American National Red Cross, 2009, "Landslide safety checklist"). The National Flood Insurance Program may be able to help you if your insurance company cannot (DHS, n.d., "Landslides & debris flow").

During severe weather, listen to the radio for instructions from officials (CDC, 2014, "Landslides and mudslides"). Clues that a landslide is imminent include sounds such as rumbling, trees cracking, and boulders hitting each other, as well as sights such as tilted trees, fences, or walls; new cracks; doors/windows sticking or jamming for the first time; and collapsed pavement (CDC, 2014, "Landslides and mudslides"; DHS, n.d., "Landslides & debris flow"; United States Geological Survey, 2000, "Landslide hazards").

Evacuation is recommended for landslides (United States Geological Survey, n.d., "Landslide preparedness"). However, if your church shelters people during a landslide, have them go to the highest floor, curl into a tight ball, and cover their heads (DHS, n.d., "Landslides & debris flow"; United States Geological Survey, n.d., "Landslide preparedness"). Listen to the radio for emergency information (DHS, n.d., "Landslides & debris flow").

After a landslide, be aware that additional landslides or flooding may occur (CDC, 2014, "Landslides and mudslides"). Report damage to authorities, and help injured or trapped people (CDC, 2014, "Landslides and mudslides"; DHS, n.d., "Landslides & debris flow").

Hurricanes

Hurricanes cause "flooding, storm surge, high winds, and tornadoes" (American National Red Cross, 2016, "Hurricane preparedness"). Hurricanes are also known as typhoons and cyclones (CDC, 2015, "Hurricanes"). It is important to know the different terms for emergency alerts so you can decide how to proceed. The American National Red Cross (2009) provided these definitions:

- Hurricane Watch: hurricane conditions are a threat within 48 hours.
- Hurricane Warning: hurricane conditions are expected within 36 hours.

2017 was ranked among the top 10 most active years for damaging hurricanes in recorded history.

Tsunamis

"'Tsunami' comes from the Japanese words for harbor ('tsu') and wave ('nami')" (Pacific Tsunami Warning Center, 2009, "Frequently Asked Questions"). Tsunamis are also called seismic sea waves and "are a series of enormous waves created by an underwater disturbance such as an earthquake, landslide, volcanic eruption, or meteorite". Asteroids and comets landing in the ocean can also create tsunamis (CDC, 2013, "Tsunamis"; National Oceanic and Atmospheric Administration, 2017, "NOAA tsunami program"; National Weather Service, n.d., "Tsunami safety home").

These series of waves are called a "tsunami wave train" (Pacific Tsunami Warning Center, 2009, "Frequently Asked Questions"). Sometimes, tsunamis are mistakenly called "tidal waves," but they are not related to tides (American National Red Cross, 2017, "Tsunami preparedness"; Pacific Tsunami Warning Center, 2009, "Frequently Asked Questions").

The deadliest tsunami in recorded history was the great Indian Ocean tsunami of 2004.
The earthquake responsible released the energy of 23,000 Hiroshima-type atomic bombs.
The tsunami eventually claimed the lives of more than 150,000 people and affected 11 different countries.

A tsunami wave train can last for hours or even days and can begin within minutes after an earthquake (American National Red Cross, 2017, "Tsunami preparedness"). Pacific Tsunami Warning Center, 2009, "Frequently Asked Questions"). Tsunamis occur about twice a year (National Weather Service, n.d., "Tsunami safety home"). Tsunamis can destroy property, cause injuries, and kill people (National Weather Service, n.d., "Tsunami safety home").

Before a tsunami occurs, encourage your congregation to pack an emergency kit; plan evacuation routes from home, work, and schools; and have a plan for pets (American National Red Cross, 2017, "Tsunami preparedness").

These terms will help you understand the alerts (Department of Homeland Security, n.d., "Tsunamis"; National Weather Service, n.d., "Understanding tsunami alerts"; American National Red Cross, 2017, "Tsunami preparedness"):

- Tsunami Information Statement: an earthquake has occurred or a tsunami watch, advisory, or warning has been issued for another part of the ocean; however, there is no determined threat of a tsunami in the identified area at this time.
- Tsunami Watch: an earthquake has occurred; tsunami has not been verified but could occur within an hour.
- Tsunami Advisory: a tsunami is expected or is occurring and is dangerous to those near water; flooding of beach and harbor areas is possible and officials may close those locations.
- Tsunami Warning: a tsunami is expected or is occurring; dangerous coastal flooding and strong currents are likely so people should move to higher ground or inland.

The National Weather Service constantly monitors tsunami conditions from two warning centers which specifically watch for tsunamis and earthquakes that could cause them (National Oceanic and Atmospheric Administration, 2017, "NOAA tsunami program," p. 1). Current tsunami threats are available at http://tsunami.gov/.

Because a tsunami may occur too suddenly for an official alert to occur, pay attention to natural warnings: strong or long earthquakes, a loud roar like a train, unusual ocean behavior such as a wall of water or sudden draining showing the ocean floor (National Weather Service, n.d., "Before a tsunami").

If there is a tsunami, people should immediately tell others of the warning—especially people who may have special needs such as infants, elderly people, and people with mobility or functional issues—and evacuate to higher ground that is ideally "100 feet above sea level or two miles away" (American National Red Cross, 2017, "Tsunami preparedness"; Department of Homeland Security, n.d., "Tsunamis"; Pacific Tsunami Warning Center, 2009, "Frequently Asked Questions").

People at the beach should not wait for an official warning but should immediately move to higher ground if they feel the earth shake (Pacific Tsunami Warning Center, 2009, "Frequently Asked Questions").

Unless your church is two miles away from the shore, you should not shelter people during a tsunami. After the tsunami, listen to officials about when it is safe to return to the area (National Weather Service, n.d., "After a tsunami").

Do not go to disaster areas until they are cleared by officials because emergency responders need time to work without interruptions of concerned citizens (Department of Homeland Security, n.d., "Tsunamis"). When authorities determine it is time to return, help injured people by following this process (American National Red Cross, 2017, "Tsunami preparedness"):

- CHECK: Check the scene to make sure it is safe to approach.
- CALL: Call for help.
- CARE: Care for the person by providing first aid if you have training.

Do not try to help people if you are not able to do so because people are often injured or killed by trying to help when they are not trained; just call for professionals to help them (Department of Homeland Security, n.d., "Tsunamis").

When allowed to return home, be careful about where the tsunami or flood waters have hit because damage may not be immediately visible (Department of Homeland Security, n.d., "Tsunamis").

Thunderstorms

Of all the natural disasters and weather-related threats that you face each year, none is more underappreciated than thunderstorms. According to the National Weather Service:

- There are 100,000 thunderstorms each year in the United States
- About 10% of all storms are classified as severe
- All thunderstorms have lightning, which causes 55-60 fatalities, 400 injuries, and more than $1 billion in insured losses each year

Thunderstorms can have straight-line winds and hail (National Weather Service, n.d., p. 1). Thunderstorms can also cause tornadoes, flash floods, and floods (see more on those events). Lightning is very dangerous, and people should immediately go inside if they hear thunder. Lightning can occur without rain, and "heat lightning" is lightning from a thunderstorm that is too far away for thunder to be heard (National Weather Service, n.d., p. 7).

Straight-line winds are winds not associated with rotation of a tornado (National Weather Service, n.d., p. 8). They can exceed 125 mph and cause as much destruction as a tornado (National Weather Service, n.d., pp. 1, 8). Hail causes more than $1 billion in crop and property damage each year (National Weather Service, n.d., p. 1). Hail only forms in thunderstorms and can fall as fast as 100 mph (National Weather Service, n.d., p. 9).

The largest hailstone ever recorded fell in South Dakota. It weighed almost two pounds and was almost 19 inches in circumference.

It is important to know the different terms for emergency alerts so you can decide how to proceed. The National Weather Service (n.d.) provided these definitions:

- Severe Thunderstorm Watch: severe thunderstorms are likely to occur in your area.
- Severe Thunderstorm Warning: severe thunderstorms are occurring or likely to occur. There is an imminent danger to life and property.

Tornadoes

Tornado Facts:

Can move up to 70 mph.

Rotating winds as fast as 200 mph.

Kill up to 65 people per year.

At least 1,500 tornadoes per year in the US.

The American National Red Cross (2016) defines a tornado as "a violently rotating column of air extending from the base of a thunderstorm down to the ground ("Tornado"). There are about 1,200 tornadoes each year that cause 60-65 fatalities and 1,500 injuries (National Weather Service, n.d., p. 3).

Tornadoes occur throughout the year, at any time of the day (National Weather Service, n.d., p. 3). Tornado intensities are rated on the Enhanced Fujita Scale between EF0 (weakest) to EF5 (strongest)" (National Weather Service, n.d., p. 3). Tornadoes move at an average of 30 mph, but can be still or as fast as 70 mph (Department of Homeland Security, n.d., "Tornadoes"). Rotating winds can be more than 200 mph (National Weather Service, n.d., p. 5). Tornadoes that form over water are call waterspouts (Department of Homeland Security, n.d., "Tornadoes").

There are several indications that a tornado may form:

- A dark or green-colored sky (CDC, 2014, "During a tornado")
- A large, dark, low-lying cloud (CDC, 2014, "During a tornado")
- Wall cloud, an isolated lowering of the base of a thunderstorm (American National Red Cross, 2016, "Tornado")

- Cloud of debris (American National Red Cross, 2016, "Tornado")
- Large hail (American National Red Cross, 2016, "Tornado"; CDC, 2014, "During a tornado")
- Funnel cloud, a visible rotating extension of the cloud base (American National Red Cross, 2016, "Tornado")
- A loud roar that sounds like a freight train (CDC, 2014, "During a tornado")

It is important to know the different terms for emergency alerts so you can decide how to proceed. The American National Red Cross (2016) provided these definitions:

- Tornado Watch: tornadoes are possible.
- Tornado Warning: a tornado has been sighted or indicated by weather radar.

During a tornado, "the safest place to be is an underground shelter, basement or safe room" (American National Red Cross, 2016, "Tornado"). The CDC (2014) recommends the following, provided verbatim below:

- Move away from windows and glass doorways.
- Go to the innermost part of the building on the lowest possible floor.
- Do not use elevators because the power may fail, leaving you trapped.
- Protect your head and make yourself as small a target as possible by crouching down ("During a tornado").

Avoid big rooms (e.g., gymnasiums, cafeterias, or theaters) because those areas generally have roof structures "supported solely by the outside walls. Most such buildings hit by tornados cannot withstand the enormous pressure. They simply collapse" (CDC, 2014, "During a tornado").

Winter Storms

Winter storms can vary from snow lasting a couple of hours to white-out conditions that last days. They are also often "accompanied by dangerously low temperatures and sometimes by strong winds, icing, sleet and freezing rain" (American National Red Cross, 2016, "Winter storm"). It is important to know the different terms for emergency alerts so you can decide how to proceed:

- Winter Storm Outlook: storm conditions are possible in the next two to five days (American National Red Cross, 2016, "Winter storm").
- Winter Weather Advisory: conditions (e.g., snow, freezing rain, and sleet) are expected to cause significant inconveniences and may be hazardous (American National Red Cross, 2016, "Winter storm"; CDC, 2015, "Winter weather").
- Winter Storm Watch: storm conditions possible within the next 36 to 48 hours (American National Red Cross, 2016, "Winter storm").
- Frost/Freeze Warning: expect below-freezing temperatures (CDC, 2015, "Winter weather").
- Winter Storm Warning: life-threatening, severe winter conditions have begun or will begin within 24 hours (American National Red Cross, 2016, "Winter storm"; CDC, 2015, "Winter weather").
- Blizzard Warning: storm occurring—snow and strong winds, near-zero visibility, deep snow drifts, and life-threatening wind chill (CDC, 2015, "Winter weather").

If your church is sheltering people during a winter storm, prevent pipes from freezing by keeping faucets running and opening cabinet doors (American National Red Cross, 2016, "Winter storm").

Acting as a Receiving Facility

If your church is considering sheltering people during severe weather events, the Department of Homeland Security (2014) provided information for churches planning to build "safe rooms" or other spaces for people to shelter in place during tornadoes, floods, and hurricanes.

When acting as an emergency shelter, there are special issues to address, including knowing the fire codes on how many people the church can hold; how to provide security, food, and janitorial services; and how to store people's possessions including weapons (Brotherhood Mutual Insurance Company, 2016, "Guidelines").

When sheltering people from a tornado, have them face an interior wall with their elbows on their knees and their hands over the backs of their heads (National Weather Service, n.d., p. 13).

Volcanoes

"A volcano is a mountain that opens downward to a reservoir of molten rock below the surface of the earth. Unlike most mountains, which are pushed up from below, volcanoes are vents through which molten rock escapes to the earth's surface. When pressure from gases within the molten rock becomes too great, an eruption occurs" (DHS, n.d., "Volcanoes").

In volcanoes, rocks melt and become magma. The magma rises and pushes out of vents in the volcano; after eruption, the magma is called lava (United States Geological Survey, 2017, "How do volcanoes erupt").

Volcanoes can be explosive—and thus more dangerous—when the magma is thick and sticky (United States Geological Survey, 2017, "How do volcanoes erupt"). If the magma blasts into the air and breaks apart, the pieces are called tephra and can be tiny ash or house-sized boulders (United States Geological Survey, 2017, "How do volcanoes erupt").

50 to 60 volcanoes erupt per year around the world, with an average of one per week.

Defending the Flock

Although some people think that volcanoes are caused by earth-quakes, that is not true; earthquakes merely indicate a "geologically active landscape" in which volcanoes are also likely (American National Red Cross, 2017, "Volcano preparedness"). Volcanologists are unable to predict when a volcano will become "restless" but they can make educated estimates about when the volcano will erupt once activity begins (American National Red Cross, 2017, "Volcano preparedness").

Lava flows are the most dangerous aspect of volcanoes in Hawaii, but in most places, the volcanic ash and volcanic mudflows (lahars) are more dangerous (American National Red Cross, 2017, "Volcano preparedness"). Ash can damage vehicles, machinery, and utilities and clog water treatment facilities (American National Red Cross, 2017, "Volcano preparedness"; Environmental Protection Agency, n.d., "Volcanoes").

Volcanic ash can also hurt infants, elderly people, and people with respiratory diseases (CDC, 2012, "Key facts about volcanic eruptions"; DHS, n.d., "Volcanoes"; Environmental Protection Agency, n.d., "Volcanoes"). Volcanic ash can scratch people's eyes and "be hazardous to grazing livestock" (Environmental Protection Agency, n.d., "Volcanoes").

Lahars can destroy bridges, buildings, and burn or smother people (American National Red Cross, 2017, "Volcano preparedness"; CDC, 2012, "Key facts about volcanic eruptions"). Additionally, volcanic gases such as sulfur dioxide can cause acid rain and other gases can "cause rapid breathing, headache, dizziness, swelling and spasm of the throat, and suffocation" (CDC, 2012, "Key facts about volcanic eruptions"; Environmental Protection Agency, n.d., "Volcanoes").

Sideways volcanic explosions are called lateral blasts and can kill through impact, heat or burial. These blasts have sufficient strength to level forests.

Before a volcano erupts, pack an emergency supply list and make a family emergency plan. Listen to local authorities regarding whether you should evacuate or shelter (CDC, 2012, "Key facts about preparing for a volcanic eruption"). If you evacuate, make sure you take an emergency supplies kit (CDC, 2012, "Key facts about preparing for a volcanic eruption"). During a volcano eruption, "avoid river valleys and low-lying areas" (DHS, n.d., "Volcanoes") during any form of travel.

If your church shelters people during a volcano, do the following (CDC, 2012, "Key facts about preparing for a volcanic eruption"):

- Close and lock all windows and outside doors
- Go into an interior room without windows that is above ground level
- Turn off all heating and air conditioning
- Close the fireplace damper (if applicable)

In addition to the emergency supplies, also have goggles and face masks available to protect people (CDC, 2012, "Key facts about preparing for a volcanic eruption"). If people are indoors, they should close all windows, doors, and fireplace/woodstove dampers (CDC, 2012, "Key facts about protecting yourself during a volcanic eruption").

If people are outdoors during an eruption, they should try to get inside; wear clothing that covers all skin; wear protective items such as goggles and masks; cover their heads; and seek immediate care for burns (CDC, 2012, "Key facts about protecting yourself after a volcanic eruption"; CDC, 2012, "Key facts about protecting yourself during a volcanic eruption"; DHS, n.d., "Volcanoes").

When authorities say it is safe to do so, remove ashfall from your roof because ash is very heavy and can cause buildings to collapse, especially if rain has made it heavier (American National Red Cross, 2017, "Volcano preparedness"; CDC, 2012, "Key facts about protecting yourself after a volcanic eruption"; DHS, n.d., "Volcanoes").

Finally, volcanic eruptions can cause acid rain, floods, landslides, mudslides, power outages, contamination of drinking water, and wildfires. (CDC, 2012, "Key facts about protecting yourself after a volcanic eruption"; CDC, 2012, "Key facts about volcanic eruptions"; DHS, n.d., "Volcanoes").

If the Church Is Destroyed

Severe weather may not only cause temporary inconveniences in deciding how to shelter people, but it may also damage your church. This worksheet (https://www.brotherhoodmutual.com/resources/safety-library/risk-management-forms/ministry-continuity-worksheet/) from the Brotherhood Mutual Insurance Company will help you to create a plan how to continue ministry if the church is destroyed by a severe weather event.

Teaching the Content

We estimate that teaching the content covered in this chapter should take between two and two and a half hours. Don't forget that, as always, the content can and should be customized to meet your church's specific needs and situation. In this instance, geographic location and geo-specific natural disasters common to that area should be your focus.

Explain to your learners that severe weather emergencies can happen at any time. Should a severe thunderstorm or other natural emergency happen while worship is in session or while members are in the church, it will be up to the Church Safety Team to help congregation members take care of themselves. Church Safety Team members might have to monitor conditions, help church members find appropriate shelter, and keep church members safe until authorities issue an "all clear."

In most of these emergencies, you would have to keep members indoors and protected until conditions changed or the threat was gone. In some cases, the hazardous conditions might continue for an extended period of time—like, for example, a snowstorm—so we'll also consider how you might plan for having to shelter people for an extended period of time. Hopefully, none of the situations we will be discussing today will ever impact your church. The purpose of this training, however, is to make sure you are ready if they do. It's better to be prepared than to be caught off guard.

Overview: Types of Hazards

We will discuss two types of hazards within this section, as well as how to prepare for them. These are emergency natural hazards and predictable natural hazards. Man-made hazards are covered individually in separate chapters of this book.

Emergency Natural Hazards

Emergency natural hazards are "acts of God" emergencies—weather-related or natural disaster emergencies that happen with little or no advance warning. Tornadoes and flash floods fall into this category. In these situations, you may have only a matter of minutes to get church members to safety. Advance planning, practice, and drills will be important because you will have to give directions and move people quickly.

Predictable Natural Hazards

These are also "acts of God" natural events, but they will not happen suddenly. You will have time to plan or even to suspend regular church activities so that people can seek appropriate shelter on their own. Hurricanes and extreme heat are examples of this type of hazard. Predictable natural hazards might impact your church if some church members or people in the community lack the resources to get to shelter. For example, in periods of extreme heat, the church may be called upon to operate as a "cooling center" for people who lack air conditioning in their homes.

Ice Breaker Activity

Explain to your learners that in the training today, you will be talking about how the Church Safety Team will protect the church and its members from all types of natural hazards. Although this is not a Bible class, be mindful throughout the class of how natural emergencies like tornadoes and earthquakes are always under God's control.

Step 1. Ask someone to read aloud Job 37:9-13 (New International Version) 9 The tempest comes out from its chamber, the cold from the driving winds. 10 The breath of God produces ice, and the broad waters become frozen. 11 He loads the clouds with moisture; he scatters his lightning through them. 12 At his direction they swirl around over the face of the whole earth to do whatever he commands them. 13 He brings the clouds to punish people, or to water his earth and show his love.

Step 2. Ask each learner to get a partner, preferably someone they don't know well or haven't met.

Step 3. Ask the partners to think about how God uses weather. For example, why does God create dangerous and destructive weather events? What purpose might they serve? Does the Bible text we just read give us any clues?

Step 4. Give the partners two to three minutes to discuss and come up with a possible answer.

Step 5. Call on several of the partners to share what they came up with. Ask other class members to comment or share their own perspective. Explain that we can't always know God's reasons. We can't always understand the mind of God. However, we do have God's promise that He will never leave us nor forsake us. (Hebrews 13:5) That includes during times of dangerous weather and uncertainty.

As we discuss our topic today, always keep this in mind: We will be looking for ways to protect God's people and keep them safe; meanwhile God is looking after us all.

Preparing for Emergency Natural Hazards

By Emergency Natural Hazards, we mean "acts of God" that happen with little or no advance warning, and that require immediate action to get people to safety.

Types of Hazards

Emergency natural hazards include:

- Thunderstorms
- Flash Floods
- Tornadoes
- Earthquakes

The planning required for each of these is a little different as is the response during the actual emergency. In addition, some geographic areas are more prone to certain kinds of emergency natural hazards than others. We'll take these hazards one at a time and, for obvious reasons, we'll spend the most time on the ones that are more likely to happen in our area.

Thunderstorms

Thunderstorms are the most common kind of natural hazard. they create more than $1 billion worth of insurance-reported damage each year in the U.S. All thunderstorms are dangerous—even small ones that pass quickly. It's the lightning, wind, and hail that make them dangerous.

Lightning is one of the top 3 storm-related killers in the U.S. On average, more than 50 people are killed in the U.S. each year by lightning, and another 400 or so are injured. Lightning can strike as much as 10 miles from where rain is falling, even when there is no rainfall. A rule of thumb is this: if you can hear thunder, you are close enough to the storm to be struck by lightning and you should seek shelter.

High wind is another dangerous aspect of thunderstorms. A

thunderstorm can have winds in excess of 100 mph and can cut a path of damage that extends for many miles; it's wind that creates most thunderstorm damage. Note that there does not have to be a tornado present for winds associated with a thunderstorm to be destructive.

Hail is a form of precipitation that can occur during thunderstorms; updrafts of wind can move raindrops upward so that they freeze before falling back to earth. Hail can fall in excess of 100 mph, damaging crops and injuring livestock and people.

Know the Difference

Weather conditions should be monitored anytime worship is in session and anytime people are in the building. Monitor weather especially closely if visual cues like dark clouds or heavy winds suggest a storm might be approaching. Also, be sure you know the difference between a Severe Thunderstorm Watch and a Severe Thunderstorm Warning.

Severe Thunderstorm Watch: A Severe Thunderstorm Watch means severe weather conditions are possible. It means the conditions are right for a storm having high winds and large hail. It means you should be vigilant and be prepared to seek shelter, if necessary. Inside the church, you should alert all Safety Team members on duty. If church members are engaged in outdoor activities, you may consider having them move indoors. The most important thing is to monitor radio transmissions closely for worsening weather conditions.

Severe Thunderstorm Warning: A Severe Thunderstorm Warning, on the other hand, means severe weather with life-threatening conditions has been spotted in your area, either by eyewitnesses or by radar. It means you should be prepared for high winds, damaging hail, lightning, flash floods, and tornadoes. It also means you should seek shelter immediately.

Response to Thunderstorms

If a Severe Thunderstorm Warning is announced for your area, take action.

Get People Inside: Lightning poses a major threat to people outdoors during, before, and after a thunderstorm. Make sure there is no one in the parking lot or outside on the grounds of the building. If church is just letting out, you may want to move people to shelter indoors rather than allowing them to leave. If members are just arriving as the Severe Thunderstorm Warning is issued, it may be safer for them to stay in their vehicles than to leave their cars and try to run to the building.

Move People to Interior Shelter: Quickly move members to interior spaces in the building away from doors and windows, the same as you would for a tornado.

Avoid Use of Corded Phones, Electrical Equipment, and Plumbing: Electrical equipment and corded telephones can conduct electricity, as can plumbing. Discourage the use of electrical equipment and lavatory facilities while under the Severe Thunderstorm Warning.

Monitor Weather Conditions: Monitor conditions for additional threats such as tornadoes or flash floods. Do not allow members to leave the shelter area until the Severe Thunderstorm Warning has been lifted.

Floods & Flash Floods

Floods can occur any time there is heavy, sustained, or frequent rainfall, or during the spring thaw season. Floods happen relatively slowly—over the course of several days or several hours—giving the Church Safety Team time to alert church members or move people and equipment to higher ground.

Flash floods are rapidly occurring flooding conditions, often accompanied by fast-moving water. Flash floods can happen when there is excessive rainfall, when a levee or dam overflows or is breached, or when water is suddenly released because an ice jam has broken or melted.

Flashfloods can also happen in low-lying areas when water from a heavy rainfall cascades down the sides of mountains.

Floods can occur anytime, but they are more likely to occur in certain seasons, depending on the location of your church. Early spring and the thawing of winter snow typically bring the threat of floods to the Midwest and Upper Midwest. In coastal areas, floods are more likely during or after hurricanes. In some parts of the country, heavy rain creates the possibility of mudslides as well.

Understand Flood Danger

Fast moving water is deceptively dangerous. People often drown during floods because they underestimate the danger of fast-moving water. As little as six inches of fast-moving water can knock a person off his feet and sweep him away, and 12 inches of fast-moving water can carry a vehicle away.

The best advice is to stay out of fast-moving water, if at all possible. People traveling in a vehicle should not cross a bridge over fast-moving flood water. Fast-moving water can quickly erode a bridge's foundations, making the bridge unstable and unsafe to cross. Never touch electrical equipment if you are wet or standing in water. Electrical equipment should be shut off before the flood, whenever possible.

If people are sheltered in your church, be careful never to serve food or water that has come into contact with flood waters. In fact, all food (including canned goods), water, plates, utensils, medical supplies, baby supplies, etc. that have come into contact with flood waters should be thrown out.

Response to Floods

Obviously, some churches will be more prone to floods than others. The Church Safety Team should ask these questions and develop plans accordingly.

- Is your church in a known flood plain?
- Is your church near a river, stream, or body of water that could overflow or be subject to a storm surge?
- Is your church in a coastal or low-lying area?
- Are hurricanes common in your area?
- Does your area have a "rainy season" or a period of the year when excessive rainfall is common?

Whether or not you answered yes to any of the above questions, the Church Safety Team should monitor weather conditions and be aware when there is a Flood Watch or Flood Warning in your area. If you know that floods or flash floods are a possibility at your church and a Flood Watch is in effect, the Church Safety Team should alert the pastor and/ or church leaders about the possible need to evacuate the church or get people quickly to safety.

Note that "watch" and "warning" are used for floods just as they are for severe thunderstorms. A Flood Watch means to be prepared, especially if you know you are in the possible path of flood water. A Flood Warning means a flood is imminent or is actually happening.

In a flash flood situation, there is often a very short window of time for people to get to safety. Depending on the location and structure of your building, there may be no safe place inside for people to escape flood waters. Church members may have to evacuate—on foot or by vehicle—to higher ground. If you have a large number of people, a plan like this might not be feasible. It may be more prudent to cancel church activities than to try to protect people from rapidly moving flood waters.

The Church Safety Team leader should not hesitate to contact the pastor or appropriate church leader is he/she believes it would be better to, say, cancel worship service rather than risk the safety of church members in a rapidly changing situation, such as a possible flash flood.

Even with monitoring and good advanced planning, emergencies can still happen. Have a back-up plan for what you would do if church activities could not be cancelled and church members could not be evacuated in time to avoid fast-moving or rapidly rising flood waters.

Tornadoes

Tornadoes take place on every continent except Antarctica. However, most of the world's tornadoes take place between the Appalachian Mountains and the Rocky Mountains, in the central and southern U.S. This area, that includes northern Texas, Oklahoma, Nebraska, Kansas and Arkansas, is often referred to as "Tornado Alley" because of the frequency of tornadoes.

Churches in these areas need to pay special attention to tornado safety planning. However, it's important to remember that tornadoes can strike anywhere; every church should have a plan.

Response to Tornadoes

Paying attention to local weather conditions, even when there are no obvious or known threats, is an important part of keeping the church and its members safe. This is similar to Severe Thunderstorm Watches and Severe Thunderstorm Warnings.

Make sure that your team understands Tornado Watch vs. Tornado Warning.

Tornado Watch: A Tornado Watch means conditions are right for the development of a tornado. It means you should monitor weather conditions closely and be ready to take shelter if necessary.

Tornado Warning: A Tornado Warning means a tornado has been sighted in your area by an eye witness or on radar. You should seek shelter immediately.

If your church comes under a Tornado Watch, require members engaged in outdoor activities to come inside. If there are separate, less sturdy buildings on church property, require people in those building to move to the sturdiest building and/or a building that has a tornado shelter. These precautions would make it easier to get people to a safe area quickly in the event of a tornado.

Similarly, if there are young children in the building and it might take a few minutes to move them to the tornado shelter area, consider not waiting for a Tornado Warning, but having them move and continue their activities in an area of the church that could provide tornado shelter if necessary.

Figure out in advance how you will alert church learners and members throughout the building if a Tornado Warning goes into effect. There may be tornado sirens in your that will make it obvious. If there are not, come up with a plan, such as:

- If a Tornado Watch is in effect when worship or other church activity lets out, the Church Safety Team should alert members and discourage them from leaving the building.

Obviously, time will be of the essence in a Tornado Warning situation. You might have only a couple of minutes' lead time—perhaps less than that. You should figure out in advance where the best tornado shelter areas are in your building and the best ways to get people there.

Come up with some easy-to-follow instructions in case worshippers must be moved from the sanctuary to a shelter area in another part of the church. For example, "I need everyone in these six rows to exit down the center aisle and follow Dave to the basement. Meanwhile, I need everyone in these six rows to exit to your right and follow Marla down that side aisle to the pastor's conference room. Leave your purses and belongings. Walk quickly, but don't run."

Once in the shelter areas, members should be instructed to sit on the floor in rows facing the wall, bent over with their heads close to their knees, arms and hands covering their head.

If there's no time to move people to designated shelter areas, do the best you can to have them take shelter where they are—on the ground, arms and hands covering their heads, under pews or heavy furniture, if possible.

Appropriate Tornado Shelter

Tornado response requires advance planning, especially if your church has a large congregation. Well in advance, the Church Safety Team should identify the possible tornado shelter areas in the building. Flying debris creates the greatest hazard during a tornado. For this reason, tornado shelter areas should be on lower floors of a building and need to be away from doors and windows. Acceptable areas might include:

- Interior rooms and hallways Interior hallways work well.
- Rooms and offices with no windows & no exterior doors.
- Interior classrooms, offices, and meeting rooms, if they have no windows, and no exterior doors.
- Basement areas, but be cautious if your church is in a low-lying area where heavy rain might cause the basement to flood.
- Don't overlook obvious spaces like lavatories. In some buildings, lavatories are interior spaces with no windows and, therefore, could provide shelter from tornadoes.

Large indoor spaces with no roof support beams, (e.g., most gymnasiums and auditoriums) do not provide good shelter. The walls or roofs of such spaces can collapse. The sanctuary of your church may be unacceptable as a tornado shelter for this reason. Seek the advice of emergency planning experts or a structural engineer before deciding to use your sanctuary as a tornado shelter.

The Church Safety Team leader should continue to monitor weather conditions until an "all clear" is sounded. Keep in mind that there is no 100% safe space during a tornado. Your goal as a Church Safety Team member is to have a plan in place that will minimize the possibility of injury or death in the event of a tornado.

Earthquakes

Some areas of the country are more prone to earthquakes than others. If your church is in a high-risk earthquake area, your Church Safety Team should plan have a plan for earthquake preparedness. Keep in mind that earthquakes—like tornadoes and other natural hazards—can happen even in low risk areas. High risk areas include:

- Western States: California, Oregon, Washington, Alaska
- New Madrid Fault Area: Missouri, Arkansas, Tennessee, and Kentucky
- East Coast: Mid-Atlantic coast, costal North Carolina, New England

Response to Earthquakes: Before the Quake

There is never any advance warning for an earthquake; earthquakes always hit by surprise. Therefore, advance planning is critical.

Buildings in earthquake risk areas should be free as possible of heavy items on shelves, hanging on walls, and even inside cabinets. These items could fall on someone or become projectiles during a quake. File cabinets, bookshelves, and other tall, heavy furniture should be anchored to walls so they cannot fall. Canned goods, utensils and other kitchen items should also be safely stored, so that they do not fall or fly off shelves.

Because there will be no time to give members instructions before the earthquake strikes, members will have to already know what to do. Hopefully, most people living in earthquake zones know how to respond to a quake, but it's worth reviewing with your church members; many of the old responses people may have learned as children (e.g., run outside or stand in a doorway) are not correct. An all-church drill at least once a year may be an excellent way to make sure people are informed and ready.

Response to Earthquakes: During the Quake

Most earthquakes last one minute or less. The Federal Emergency

Management Administration (FEMA) recommends the following response during an earthquake: drop, cover, hold on.

1. Drop: At the first sign of an earthquake, drop to the floor to keep from falling or being knocked over. If you can get under a desk or heavy table, do so. The pews in the sanctuary may offer some protection.
2. Cover: Cover your head and the back of your neck with your hands to protect yourself from falling items and debris.
3. Hold On: If possible, hold on to something stable and sturdy so that you remain steady during the quake.

People in wheelchairs and scooters may not be able to get to the ground. A wheelchair-bound person should make sure their device is locked, then bend forward in the seat, bringing their face as close to their knees as they can. They also should cover their head and back of their neck with their hands.

Response to Earthquakes: After the Quake

Once the earthquake is over, the Church Safety Team will have much to do.

Evacuate, if necessary: Quickly assess damage to the building. If there is obvious or even minor structural damage, it may be best to evacuate until you are certain that the building is structurally sound and safe.

Care for the injured: Anyone injured during the quake will need first aid until medical help can arrive. If the earthquake was extensive or severe, emergency response may be compromised; you may have to keep the injured comfortable for a considerable period. Members of your congregation who are medical professionals may be able to assist.

Monitor local conditions: Keep abreast of local emergency information to learn the seriousness of the quake. This will help you advise church members whether they should try to go home or whether to keep sheltering in the church for the time being. Also, be prepared for aftershocks.

Provide shelter-in-place options, if necessary: If the earthquake was extensive or damage was great, members may not be able to go home, at least not right away. Your emergency preparedness plan should include guidelines for how and where members could be sheltered in the church.

Discussion: Emergency Natural Hazards

Create a brief discussion about the natural hazards you have discussed so far. Ask any or all of the following questions to get learners thinking and talking: What have you learned so far about natural hazards that you didn't already know? In your opinion, is this church adequately prepared for a tornado? Why or why not? If we had to shelter two-thirds of our congregation in interior rooms and hallways, where would we put everyone? Given the geographic location of this church, which of these other emergency natural hazards should we be preparing for? What does this church need to do to be ready for some of these other hazards?

Preparing for Predictable Natural Hazards

So far, we've only talked about some of the deadliest kinds of natural hazards—the kind that happen with little or no advance warning. In this next section, we'll look at some kinds of "non-emergency" natural hazards. These are natural events that usually give you plenty of warning, but still have the potential to impact your church and its members.

Types of Hazards (Predictable Natural Hazards)

Predictable natural hazards include:

- Hurricanes
- Blizzards and Snowstorms
- Extreme Heat or Cold
- Wildfires

With rare exceptions, you will probably know when the church is about to be affected by one of these hazards. That will give you time to put your emergency preparedness plan into operation. Although these hazards are all different, the planning and preparation will often be similar.

Let's take a look at how you might prepare for predictable hazards.

Preparing for the Predictable

In the case of hurricanes, snowstorms, and wildfires, it is imperative that members of the Church Safety Team monitor conditions on a regular basis to be aware of impending events. Being aware of an impending event and being prepared for its severity or duration is important to keeping your church and its members safe.

Monitor Conditions: Hurricanes and their paths can be predicted relatively accurately. You will often have anywhere from three to seven days advance warning of an impending hurricane. Blizzards and snowstorms are also often predicted in advance, although occasionally a heavy snowfall will catch everyone by surprise. Wildfires can be very unpredictable and may require around-the-clock monitoring. Usually, you will know that conditions are right for wildfires or that the authorities are battling fires in your area.

Extreme heat or cold are the only weather conditions that may not require constant monitoring. Temperature change tends to happen slowly and rarely threatens the safety of members the way the other three hazards might. Nonetheless, extreme temperatures may affect operations at your church and may put some members at risk.

Cancel Activities: For most predictable hazards, the best way to keep church members safe will be to cancel church activities and encourage members and their families to seek appropriate shelter. Work with your church leadership to set up a protocol for canceling church activities. Determine how and at what point in a pending emergency you should confer with church leaders about canceling worship service or closing the church. Determine how members will be alerted that the church is closed so that no one shows up at your building seeking shelter.

Extreme heat or cold are the only events that may not require cancelling activities. If your church's heating and cooling systems work well enough for extreme conditions, church leaders may choose to continue with all church activities as planned or consider rescheduling them. Even if activities are cancelled and the church is closed, the building itself may be vulnerable to damage from one of these hazards. The Church Safety Team may assist or even take the lead in preparing the building for some of these predictable events.

Prepare the Building: To prepare the building for wildfires, work with custodial staff to ensure that there are no combustible items (e.g., dry leaves, newspaper, woodpiles, etc.) within about 30 feet of the building. Landscaping should be arranged so that there is no vegetation within about 100 feet of the building. Also, make sure that important church documents (e.g. baptism records, financial records, insurance records, etc.) are stored safely off the premises. Obviously, some of these preparations will have to be done well before your church is in a fire watch area.

To prepare the building for a hurricane, windows and glass doors should be boarded up. Outdoor furniture or equipment should be secured. Flooding is a possibility, so be certain that important items like church records are safely stored away from possible flood water. In some locations, the authorities encourage building owners to disconnect or turn off utilities. Be sure to follow any preparation instructions issued by the authorities.

In order to be ready for extreme heat or cold, the church's heating and cooling systems should be serviced and tuned-up at least once a year. Should the heating system fail during a period of extreme cold, steps should be taken to prevent pipes from freezing.

Shelter-in-Place: An unexpected snowstorm may require church members to shelter-in-place at the church until conditions improve. This is particularly true if roads are impassable or members' vehicles are not equipped for the weather. Extreme heat or cold may also cause the church to offer itself as a warming center or a cooling center to members whose homes are not equipped for the severe conditions.

For example, if you know there are many in your community who cannot afford air conditioning, you may want to open your building during the day as a "cooling center" where seniors, disabled people, or families with young children can spend the hottest part of the day. Advance planning is necessary in order for your church to be able to shelter people.

After the event, assess the damage and begin the work of cleaning up or digging out. Get the help of the custodial staff and church members if there is extensive work to be done.

Discussion

Start a discussion about the likelihood of any of these predictable events occurring near your church and ask the following questions: Which of these predictable hazards do we have to be most concerned about? Who is responsible for monitoring for these hazards? In what months/seasons should this monitoring take place? What's the procedure for notifying the Church Safety Team and church leaders of an impending hazard? Who can make the decision to cancel worship service at our church? Who can make the decision to cancel other activities and/ or to close the church? Who can make the decision to allow members to stay in the church because conditions on the outside have deteriorated or are unsafe (i.e., who makes the decision to allow members to use the church to shelter-in-place)?

Planning and Preparation

In this section, we'll take a look at what your church needs to do in order to be prepared for the hazards we've been discussing. Let's begin by taking a look at what might be involved in sheltering members from some of these hazards.

Can Your Church Be a Shelter?

As we've seen, this church might be called upon to shelter people during certain kinds of emergencies—and you might have to do so at a moment's notice. Clearly, this church can only shelter members safely if you have planned for this in advance. Here are some things you should be considering.

What are the building's occupancy limits? You must be careful to not violate building occupancy limits. These limits have been set for public health and public safety reasons; you risk creating additional safety or health hazards if you ignore these limits. So, the first thing you would need to know is: how many people can your building hold and still be safe? You would also need to know how many people can be housed in any given room.

The next issue is this: Even if you are meeting occupancy limits, you may not have comfortable space for many people. Keep in mind that families will need to spread out. They will need space for their belongings and space to stretch out and sleep. They will need privacy. They will need space for small children to be active.

What was, perhaps, supposed to be an overnight stay might become a days' long shelter situation if conditions on the outside deteriorate or an "all clear" is not sounded. Stress levels will increase if people are confined for an extended period. Do you honestly have the space to accommodate a significant number of people for several days—if it came to that? And do you have enough SAFE space? You need areas away from windows and doors. Depending on the type of emergency, you might not be able to use large spaces like a gymnasium or the sanctuary. Can interior hallways and basement areas accommodate a large number of members and their families?

Another major concern would be sanitation. You would need an adequate number of toilets. And if the lavatories were not in the safe area of the building—that is, in the building interior away from windows and doors—you might have to set up make-shift toilets. What about bathing?

People could get by with moist towelettes for a couple of days, but beyond that, you might need a way for people to shower or bathe.

Of course, you would have to provide food. How much food can your church keep on hand for emergencies? Where would you store it? Who would be responsible for regularly checking expiration dates and making sure the food on hand was fit for human consumption in the event of an emergency?

Additional Considerations

Here are some additional issues you need to consider.

People: If you determine that you're able to shelter people, should you limit it to your immediate members, or should you make your building available to people who live nearby? For example, if a tornado were bearing down on your church and you had the space and supplies to protect some of the people who live nearby, should you allow them in?

Pets: What about pets? Most families will want to bring their pets if they come to the church seeking shelter. You should, without question, accept service animals, but what about family pets that are not service animals?

Crowd control/personal safety: What kind of personal safety could you provide? How might tempers flare if people were cooped up for two or three days in close quarters with perhaps no electricity and not much to do?

Can Your Building Withstand a Storm?

Maybe the most important question of all is whether your building is storm-worthy enough to protect against severe weather conditions.

- No structure is 100% safe: When church members are sheltered in interiors rooms or church basements during a tornado, you are offering the best available shelter at the time. Without question, placing people in basements or hallways away from windows is safer than doing nothing, but no building offers absolute protection during a tornado or hurricane. The building roof may be torn off, building walls may collapse, or heavy rainfall may flood the building.

- FEMA offers guidelines for safe room construction: The Federal Emergency Management Administration (FEMA) offers guidelines for the creation of safe rooms. Safe rooms are constructed of reinforced steel and concrete, and are built underground, inside of, or adjacent to main buildings. Many schools and government buildings in "Tornado Alley" now have safe rooms, and some towns in areas repeatedly hit by tornadoes require safe rooms to be built into all new construction homes.

    Safe rooms in homes are often the size of a walk-in closet, designed only to keep family members safe. However, in schools and other large buildings, engineers can design attractive, multiuse spaces that also meet FEMA guidelines. These can protect several hundred people at a time. More and more churches are building safe rooms. Here are things to consider:
    - Should your church have a safe room?
    - How great is the risk in your area?
    - Can your members be convinced of the need?
    - Can your members raise the funds?
    - How old is your building?
    - Would extensive renovations be required?
    - Is grant assistance available to help cover the cost?

Emergency Equipment and Plans for Sheltering

Even if your church doesn't have a safe room, you need to be prepared for the possibility that members might have to shelter-in-place for a few hours or even a few days. The area that you set aside for sheltering should have emergency equipment and supplies. Follow the instructions for creating an emergency preparedness plan.

Review of Hazards Activity

Step 1. Assign one of the hazards to each of the learners. If the class has more than 12 learners, have them work in pairs or small groups. If the class has fewer than 12 learners, assign only the most likely hazards.

Step 2. Give learners one to two minutes to come up with answers to the following questions about their assigned hazard.

Step 3. Call on as many learners as time permits to share their answers. Once someone has shared their answers, get ideas from others in the class. Try to get the group thinking and talking about what their next steps might be to better prepare for each hazard.

Step 4. As learners share and discuss, make a master list on a flipchart or chalkboard of the best ideas for improving the church's preparation for all the hazards.

Step 5. End the discussion by thanking everyone for their input. Make sure someone writes down or otherwise keeps a copy of the "best ideas" list so the Church Safety Team can begin implementing some of the ideas that were generated. Close with a prayer.

Unit 5 Overview: Attack/ Threat Preparedness

Preparedness for threats and attacks requires the right tools, and an understanding of the correct actions to take for a specific situation, threat, or attacker. In this unit, we will cover:

Your Rights, the Use of Force and Citizen's Arrest: In this chapter, we discuss how to deal with altercations and escalating situations on church property. We also discuss laws dealing with self-defense and the use of force, citizen's arrest and other important information that you and your team must know in order to successfully diffuse a situation and avert violence safely.

Verbal De-Escalation and Disruptive Individuals: In this chapter, we'll discuss the actual techniques and strategies you and your team should employ when dealing with an escalating situation, including control techniques and more.

Chapter 14:
Your Rights, the Use of Force, and Citizen's Arrest

The United States allows people to act in self-defense, i.e., use force (even deadly force) to protect themselves, other people, or property. The laws explained below can also be applied to church security team members defending their congregations and church property. Reinhart (2007) noted that most states also include language so that people who act in self-defense have immunity from criminal prosecution and may even be entitled to compensation for attorney's fees and lost income if prosecuted (p. 3).

Self-Defense

Laws vary from state to state, and it is best to check your state legislation to learn your specific rights. The following are general guidelines about using self-defense.

> Merriam Webster defines self-defense as, "The act of defending oneself, one's property, or a close relative".

You'll find a myriad of different self-defense techniques out there, from traditional martial arts like karate and judo to MMA-inspired options like Brazilian jiu-jitsu, and options like Krav Maga to name just a few. Our recommendation is that all of your Church Safety Team members complete a self-defense course of your choosing, and that they regularly receive refresher training, or practice with other team members.

Firearms

The choice to allow Church Safety Team members to carry firearms on church grounds is one that your church and its leadership will need to discuss at length, and decide for yourselves. There are pros and cons to having armed team members. However, if you decide that arming your team is the best option, it is absolutely VITAL that every single member complete a basic firearms training program. It's also important that they be licensed by your state to carry firearms.

A basic program will teach things like gun safety, carrying, cleaning and other important topics. There are plenty of places to find such training, as well. In some instances, your local law enforcement office may be able to help (police or sheriff's department, for instance).

In others, you may need to look farther afield. You'll also find options available from the NRA (National Rifle Association). The NRA's website offers online training courses (found at https://onlinetraining.nra.org), as well as a list of other courses and classes available (https://firearm-training.nra.org).

Ensure that every single member is fully trained before being allowed to carry a firearm on church grounds. You may also wish to institute stricter requirements for training.

Use of Force Continuum

The National Institute of Justice (2009) explained that law enforcement agencies have policies and expectations to guide their use of force in resolving violent situations. An example is as follows:

- Presence: Officer presence deters violence, and no force is used.
- Verbal De-escalation: The officers make statements such as "Let me see your license and registration." They may increase volume and issue commands such as "Stop."
- Empty-Handed Control: The officer may restrain the individual through grabs, punches, and kicks.
- Less-Lethal Methods: The officer may immobilize an individual with a baton, chemical (such as pepper spray), or conducted energy device (such as a stun gun).

- Lethal Force: An officer may use deadly force (such as using a firearm) to stop an individual. (National Institute of Justice, 2009)

Your church security team should create policies such as those detailed below to deal with violent offenders before situations arise. Know what your use of force continuum should be. The following information explains the legal right to act in self-defense.

Imminent Threat

Self-defense laws generally require that force be used only when there is an imminent (immediate) physical threat to oneself or a third person (such as a spouse or child). It is not justified to use force against someone who makes a verbal attack with no "accompanying threat of immediate physical harm" ("Self-Defense Overview," 2016).

Reasonable Belief

Reasonable belief refers to what the person who uses self-defense could have reasonably believed under the circumstances. For example, if a stranger seems to be suddenly about to strike your head, it is reasonable to defend yourself. If that stranger is only to trying to swat away a bee, your reaction can still be viewed as reasonable ("Self-Defense Overview," 2016). If a person has an unreasonable belief of threat, he or she could be prosecuted for assault or even murder but may plead "imperfect self-defense" and have the charges and penalties reduced ("Self-Defense Overview," 2016). Not all states recognize this defense.

Proportional Response

This criterion means that when someone acts in self-defense, he or she must react in a way that matches the threat. If someone is attacked but his or her life is not threatened, the defender cannot respond with deadly force. Likewise, if the attacker is neutralized easily, then continuing to fight the attacker would be considered retaliation and not self-defense ("Self-Defense Overview," 2016).

For example, if you find someone stealing from the offering, it is not a proportional response to shoot that person. Sheepdog Church Security recommends that firearms are not permitted until and unless full training has occurred and the firearms are approved by church leadership. Any team member who carries a firearm without permission should be dismissed immediately.

Duty to Retreat

Many states require that a person try to escape from an attacker before using force as self-defense. Some states stipulate that a person may use force as self-defense but may not use deadly force without first trying to flee the situation ("Self-Defense Overview," 2016). Find out what your state recommends before training your Church Security Team members.

Castle Doctrine

In contrast to the Duty to Retreat laws is the Castle Doctrine, a common law in many states that allows people to defend themselves in their homes. The concept comes from English Common Law and the idea that "one's abode is a special area in which one enjoys certain protections and immunities" (State of New Jersey, 2008). The concept got its name from Florida lobbyist Marion P. Hammer and comes from the phrase "one's home is one's castle" (Reinhart, 2007, p. 1).

Randall and DeBoer (2012) explained that the Castle Doctrine allows defenders to not retreat as is required by many states (p. 1). The Castle Doctrine extends not only to protecting oneself and family or guests from bodily harm but also to preventing theft of property (Randall & DeBoer, 2012, p. 1). The stand-your-ground laws are variations of the Castle Doctrine. These laws have been passed by 20 states and allow people who are legally in a location to use force without first attempting to retreat (Randall & DeBoer, 2012, p. 2). Again, Sheepdog Church Security does not recommend using physical (especially lethal) force to prevent the theft of church property.

Defense of Others

It is legally defensible to defend others but only to the extent that the person would legally be able to defend himself/herself. This means that if two people are fighting, a third person may legally come to one party's defense and use force to stop an assault. The third person can only use as much force as necessary to stop the assault so lethal force would not be justified if the assailant could have been diverted by verbal de-escalation ("Defense of Others," 2016). In other words, if an intruder is threatening a church member but could be deterred by a verbal intervention, then the Church Security Team member would not be within his/her rights to use a chemical weapon (such as mace) or physically attack the intruder.

Defense of Property

Reinhart (2007) explained that people can use force to stop the theft of property or to immediately recover stolen property, but that deadly force can only be used to "defend a person from the use of or imminent use of deadly physical force or infliction or imminent infliction of great bodily harm" (p. 4). In other words, if your church decides against the advice of Sheepdog Church Security, to allow Church Security Team members to carry lethal weapons, then use of those weapons would only be legal to stop an attack against a person in which great bodily harm or death could have occurred. Sheepdog Church Security does not recommend using force to stop the damage or theft of church property.

Defense Policies

Your Church Security Team should draft policies that work for your team, but the examples of defense policies below can help illustrate potential options. Church Security Team leaders should approve the use of all weapons before the team can carry them.

The team leader or pastoral staff leader will issue a list identifying (1) approved defensive weapons and restraints, (2) the requirements for certification in the use of each type of weapon or restraint, and (3) the list of people approved to carry each kind of weapon or restraint. Anyone who carries a weapon without prior authorization should be dismissed from the team.

Use of force should be limited to the minimum necessary to stop the aggressor. Weapons should not be used to stop the theft or damage of church property or funds.

Use of Restraints

Restraints should only be permitted in situations when a violent person has assaulted someone and would immediately attempt to re-engage the fight if not restrained. Once a person is placed in restraints, a citizen's arrest has taken place. Restrain the person until the police arrive to take him/her into custody. Church Security Team members are responsible for the safety of the person in restraints.

Use of Chemical Sprays

Church Security Team members will not use any type of chemical (including pepper spray) on any person involved in an altercation in the church unless the use of a chemical is required to prevent serious injury.

Use of Weapons

Church Security Team members may carry weapons as approved by the Church Security Team leader. Only use the minimum amount of force necessary to stop an aggressor.

Use of Lethal Force

Church Security Team members who carry firearms should conceal them to prevent church members from being fearful or accidentally touching them.

Church Security Team members will not use lethal force unless it is necessary to prevent the aggressor from causing serious bodily harm or death to another person. If there is any way to stop the aggressor using less than lethal force, the Church Security Team should do that instead.

To prevent injury to other people, Church Security Team members should ensure that discharging the weapon will not cause injury to someone else. If necessary, the team member should consider kneeling to make a shot if this will clear the background. If lethal force has been used, the Church Security Team leader should be notified immediately.

Teaching the Material

When teaching this chapter to your Church Security Team, make sure to customize the content to meet your specific needs, requirements and situation. Also, explain to your learners that people studying these topics—use of force and citizen's arrest—always want to know exactly what they can and can't do.

Unfortunately, the law in these areas is not always black and white; there are a lot of gray areas. Much will depend on the situation and sometimes a judge or a jury end up making the determination. That means, as we go through the course, you won't always be able to give an exact answer. It may depend on other factors.

So, one purpose of the teaching section is to help you know where these gray areas are, and help you know what legal aspects to consider if you find yourself in a threatening situation.

Ice Breaker Activity

Explain to your learners that there are no physical fitness requirements to be a member of the Church Safety Team. However, as you will learn today, you may be called up on from time to time as a Church Safety

Team member to act quickly or to even respond to a physical attack from a trouble maker. It will be easier to respond appropriately if you are relatively fit. Introduce yourself to someone in the class and talk with them about your level of physical fitness. There are three questions to answer:

- How many push-ups can you do?
- How many sit-ups can you do?
- Can you run a mile, and if so, how long would it take you?

Note that if this group is typical, there will be many people who have to admit that they don't exercise as much as they should. In fact, these questions will likely spark a good bit of laughter and joking around—which is OK. Ice breakers are designed to get people relaxed and talking. By the way, you as the instructor should lead off introducing yourself and admitting how many of the things on the screen you're able to do.

Activity

- Step 1. Ask each person to find a partner, preferably someone they don't know well.
- Step 2. Ask the partners to introduce themselves to one another and to share their answers to the three questions with one another.
- Step 3. Give them about two to three minutes to do this.
- Step 4. Call on one set of partners. Ask them to introduce themselves to the group and to tell what they learned about each other's level of fitness.
- Step 5. Call on one or two other sets of partners to do the same thing as time permits.

Starting today, you may want to challenge each other to set and meet fitness goals; some of you may even want to start working out together. Work together and help each other along, because, of course, the entire Church Safety Team benefits.

Security vs. Safety?

What we call our team is very important. Are we a "security team" or a "safety team"? Many states license "security" professionals. If we call our team a "security team," we may mistakenly be claiming to be something we're not. We're not licensed as "security" professionals.

Note that even in states that don't currently license security professionals, the laws could change; a "security team" would then have to change its name.

"Security" is misleading to members and visitors. "Security" implies that your church has licensed security professionals protecting its members. Someone in need of protection from, say, an abusive family member, may choose your church thinking it offers a more secure environment than some other church.

The term "security" also increases civil liability. A misperception about the level of protection offered by your church could lead to law suits. On the other hand, "safety" is a ministry. Serving Christ and His church as a sheepdog is a calling and a gift from God. When we serve Him, we are ministering to His people. So, be thoughtful about what you call the work we are doing in this ministry. Be mindful that our job is to keep God's people safe so they can worship, study the Word, and do the ministry work God calls them to do.

Throughout this course, you will be asking questions of the learners and they will likely be asking questions of you. Don't be afraid to say, "I don't know" if someone asks a question you can't answer. Help learners think through what they should do when they're on duty and they're not sure of their legal options. Encourage them to avoid taking unnecessary risks unless they or someone else is clearly in danger. Help them identify the most reasonable thing to do in a given situation. Encourage them to use their verbal de-escalation skills whenever possible and to let local law enforcement handle the difficult challenges, assuming the situation permits.

What Is Citizen's Arrest?

We've all heard of the concept of "citizen's arrest," but most of us don't really know what it is or how it works. In this section, we will review what's involved in a "citizen's arrest" so that you will understand how to lawfully carry one out if you ever need to.

What Is an Arrest?

In most states, "arresting" someone means taking the person into custody so they may be held to answer for a public offense. This can be done either by using restraint or simply getting the subject to submit. Usually, this is done by a law enforcement officer, but most states give private citizens the power to make what's known as a "citizen's arrest.

Before attempting a citizen's arrest, it's important to know the rules that govern them. Improperly arresting or detaining someone could result in civil or criminal penalties against the person making the arrest.

The exact laws regarding citizen's arrest vary from state to state, but there are some general rules that apply in almost all jurisdictions. Generally, a private citizen may make an arrest in any of these circumstances:

1. Public offenses committed or attempted in the arresting person's presence.
2. When the subject has committed a felony, although not necessarily in the arresting person's presence.
3. When a felony has, in fact, been committed and the arresting person has reasonable cause for believing the subject has committed it.

A "public offense" is any violation punishable by fine or imprisonment, including petty misdemeanors. Important note: For #2 and #3, the citizen making the arrest must be certain a felony has been committed. If it is later determined that the subject did not in fact commit a felony, the person who did the arresting may be subject to civil or criminal penalties.

A person who has made a citizen's arrest must take the arrested person before a judge or to a peace officer "without unnecessary delay." That is, you must immediately notify the law enforcement authorities and you must immediately release the detainee to those authorities. Failure to do so can be considered false imprisonment and can subject you to civil or criminal penalties.

You may use force to detain the subject, but you may only use the amount of force that is reasonable and necessary to apprehend and detain the subject. That will, of course, vary from situation to situation.

If the person arrested escapes, the law allows you to immediately pursue and retake the escapee, at any time and in any place in the state. Do so, of course, with caution.

The law does not allow you to conduct an investigation. For example, you cannot conduct a field sobriety test.

On a related note, a private person is required to participate in making an arrest under certain circumstances:

- If a peace officer requests, a private person must aid the officer in executing a warrant.
- If a judge lawfully directs a person to arrest another, it is a misdemeanor to willfully neglect or refuse to do so.
- A person is guilty of a misdemeanor if he willfully neglects or refuses to aid a peace officer after being "lawfully directed" to aid the officer in making an arrest, retaking a person who has escaped from custody, or executing a legal process.

Think Twice... Make that 3 Times

Even with the information we've just discussed, you should think twice before attempting a voluntary citizen's arrest. Personal and public safety should be significant concerns. Arrests later found to be unlawful can subject you to criminal or civil liability for false imprisonment. You could end up being arrested!

Let's say there's a man causing a disturbance in the church lobby.

He's talking loudly in a nonsensical manner. Because Sunday service is taking place, you ask him to please lower his voice. He answers you that he has a First Amendment right to speak if he chooses and continues talking loudly.

You ask him to leave the building, but he answers that he has a First Amendment right to worship as he pleases. So, you ask him to sit on a bench near the door while you call the police. He agrees to that. Each time he attempts to get up from the bench, you tell him the police are on the way and you instruct him to sit back down—which he does.

- Is this a citizen's arrest? Keep in mind that an arrest does not require restraint. It could be an arrest even if the subject willingly submits.
- Has the subject committed a felony? Keep in mind that for an "arrest" to be lawful, the subject must have actually committed a crime.

When carrying out a citizen's arrest, it's best if you are certain about what you are doing. This may be a good time to remind learners what you said earlier about the law not being clear cut. Remind them that when in doubt about the law, they should at least be certain that their actions are reasonable and their intentions good.

If you are not absolutely certain the subject has committed a crime, you probably should not attempt to detain him. As we noted above, "arresting" him improperly could subject you and the church to criminal or civil liability. In this situation, your best bet may be to encourage the subject to leave the building peacefully. Try to accomplish this using your verbal de-escalation skills.

Use of Force

In this section, we will be looking at what constitutes "force" and when the law allows you to use force.

Bodily Harm

Let's start by defining some terms and explaining some important concepts.

- Bodily Harm: By "bodily harm", we mean physical pain or injury.
- Great Bodily Harm: "Great bodily harm" is bodily injury that creates a substantial risk of death or which is likely to cause serious permanent disfigurement or loss, or extended impairment of the function of any body member or organ.

One of the things we'll discover as we get into this discussion of the use of force is that legal definitions vary. Definitions vary from state to state, and also based on the situation. In some situations, any reasonable person would agree that a given subject has suffered great bodily harm, but in others, we might not be so sure.

For example, if someone does something to a subject to cause the subject paralysis or brain damage, most people would agree that great bodily harm had been inflicted on the subject. But what if someone does something to a subject that breaks the subject's wrist or knocks out a tooth? Has the subject suffered great bodily harm according to the definitions on the screen?

What if the subject is a young person who recovers quickly from the broken wrist and within a few weeks is fine with no apparent lasting disability? Did his broken wrist constitute great bodily harm? What if the subject is a professional tennis player whose broken wrist never heals properly and who, as a result, is never able to play at his previous level and is forced to retire early? Did his broken wrist constitute great bodily harm?

Often whether something is or is not considered "great bodily harm" gets decided in court by a judge or a jury. They review the facts, listen to the arguments on both sides, and make a determination. The point we're making here is that there are many gray areas in the law when it comes to concepts such as these.

Deadly Force

Deadly force is force used by a person that they know, or reasonably should know, creates a substantial risk of causing death or great bodily harm. The law allows the use of deadly force under these circumstances:

- To protect yourself or another person from imminent death or great bodily harm.
- To carry out the arrest or capture of a person you know to have committed a violent felony, or to prevent the escape of that person.
- To carry out the arrest or capture of a person you have reasonable grounds to believe is about to commit a violent felony, or to prevent the escape of that person.
- Note: If feasible, you should give a verbal warning before using or attempting to use deadly force.

Certain actions will almost always be considered deadly force. For example, the intentional discharge of a firearm in the direction of another person, or at a vehicle in which another person is believed to be, constitutes deadly force. The use of a firearm as a weapon, the use of a knife as a weapon, even the use of a vehicle as a weapon—all would likely be considered deadly force. "Household items," such as a baseball bat, a crowbar, or a golf club, could be used in a way that a judge or jury would consider it deadly force.

Some actions will obviously be deadly force, but some will be a matter of interpretation. As with great bodily harm, it may be up to a judge or jury to ultimately decide if an action taken by someone was or was not deadly force.

Other Than Deadly Force

Other than deadly force is force used by a person that does not have the purpose of causing, nor creates a substantial risk of causing, death or great bodily harm. The law allows the use of other than deadly force:

- To carry out a lawful arrest
- To execute a legal process or enforce an order of the court (e.g., to serve a warrant)
- To defend yourself or another person

When Is Force Acceptable?

Whether you can legally use force to defend yourself depends on a number of factors.

Imminent Threat: The law only allows you to use force to defend yourself when there is an imminent physical threat to yourself or to someone else (e.g., your spouse or a child). A verbal attack with no threat of immediate physical harm is not enough.

Reasonable Belief: In order to legally use force for self-defense in some states, it must be judged that you had a reasonable belief that you were being threatened. Even if you weren't really being threatened, if the judge or jury determines that it was reasonable for you to believe there was a threat, force as part of self-defense may be allowable. For example: Imagine a would-be mugger stepping out of the shadows and threatening your life with a gun. You use force to protect yourself. Later, it is learned that the gun was a toy. A jury might be called upon to decide if it was reasonable for you to believe your life was being threatened even though, as it turns out, it was not.

Duty to Retreat: The law in many states requires you to try to escape from your attacker before you are allowed to use force in self-defense. In some states, you can use force, but you cannot use deadly force unless you have first tried to flee. There are some exceptions to the duty to retreat, including:

- If an attack is sudden. In such a case, retreat might be unrealistic or create a risk of bodily harm.

- If it is judged that there was no reasonable option to flee and no reasonable alternative other than the use of force to protect yourself, your loved ones, or your property.

Proportional Response: Proportional response says that when you do use self-defense, you must use force that matches the threat. For example, if someone attacks you, but does not use deadly force, you are not legally allowed to respond by using deadly force. Similarly, if the attacker surrenders, but you continue to fight him, your actions are no longer self-defense. They now might be considered retaliatory and you might find yourself subject to criminal or civil penalties.

More Aspects of Self-Defense

From time to time, court cases or state laws add refinements to self-defense laws. Here are some additional refinements to be aware of:

Castle Doctrine: Laws in many states allow you to defend yourself in your home. The so-called "castle doctrine" draws its name from the old phrase: "a man's home is his castle." It relates to the idea that your home is a special area in which you enjoy certain protections and immunities. In states that have passed Castle Doctrine laws, you do not have a duty to retreat when you are in your home and you can use force in your home to protect yourself, your family, your guests and your property.

Stand-Your-Ground Laws: Stand your ground laws have been passed in some 20 states and allow you to defend yourself without any duty to retreat, as long as you are somewhere you have a legal right to be.

Defense of Others: The law allows you to use force to protect others as long as you reasonably believe them to be in imminent danger. Just as with self-defense, you must have a reasonable belief the other person is in danger and the force you use must be proportional to the level of threat.

Reasonable Force

Somewhat similar to the concept of proportional response is the concept of reasonable force. Reasonable force explains how much force law enforcement officers are allowed to use in the process of carrying out their duties. The law allows police and other law enforcement officers to use force while lawfully arresting and detaining suspects or serving warrants.

The amount of force that can be used must be commensurate with the perceived level of threat at the time. That is, an officer may only use the amount of force that is "reasonable and necessary" to carry out the arrest or detention. Here again, the determination of whether the actions of a police officer were "reasonable force" or "excessive force" are often made after the fact, by a police review board or in a court of law.

The Supreme Court in its 1989 case, Graham vs. Connor, has articulated three questions that should be asked to determine whether the force used by a police officer was reasonable:

1. How severe was the crime the officer believed the suspect had committed or was committing?
2. Did the suspect present an immediate threat to the safety of officers or the public?
3. Was the suspect actively resisting arrest or attempting to escape?

These questions must be reviewed based on what the officer knew or could perceive at the time—not what we know about the situation today. In other words, with 20/20 hindsight, it may be obvious the officer should not have acted in a particular manner. The Supreme Court decision indicates that this kind of analysis would be unfair to the officer.

The review must be based on what was happening at the time. For example, was the officer under fire? Was the officer outnumbered or surrounded? What could the officer reasonably have known at the time?

Pose the following to your learners: You are not a law enforcement officer when you are carrying out your duties as a Church Safety Team member. Why, then, do you suppose it's useful to learn about this reasonable force standard?

While there are no right or wrong answers, one of the best suited is: Even though Church Safety Team members are not acting as police officers, the Church Safety Team must have some standards about how to act and how to handle tough situations. The reasonable force standard provides a good starting place for the Church Safety Team. We may choose to adopt this same standard; we may choose to develop an even stricter standard that severely limits the use of force.

Deciding When to Use Force

Law enforcement officers must often make split-second decisions about whether force is appropriate and if so, what kind. In this section, we will look at what determines whether force should be used and if so, what determines how much force should be used.

Use of Force Continuum

Most police departments have policies regarding the use of force. It is often presented to officers in the form of the Use of Force Continuum. From the base/least deadly reaction, to the use of deadly force, the continuum is as follows:

Level 1: Officer Presence – The physical presence of a law enforcement officer is all it takes to get a subject to stop engaging in criminal behavior and/or to not engage in criminal behavior in the first place. The officer's demeanor is confident, professional, and non-threatening. The subject is compliant and no physical force is used.

Level 2: Verbal Commands – The officer issues non-threatening, verbal commands. For example: "May I see some ID?" Also included in this category are short, loudly spoken commands, such as "Stop" or "Hold it right there". This level can be appropriate if subject is verbally non-compliant.

Level 3: Soft Techniques – The officer is empty handed. He or she uses grabs, holds or joint locks to restrain subject. This can be appropriate if the subject is passively resistant (i.e., refusing to follow verbal commands).Also in this category: the officer uses punches or kicks to restrain subject. (note that some experts place punches and kicks in the Hard Techniques category.)

Level 4: Hard Techniques – The officer uses non-lethal tools (e.g. baton, pepper spray, Taser) to restrain the subject. This can be appropriate when subject is actively aggressive.

Level 5: Lethal Force – The officer uses a deadly weapon to gain control of situation. This is appropriate only if subject poses a serious threat to officer or another individual.

Remember, when acting in your capacity as a Church Safety Team member, you are not "law enforcement" and you are not "security." We are reviewing this information so you will know your options and will be able to act in a lawful manner. Hopefully, you will be able to contact law enforcement authorities when situations require higher levels of force.

Reading the Situation

Deciding whether you should use force requires you to analyze the situation quickly and accurately:

- Does the attacker have the INTENT to cause great bodily harm or death to you or someone else?
- Does the attacker have the ABILITY to cause great bodily harm or death to you or someone else?
- Does the attacker have the OPPORTUNITY to cause great bodily harm or death to you or someone else?

Other Factors to Consider

Every situation will be different and there will be many different factors to consider as you decide what level of force is appropriate. We've categorized some of these factors into:

- What you know or can observe about the subject (i.e., the attacker).
- What you know or can observe about the situation.
- What you know about yourself and the resources available to you.

What you know or can observe about the subject:

- The subject's age, size, relative strength, skill level, injuries already sustained, exhaustion or fatigue.
- The subject's conduct: How is the subject behaving? What is the subject doing?
- The subject's mental state or mental capacity? Is the subject under the influence of drugs or alcohol?
- Is the subject a known violent offender? Someone who has killed before?
- Does the subject have access or is in close proximity to weapons or items that can be used as weapons?
- Is the subject resisting? Trying to flee?
- Has the subject stopped being a threat?

What you know or can observe about the situation:

- The immediacy or severity of the threat
- The seriousness of the offense
- Are there innocent bystanders or people who could be hurt? Are there hostages?
- Is there a need for a prompt resolution of the situation?

What you know about yourself and the resources available to you:

- Your age, size, relative strength, skill level, injuries already sustained, exhaustion or fatigue.
- Your level of training or experience.
- Potential for injury to yourself or others.
- Do you have help? Is backup available?
- Are lesser means of force available?

Authorized Use of Force

The law in most states gives private citizens the authority to use force in certain situations. This is important for you because when you are on duty as a Church Safety Team member, you are a private citizen. For the purposes of this discussion, we are using the laws as they are written in the state of Minnesota, but most states have similar laws.

Private citizens may use force:

To carry out a citizen's arrest. Use of force when carrying out a citizen's arrest is authorized provided that it is a legally executed citizen's arrest and provided that the person arrested is immediately turned over to the proper authorities.

To resist an attack or aid someone who is resisting an attack. Again, the use of force must meet the guidelines we've discussed earlier; it must be proportional to the force the attacker is using and there must be a reasonable threat.

To protect your own property, or to assist in the protection of another's property.* We've put an asterisk by this one because it speaks directly to much of the work you will be doing as a Church Safety Team member.

Protection of Property

We've reprinted the complete law as it appears in the statues for the state of Minnesota:

When used by any person in lawful possession of real or personal

263

property, or by another assisting the person in lawful possession, in resisting a trespass upon or other unlawful interference with such property.

In short, you are authorized to use force when you are protecting property or real estate that is legally yours. You are also authorized to use force when you are assisting in the protection of property or real estate that belongs to someone else. You are also legally authorized to use force to prevent someone from trespassing upon such property or prevent someone from unlawfully interfering with such property.

In other words, in your duty as a Church Safety Team member, the law allows you to use force to protect church property or to prevent trespassing on church property. Keep in mind, though, what we've learned earlier: The threat has to be reasonable (i.e., any reasonable person would have determined that the subject was trespassing or interfering with church property). Also, the force you use has to be proportional to the threat. If the subject is not threatening you physically, you are not allowed to use physical force against him.

Private citizens may also use force:

- To prevent the escape of a lawfully held detainee, or to recapture an escaped detainee.
- When used by someone in authority to compel compliance with reasonable rules of conduct.
- When used by a parent, teacher or other lawful custodian of a child, to correct or restrain the child.
- To restrain a person who is mentally ill or mentally defective from self-injury or injury to another.

Our Church's Policies

Note: If your church has written policies for the Church Safety Team regarding use of force, authorized used of weapons, allowable non-deadly force, etc. these policies should be discussed in this section of the course. If your church has no such policies, this section is a good place for Church Safety Team members to begin to think about or discuss possible policies.

Defensive Weapons

Explain to your learners what is meant by an authorized device: A legally possessed device you have received permission from the church to carry and use in your assigned duties, and for which you have obtained training in the technical, mechanical and physical aspects of; and have developed a knowledge and understanding of the law, rules and regulations regarding the use of.

The Church Safety Team leader or pastoral staff leader should issue a list identifying authorized defensive weapons, requirements for certification in the use of each type of weapon, and people approved to carry each kind of weapon.

Regarding authorization: The Church Safety Team leader and/or the pastoral staff should approve the use of all weapons before anyone on the team is allowed to carry them. Anyone who carries a weapon without prior authorization should be dismissed from the team.

Use of Deadly Force

Church Safety Team members who carry firearms should keep them concealed. Church Safety Team members should not use deadly force unless it is necessary to prevent the aggressor from causing serious bodily harm or death to another person. If there is any way to stop the aggressor using less than deadly force, the Church Safety Team member should do that instead.

To prevent injury to other people, Church Safety Team members should ensure that discharging the weapon will not cause another person to be injured. If necessary, the Church Safety Team member should consider kneeling to make a shot if this will prevent possible injury to others. If deadly force must be used, the Church Safety Team leader should be notified immediately.

Weapons should not be used to stop the theft of church property or funds. Use of force should be limited to the minimum amount of force necessary to stop the actions of the aggressor.

Use of Restraints

Church Safety Team members should not use any type of restraint (including handcuffs) on any person involved in an altercation in the church unless it is determined that the use of a restraint is required to prevent serious injury to the person or someone else. Use of physical restraints should be limited. Note that once a person is placed in restraints, a citizen's arrest has taken place.

The Safety Team members are responsible for the safety of the person in restraints. Furthermore, the law requires that the person be turned over to the proper authorities without delay. Restraints should be permitted in extreme situations, such as:

A violent person has assaulted a church member and has been stopped by the Church Safety Team. The person continues to fight and causes additional injury to the church member or Church Safety Team member. It is clear that the aggressor would immediately attempt to re-engage the fight if released.

In this case, the person should be restrained until the police arrive to take him/her into custody.

Use of chemical restraints should be limited. Church Safety Team members should not use any type of chemical (including pepper spray) on any person involved in an altercation in the church unless it is determined that the use of a chemical is required to prevent serious injury. When necessary, only authorized restraints should be used.

As the instructor, create several potential scenarios that require your learners to determine whether the use of force is needed, whether deadly force is needed, whether restraints are warranted, and whether the need for chemical restraints is present.

Wrap Up

In close, explain to your learners, as you go about your work on the Church Safety Team, keep in mind that you must be like a faithful sheepdog, always at the ready. There will be threats—wolves who will attempt to harm the sheep. But God has called you and equipped you to be the Shepherd's companion, ready to serve Him by helping to protect His people. Make sure prayer and Bible study is part of your daily regimen so you can stay strong.

Assemble the group in a circle and ask someone to offer a closing prayer.

Chapter 15:
Verbal De-Escalation and Disruptive Individuals

Verbal de-escalation is an important subject for church safety. It can move a person from the edge of committing a violent act to the position of making a controlled decision. The Bible tells us, "the tongue holds the power of life and death" (Proverbs 18:21). When used properly, verbal de-escalation is a powerful tool.

What Is Verbal De-escalation?

Verbal de-escalation is a learnable skill that can be used to prevent a verbally disruptive person from becoming physically combative. It is Sheepdog Church Ministry's first and most frequently used response when dealing with verbally disruptive people. The challenge of learning verbal de-escalation is to eliminate the assumption that there are magic words or phrases that instantly calm people down. The truth is that verbal de-escalation is a set of principles and guidelines which are most effectively used by people of maturity and emotional intelligence.

Goals of De-escalation

There are four main goals of verbal de-escalation:

- Keep lines of communication open.
- Get the person talking.
- Actively listen.
- Maintain control through clear and calm communication.

Identifying Risks

Before we discuss the techniques of verbal de-escalation, we need to discuss both identifying a potentially violent person and preventing incidents.

Why Do People Become Disruptive?

It's critically important to understand why people become disruptive. In most cases disruptive behavior is a result of a personal crisis. A personal crisis happens when a person perceives an event or situation has exceeded his/her ability to cope with the problem and the emotional anguish becomes intolerable.

There are several causes of personal crises:

- Family problems: A marriage falling apart, teenagers acting out, arguments with in-laws, and countless other scenarios.
- Financial problems: Their home may be in foreclosure, they may have lost a job, they may not be able to feed their families or pay their bills.
- Substance abuse: Alcoholism and addiction can put a great deal of strain on people.
- Medical conditions: Chronic pain, a serious medical diagnosis, or even terminal illness can change people's personalities and behavior.
- Mental illness: Mental illness can also contribute to verbally combative behaviors.

It's important to remember that a person who has a personal crisis is not necessarily weak in faith or character. Everybody has hard times, so we should be compassionate and humble.

Protesters also sometimes become disruptive. Protesters are different from people in crisis because their intent is to disrupt and destroy the church's ministry and reputation. Because of this issue, we need to be aware that the media will be present and recording devices will be in use. Media are looking for that five second clip taken out of context that will embarrass the church. The good news is that the same principles of verbal de-escalation still apply. We need clear, calm communication.

Warning Signs

When someone may become verbally combative or physically violent, he or she usually exhibits several warning signs in behavior or through physical manifestations.

Changes in Behavior

The top warning sign is a change in the person's behavior. Increased frequency and intensity of the behaviors are disruptive to the church environment, especially if the person exhibits many of these behaviors rather than just a few. The following list is provided verbatim from the Canadian Centre for Occupational Health and Safety (2014).

- Crying, sulking or temper tantrums.
- Excessive absenteeism or lateness.
- Pushing the limits of acceptable conduct or disregarding the health and safety of others.
- Disrespect for authority.
- Increased mistakes or errors, or unsatisfactory work quality.
- Refusal to acknowledge job performance problems.
- Faulty decision making.
- Testing the limits to see what they can get away with.
- Swearing or emotional language.
- Handles criticism poorly.
- Making inappropriate statements.
- Forgetfulness, confusion and/or distraction.
- Inability to focus.
- Blaming others for mistakes.

- Complaints of unfair personal treatment.
- Talking about the same problems repeatedly without resolving them.
- Insistence that he or she is always right.
- Misinterpretation of communications from supervisors or co-workers.
- Social isolation.
- Personal hygiene is poor or ignored.
- Sudden and/or unpredictable change in energy level.
- Complains of unusual and/or non-specific illnesses.
- Holds grudges, especially against his or her supervisor. Verbalizes hope that something negative will happen to the person against whom he or she has the grudge.

Physical Warning Signs

The Canadian Centre for Occupational Health and Safety (2014) explains that a person preparing to become verbally combative or physically violent may show any of the following physical signs. The following list is provided verbatim from the Canadian Centre for Occupational Health and Safety (2014):

- Flushed or pale face.
- Sweating.
- Pacing, restless, or repetitive movements.
- Signs of extreme fatigue (e.g., dark circles under the eyes).
- Trembling or shaking.
- Clenched jaws or fists.
- Exaggerated or violent gestures.
- Change in voice (exhibiting signs of stress or anger).
- Loud talking or chanting.
- Shallow, rapid breathing.
- Scowling, sneering or use of abusive language.

- Glaring or avoiding eye contact.
- Violating your personal space (they get too close).

Prevention

Many schools, businesses, and churches are developing threat assessment teams. These teams are made up of top management and department heads, and they meet on a regular basis to discuss people who may be demonstrating a propensity for a violent outburst. The intention is not to gossip about the person. Rather, the meetings are opportunities for church leaders to identify who is suffering from a personal crisis so counseling and assistance can be offered.

Oftentimes, no one person sees the entire picture. It is only after leaders share information that pastors get a clear picture of what is going on in a person's life. Far too often it is discovered after a violent incident that a person was demonstrating many of the warning behaviors.

Meetings should include pastors, ministry leaders, and the church security director. The intention is to share information and educate leaders about warning signs. The Canadian Centre of Occupational Health and Safety (2014) explains that the meetings should include discussions of the following:

- History of violence
- Threatening behavior
- Intimidating behavior
- Increase in personal stress
- Negative personality traits
- Changes in mood or behavior

History of Violence

To determine if someone has a history of violence, you need to have a personal knowledge of the individual's history or talk to someone who knows him/her. The Canadian Centre for Occupational Health and Safety (2014) suggests asking these questions:

- Does the person have a fascination with incidents of violence?
- Does the person show an extreme interest in or an obsession with weapons?
- Has the person committed violence or destroyed property?
- Has the person committed violent acts before?

Threatening Behavior

To determine if the person has been exhibiting threatening behavior, the Canadian Centre for Occupational Health and Safety (2014) suggests asking these questions:

- Does the person hold a grudge against the church or someone in the church?
- Has the person demonstrated excessive behavior such as inappropriate giving?
- Is the person preoccupied with violence?
- Has the person made a threat (verbal or written) to hurt somebody?
- Have the threats been escalating?

Intimidating Behavior

To determine if the person has been exhibiting intimidating behavior, the Canadian Centre for Occupational Health and Safety (2014) suggests asking these questions:

- Is the person argumentative or uncooperative?
- Does the person display unwarranted anger?
- Is the person's level of anger mismatched to the offense?
- Has the person been impulsive in recent instances?
- Does the person seem easily frustrated?

- Is the person challenging peers and authority figures?

Increase in Personal Stress

To determine if the person has been dealing with more stress, the Canadian Centre for Occupational Health and Safety (2014) suggests asking these questions:

- Is the person in an unreciprocated romantic obsession?
- Is the person suffering from serious family or financial problems?
- Has the person had a recent job loss or personal loss?
- Is the person struggling with substance or alcohol abuse?

Negative Personality Traits

To determine if the person has negative personality traits, the Canadian Centre for Occupational Health and Safety (2014) suggests asking these questions:

- Is the person suspicious of others?
- Does the person have a sense of entitlement?
- Does the person reject criticism or helpful advice?
- Does the person feel victimized?
- Does the person show a lack of concern for the safety or well-being of others?
- Does the person blame others for his/her problems and mistakes?
- Does the person have a low self-esteem?

Changes in Mood or Behavior

To determine if the person is having changes in mood or behavior (including isolation), the Canadian Centre for Occupational Health and Safety (2014) suggests asking these questions:

- Has the person demonstrated extreme or bizarre behaviors?
- Does the person have any irrational beliefs or ideas?
- Does the person appear depressed?
- Does the person express hopelessness?
- Does the person express heightened anxiety?
- Does the person exhibit marked decline in work performance?
- Has the person drastically changed his/her belief system?
- Does the person have a history of negative interpersonal relationships?
- Does the person have a small family and only a few friends?
- Does the person see the church as a dysfunctional family?
- Has the person become obsessively involved in church politics and drama?

Skills of Verbal De-escalation

Learning the skills of verbal de-escalation feels a little bit like high school speech class. It starts with a basic understanding of communication. Remember that communication has a lot more to do with your body language, facial expression, and your voice than the words you use.

It is critically important that we understand what we are saying with our nonverbal cues because when our words and body language disagree, people will react to our body language. Therefore, follow these basic rules for body language:

- Mindful: be conscious of your body posture.
- Open: Use an open yet defensible posture (so-called interview stance)
- Move slow: Use slow and deliberate movements.
- Don't accuse: Never point your finger at anyone because it communicates accusation.
- Don't shrug: Never shrug your shoulders because it shows that you are uncaring or unknowing.

- Relax: Don't display a rigid posture by crossing your arms or puffing out your chest because shows that you are defensive or aggressive.

Your facial expression will also communicate more than your words, so follow these rules:

- Relax your facial muscles: Don't furrow your brow or frown.
- Smile: Be friendly with a natural smile. (If the situation is becoming too stressful for you, it is okay to relax your smile to avoid faking one. A fake smile is very aggravating to an already stressful situation.)
- Eye contact: Keep natural eye contact and keep your eyes open to show interest. Maintain natural eye contact. Avoid staring at the person because that can be interpreted as a challenge. Don't close your eyes or look away because that shows disinterest.

Your voice is also important, so follow these rules:

- Volume: Keep the volume of your voice soft: a soft voice is calming.
- Slow down: Keep your rate of speech natural or even slow: slow speech is soothing.
- Friendly: Keep the tone of your voice friendly and helpful.

Your thoughts, emotions, and attitudes are also expressed through means other than your words:

- Keep your emotions under control. Otherwise, they are likely to show through on your face and in your body language, complicating the situation.
- Maintain the mind of Christ. Be careful not to prejudge, criticize, argue, threaten, engage in power struggles, or disregard the feelings or position of the person.
- Remember that understanding is not agreement. A phrase I use

often is "I hear you." It communicates that I understand what the person is saying and the emotions behind it. However, I don't necessarily agree with the person's actions or interpretations.

Verbal De-escalation Techniques

The best way to show how verbal de-escalation techniques work is to create a scenario. In the following scenario, imagine a new couple has started to visit your church. There's been talk that they are separated and are working through child custody issues. They are standing in your lobby before services and loudly arguing. The man is shouting and the woman is crying. The kids are nowhere to be seen.

Pre-engagement

Your first consideration before approaching a disruptive and potentially violent person is personal safety. Your first action should be to call for backup. If your safety team uses two-way radios and our radio procedures explained in chapter 3, you would call out, "Code Orange in the lobby. Code Orange in the lobby." "Code orange" means a disruptive person. You may or may not add the "911" enhancement code depending on if you anticipate violence. The 911 enhancement code advises your team to respond quickly and call police.

Your second action should be to totally evaluate the situation and prepare to use greater levels of force to defend yourself and others. Remember the four goals of verbal de-escalation discussed at the beginning of this chapter.

Approach

Keep the lines of communication open by establishing trust. Do not sneak up on the person. He/she is already aggravated, so approach within that person's field of vision. Keep in mind that anything that identifies you as a Church Security Team member may cause alarm.

Make sure you maintain your freedom of movement in case things get violent. Use an interview stance. In an interview stance, you have your feet shoulder width apart with one foot slightly back. You should also have your hands in front of you. This is not a fighting stance. You want to look natural but ready. Folding or cupping your hands at waist level is quite natural. It is also natural to use your hands while talking.

Do not enter the person's personal space. In America, personal space is usually about three feet. When a person is aggravated or angry, that increases to five to six feet. In addition, six feet just happens to be the reactionary gap police used for an unarmed combatant (Grossi, 2013). Six feet provides enough time to evade or deflect a physical attack.

Never touch a hostile person because what you think is a friendly touch might be interpreted as a physical assault. If the person gets too close to you, you may back up to create space. It is also completely acceptable to put your hand up in a blocking manner, but do not touch the person if you can avoid it. If the person continues to invade your space, then you will want to prepare to use increasing levels of force.

Engagement

Get the person talking by introducing yourself. In our scenario, you can approach the couple and introduce yourself. Tell them you see they seem upset and have heard they are having problems. Tell them that you are there to help. An example may be, "Hi, I'm Kris. I see that you're both very upset. Is there any way I can help?" The key to remember is that introducing yourself promotes communication and you should be prepared to give a reason why you're there.

When introducing yourself, ask for their names and use them often. Be prepared for them to refuse your help or even become confrontational towards you. If it's possible, move them to a semi-private or safe location. However, you should not corner the person in an office and you should not engage the person alone. In the engagement phase, you're trying to get the person talking, but there are a few things you need to keep in mind:

- Emotional people do not think logically.
- Emotional people process information slowly.
- Emotional people have trouble remembering details.

Continue engagement with active listening. Use a low, soft, calm voice and repeat things when necessary. Active listening requires you to echo the person's statements with slightly

different wording. For example, if a person said, "I got fired!", you may say back to them, "You lost your job."

During an engagement, be patient. Time is on your side. Your goal is to prevent the situation from becoming violent. If verbal de-escalation is working, then keep using it. Let the person vent. Take as much time as you need. At the same time, you may want to reduce noise and distractions. This may mean moving to a private location or having your team members move bystanders out of the area. Maintain control through clear and calm communication.

When an emotional person tells you what's wrong he or she will start with the most upsetting detail. Imagine a triangle with the narrow part on the top and the wide base on the bottom. The closer the person is to the top, the more upset he/she is and he/she is less upset closer to the bottom. The narrow top signifies the brevity of the story and the width of the bottom signifies a longer story.

When a person tells you his/her story, at first, it'll be brief and it'll only be the most upsetting portion. Each time the person repeats the story, he/she will give more supporting details while repeating the most upsetting element. If your verbal de-escalation techniques are working, the person will continue to tell his/her story over and over again, adding more details each time.

When this happens, you will know that your techniques are working and the person is trying to calm down. Keep in mind that this process can take some time. The person may tell you the story a half a dozen times before beginning to calm down.

When talking to the disruptive person, use the word and instead of the word but. The word but is argumentative, whereas the word and adds information. Use please and thank you. If the person cannot or will not communicate, talk to witnesses to find out what's wrong. There may be a family member or friend nearby who knows what's going on.

Ask the person if he/she needs anything. Offer something to eat or drink. Food and drink has a way of calming people down. Announce your movements, especially if you're moving towards the person. Remain friendly but firm.

Accept the person's feelings, thoughts, and behavior by respecting his/her dignity regardless of their gender, race, age, religion, or sexual orientation.

Additional Tips

- Avoid intervening too quickly. People argue and it is a healthy part of relationships.
- Avoid interrupting the person. The whole point is to get the person talking and keep him/her talking to calm down.
- Don't ask why questions. Why questions are logic based. Emotional people do not think logically.
- Don't rush the interaction. Time is on your side. Don't try to hurry verbal de-escalation techniques.
- Avoid asking a lot of questions. If you do ask a question, it should be "softball" type of question.
- Avoid accusatory statements such as "act right--this is a church", "you're acting crazy", or "you need to calm down." These statements are very inflammatory.
- Avoid saying "I know how you feel", or "things can't be that bad." Their problems and their feelings are not about you, and you

can't know how they feel inside. Do not suggest that things will get better because they may not.

- Avoid shouting or giving rapid commands.
- Don't take anything personally (lying, tricking, deceiving, threatening, etc.).
- Never make promises you can't keep.

Protesters

Protesters require special mention because they are intentionally trying to provoke a response so you will do something to embarrass the church in front of the cameras. Therefore, you need to have a higher threshold before using increasing levels of force. Of course, other verbally disruptive people may use these tactics, but they are frequently used by protesters.

When faced with protesters, the important thing is to remain calm. Remember that you are not the target, so don't take things personally. Protesters may:

- Taunt you
- Call you names
- Use coarse language
- Invade your personal space
- Use bizarre or insulting gestures toward you and others

This is not the time to demand respect. Stay in control of your emotions. Remember; Jesus was called far worse things. Learn to recognize your limits. Let someone else take over if you're becoming angry and it's feasible. Set limits with them with I statements: "I really want to help you but I find it difficult because of your name calling. Will you help me and stop cursing so that I can work on helping you? Thanks, I appreciate it."

The Philosophy of Verbal De-Escalation

The philosophy of verbal de-escalation might seem somewhat illogical – it's the reverse of what most of us assume is required in such a situation. Really, it can be summed up as, if you take a less authoritative, less controlling, less confrontational approach, you will actually will have more control. Give the person a sense of control, so he/she doesn't escalate the violence.

Your job is to maintain control until police arrive.

Final Note on Escalation

Know when to act. A person may be acting dangerously but not directly threatening any other person or himself/herself. If possible, give the person time to calm down. This requires patience and continuous safety evaluation. Use force only when it is necessary to protect yourself and others.

Teaching the Content

Teaching de-escalation skills is not difficult, but it will require you to provide specific training for your team. Remember that this content should be customized to your church's specific needs and requirements.

Icebreaker

While preaching the Sermon on the Mount, Jesus said, "Blessed are the peacemakers, for they will be called children of God." –Matthew 5:9 (NIV). Explain that you want to begin today by giving some thought to what it means to be a "peacemaker."

Activity

Step 1. Ask each person to find a partner, preferably someone they don't know well.

Step 2. Ask the partners to introduce themselves to one another.

Step 3. Have the partners read Matthew 5:9 and discuss what it means to be a peacemaker. Ask them to choose a person living or dead (other than Jesus) that they consider to be a peacemaker and to be prepared to tell why they've chosen that person.

Step 4. Give them about three to four minutes to do this.

Step 5. Call on one set of partners. Ask them to introduce themselves to the group and to tell who they thought of as a peacemaker and why they chose that person.

Step 6. Call on one or two other sets of partners to do the same thing as time permits.

Step 7. Thank everyone for participating and sharing. Wrap up the activity with the following explanation.

Explain to your learners that this little activity should get you thinking about what it means to be a peacemaker. People don't often think of it this way, but much of what law enforcement professionals do is peace making; they step into dangerous or chaotic situations and restore the peace. Although you are not officially a law enforcement officer when you are working as a Church Safety Team member, you may be called upon to do some things that law enforcement officers do. One of those things is restoring peace.

What Is Verbal De-Escalation?

Verbal de-escalation is a skill used by people in law enforcement, in the medical profession, by psychologists, by school teachers, and by any-one who works with people who might at times be agitated, emotional, or difficult to deal with. We will discuss two ways you can use it.

First: Verbal de-escalation is a skill used to lower the agitation level of a disruptive or combative subject. It's the skill most frequently used by law enforcement professionals. We often think of police officers as chasing suspects and arresting people all day, but, the skill police officers use most often, day in and day out, is verbal de-escalation. When used well, verbal de-escalation can get agitated and disruptive people to calm down and cooperate with you.

Second: Verbal de-escalation is used to manage routine interactions so that subjects do not become agitated or combative. Here's an example: While patrolling the church, you spot someone doing something suspicious. There may not be a problem at all, but you want to be sure. You approach the suspect and engage him/her in a conversation. You never want a routine interaction like this to blow up into something uncontrollable. Verbal de-escalation is the skill you will use to manage this routine conversation so it doesn't become a bigger threat.

In this case, you're not "de-escalating" the situation. Instead, you're using your skills to prevent the situation from "escalating" in the first place.

Think of when police are called during a domestic dispute. If there's no violence or threat of violence, the police may simply talk with both parties, get them to calm down, perhaps suggest that one of them take a walk or spend the night elsewhere to cool off. Or, imagine the police arriving at the scene of a fender bender to find the two drivers shouting at each other—one calling the other an "idiot" for having run a stop sign. The police have to separate these two, get them to calm down, and determine what happened so they can write a report.

What Verbal De-Escalation Does

Verbal de-escalation calms the subject. People think more clearly and respond more rationally when they are calm. Verbal de-escalation reduces tensions so everyone involved (including you) can behave and respond more sensibly.

When used successfully, verbal de-escalation encourages the subject to go along willingly with any requests you make. It also reduces the likelihood of injury or violence. When subjects comply willingly, no one has to use force. When subjects comply willingly there is less chance of violence or injury.

It treats the subject with respect. Regardless of what the subject has or has not done, that person has been created in God's image. Therefore, you have an obligation to treat every person with respect, and to honor his or her dignity—even people who appear to be engaging in criminal activity.

Why Learn Verbal De-Escalation

Unfortunately, disruptive behavior is all too common in our society, and shows up even in church. Here are some examples.

Domestic Disputes: An estranged spouse may show up at church to confront his ex because he knows he will find her there. Often, he knows exactly where in the building to look for her and he knows security will not be as tight as it is at her job. The same goes for domestic abusers and controlling boyfriends.

Child custody battles may also show up at church. Non-custodial parents may try to get access to their children while the children are attending youth activities or church school. The non-custodial parent may know where the child's classroom is and may even know the church school teacher.

Substance Abuse: Church members may show up under the influence of alcohol or recreational drugs. Strangers who are intoxicated or under the influence of drugs may wander in.

Mental Illness: There may be church members who take medications to manage symptoms of mental illness. When their medications fail or are not taken properly, these individuals may become erratic or unpredictable in their behavior, and may become a danger to themselves or to others. Sometimes it's an undiagnosed mental or emotional condition, such as depression, that leads to suicidal or other unpredictable behavior.

Substance abuse, mental illness, and unpredictable behavior can show up in people—even long-standing church members—at any time. A job loss, a death in the family, work-related stress, financial problems—any of these outside pressures can cause church members to feel the need to harm themselves or to lash out at others. Churches welcome strangers and encourage troubled people to come in and begin to turn their lives around. But strangers bringing dangerous and troubling behavior can also enter.

Protesters: Churches are not immune to political and social protests. Outsiders may target the church because of the statements of its pastor or the actions of its members. Churches may find themselves in the media spotlight and may have to respond to bomb threats, death threats, or people attempting to intimidate members or disrupt worship services. Handling any of these situations requires well-trained Church Safety Team members who have good verbal de-escalation skills.

When to Use Verbal De-Escalation

It's important to understand when verbal de-escalation will be most effective as a technique and when it may not be useful at all. Every situation is different. You will have to use your best judgment about how to handle any given situation.

Goals of Verbal De-Escalation

Verbal de-escalation used successfully can do the following:
Get or keep the subject calm: If the subject is already calm, you want him/her to stay that way. Verbal de-escalation involves approaching subjects and talking with them in a way that encourages them to remain calm.
Lower the subject's agitation level: If the subject is agitated, verbal de-escalation skills can help him/her let go of that agitation.
Get the subject to cooperate: You want the subject to comply willingly

with any directives or suggestions you make. Using verbal de-escalation skills makes that outcome more likely.

Prevent the situation from escalating beyond your ability to control it: If the situation is routine and relatively non-threatening, you want it to stay that way. You never want your words or actions to trigger an emotional outburst or combative response from a subject.

Review

The situations in which you employ verbal de-escalation can vary widely and can change quickly. You will have to use your judgment. It may or may not be possible to get close enough to the subject to talk with him and use verbal de-escalation skills. In an active shooter situation, it may be most important to get people out of the building or to safety inside locked offices or behind heavy items. Hopefully, your church will never face an active shooter or someone threatening members with a weapon, but thinking and talking about it helps you prepare.

Engaging with the Subject

You will begin to use your verbal de-escalation skills the moment you spot someone behaving in a suspicious manner. How you approach that person—what you say and do in the beginning—will set the tone for the entire interaction and may determine whether things will go smoothly or whether they will spiral out of control.

So, in this section, we will look at how to engage with a subject who's behaving suspiciously—that is, how to approach the person and begin the interaction. Ask your learners, have you ever noticed how people tend to mirror the emotions and behavior of the person they're talking to? For example, if Person #1 shouts angrily at Person #2, Person #2 often responds by angrily shouting back at Person #1. Why does this happen?

Preparing to Engage

Follow these steps as you prepare to engage with a subject:

Alert other Church Safety Team members and request back-up: Try to avoid engaging a potentially difficult subject alone. Always use your radio to alert others on the Church Safety Team before you engage. Briefly describe the situation (use your codes to save time) and request back up. Depending on the severity of the situation, you may want to wait for another Safety Team member to arrive before you engage. Use your judgment about this.

Assess the situation: Determine your plan of action accordingly. Is this a low-level situation with little likelihood of danger? Or, is this a higher-level situation? Is the subject alone? Is this someone you know? Can you call him by name? Does he appear violent? Does he have a weapon? Is there something nearby he might try to use as a weapon? Are innocent bystanders in danger? Where is the nearest exit?

Pray for God's guidance: Always say a quick prayer asking God to guide your thoughts, your words, and your actions during your interaction with the subject.

Approach Carefully

Approach the subject in a way that will not appear to them as threatening or hostile. Make no sudden movements. Walk slowly but confidently. Avoid shouting at the subject and avoid sneaking up on the subject. Approach from within the subject's field of vision

Pay Attention to Personal Space

In everyday interactions, we tend to keep a "personal space" circumference around ourselves. In American culture, the comfortable distance for everyday conversations and business transactions is about three feet. If someone other than a family member or intimate partner steps inside that three-foot perimeter, it tends to make us uncomfortable.

Depending on the situation, we may regard the person stepping inside our personal perimeter as hostile. Keep this in mind when approaching a subject:

Stand about three feet away: Standing closer than three feet can be read as hostile or menacing. In other cultures, the acceptable distance is different. If the suspect is a different ethnicity than you, be aware of any possible differences. Increase this to five to six feet if the subject is agitated or angry. Six feet gives you enough space to avoid or deflect a physical attack.

Avoid touching the subject: Putting your hands on the subject definitely invades his space and may be interpreted as an attack. Exception: If this is a low-level interaction where you just want to have a conversation with someone to be sure everything is OK, you may want to offer a handshake as you introduce yourself. Use your judgment about how hostile or agitated the subject is before doing this.

Do not allow the subject to crowd your space: Put up your open hand in front of you, palm facing outward, to signal to the subject not to come any closer.

Lower the Threat Level

Take these additional steps to avoid making the subject feel threatened.

Reduce noise and distraction: A loud or busy environment may contribute to the subject feeling threatened. Do what you can to quiet the surroundings.

Avoid trapping the subject: Don't back him toward a wall or otherwise give him the feeling that he's trapped with no way out. People who feel trapped often lash out or attempt to fight.

Let one Church Safety Team member do the talking: The subject may easily become confused or agitated if several people are talking to him at the same time or if different people are asking him different questions. If there are several Church Safety Team members involved, designate one person to do the talking.

Avoid making it feel like an interrogation: Avoid asking questions one behind the other in rapid succession. Avoid demanding that the subject speak or answer right away. Make your interaction as much like a normal conversation as you can.

Move to a private space, if possible: A subject who feels humiliated or embarrassed may lash out. A subject who feels he has to protect his "macho image" may be less likely to back down or cooperate if others are watching. Help the subject save face by inviting him to talk in a private or quiet space, if feasible. Use your judgment as to when this is a sensible and safe alternative.

Be Aware of Body Language

Be aware that more than 90% of what we communicate is "said" without words. That is, when we are talking to someone, the other person picks up the message by listening to our words as well as by observing our facial expression and eyes, our body language, and the tone of our voice.

What we "say" with our face, our eyes, our body language and our tone of voice counts for more than what we say with our words. In other words, if we are saying something and our non-verbal communication does not match what we are saying, the listener will believe our non-verbal communication rather than our words.

When someone is talking and their words and non-verbal communication don't match, you always go with what their non-verbal communication is communicating. So, when you're engaging with a subject, make sure your body language, including your movement and tone of voice, agrees with your words.

Posture and Movement

Adopt a confident yet "ready" stance: Place your feet shoulders' width apart with one foot slightly behind you. This way you are well balanced and can move easily if necessary. Keep your hands in front of you where the subject can see them. Keep them at waist level so you can react quickly, or do something with them that looks relaxed and natural. For example, fiddle with your watch or your ring, or talk with your hands

Move slowly and deliberately: Avoid crossing your arms. This looks aggressive. Avoid shrugging your shoulders. It communicates that you don't care. Avoid pointing your finger at the subject. It suggests you're accusing them of something.

Eye Contact

Use direct eye contact, but look away occasionally to avoid giving the subject a hard, cold stare. Look at the subject when he's talking to show you're paying attention.

Remove sunglasses or anything else that hides your eyes. Make sure the subject can see your eyes. Talking to someone whose eye are hidden can be intimidating.

Avoid rolling your eyes or otherwise making fun of the subject. Make sure that your eyes never convey disrespect for the subject. For example, never roll your eyes upward as if you're annoyed or bored with what the subject is saying. Never look at another Church Safety Team member and roll your eyes as if to say, "This guy's crazy." Subjects will see and respond to any such non-verbal communication.

Facial Expression

Show empathy and understanding: Use your face to communicate that you are there to help (and not to arrest, or punish, or fight). In low-level interactions, let your face convey that you just want to talk with the subject—nothing serious.

Be careful of "micro-expressions": Micro expressions are those tiny facial movements that give away someone who is lying or trying to keep a straight face. These can be things like a subtle turning down of the corners of the mouth, a slight narrowing of the eyes, or miniscule worry lines that come across the forehead. Make sure your face doesn't show any tiny muscle movements like these, because the subject can pick up on them.

Avoid showing partiality to disputing parties: If you find yourself mediating between two parties in a dispute or in a he-said/she-said accusation, avoid showing partiality to either side—even if you strongly believe one party is telling the truth. Give both parties an opportunity to talk and listen impartially to both sides. Avoid, for example, smiling and nodding while one party talks and then giving a hard, cold stare while the other party talks.

Voice

Lower your volume: Speak quietly to help keep the situation calm. An agitated subject will often begin to mimic your quiet demeanor. Avoid shouting or raising your voice as this tends to escalate the situation.

Speak slowly and calmly: Again, the subject will often imitate whatever you do. Work on sounding reassuring, sympathetic, yet commanding. Be tactful, patient, and respectful.

Verbal Strategies that Work

We've looked at how to approach the subject and how to make sure your body language will be interpreted as non-threatening. Now it's time to look at some specific strategies for de-escalating a situation. Start with a five-step process that you can memorize and follow, so that when you're in the middle of a situation you'll be able to remember what to do.

Verbal De-Escalation and Disruptive Individuals

The main strategy for de-escalating a tense or potentially tense situation with a subject is conversation. You're going to talk to the subject and listen to the subject in a particular way. There are five steps you'll go through as you talk to the subject. To remember the steps, just remember the memory keyword: LEAST. The steps are:

- Listen
- Empathize
- Ask questions
- Summarize
- Talk about solutions

Let's look at each step and how to use it.

Listen

Verbal de-escalation involves conversation. It's important that you talk to the subject. It's even more important that you listen to the subject. Listening is your most important tool for calming someone down. Often, all an agitated person wants is for someone to listen to them. So, let them talk—and really listen. Use body language and verbal cues to show you're listening.

How can you use your body to show you're listening?

- Good eye contact
- Look earnestly at person
- Avoid distractions
- Avoid spacing out
- Nod head and smile
- Tilt head slightly to one side
- Face shows concern, interest
- Hands relaxed in front of you

What "verbal cues" show you're listening? Verbal cues are sounds, words, or phrases we use to show we're listening. They can include "Yes, go on", "I'm listening", "I see" or "I understand", "Then what happened?", "Uh-huh" or "uh-hmm". Show you're listening by looking earnestly at the person, smiling, nodding, and using verbal encouragement like, "Go on. I'm listening."

Get the Subject Talking

You'll probably have to do something to get the subject talking.

- Introduce yourself: If it's a lower level threat, you can start the conversation by introducing yourself (and even extending your hand for a handshake.
- Get and use the subject's name: Ask the subject's name if he doesn't volunteer it. Use it during the interaction. Being able to call someone by name personalizes the conversation and encourages them to be cooperative.
- If you've never seen him in the church before, you might say something like, "You must be a new member. I don't think I've met you." Notice that's much less threatening than, "You're not a member of this church, are you?" or "What are you doing here?" For higher-level threats, you may have to dispense with the introduction and handshake, but still try to get the subject's name.
- Keep your body language open and non-threatening.
- Ask the subject to describe what happened (or ask an open-ended question about what he's doing).

Empathize

Remember: Our memory key is the word LEAST. The "L" stands for listen. Now we're on "E". The "E" stands for empathize.

Show That You Understand

The surest way to calm an agitated person is to help them feel that they're understood. So, don't just listen—help them feel understood.

Do the best you can. Understanding may be difficult if the subject's conversation is rambling or illogical (e.g., a mentally ill person). See it from their point of view. Do your best to see it the way they see it. That doesn't mean you agree that they're right. It just means that you're willing to put yourself in their shoes for a moment to try to feel what their situation feels like.

Begin to echo back. Continue to use the "listening" body language and also start to echo back some of the emotion the subject is expressing. Examples: "So, that made you angry." "She humiliated you." "It's been tough since you lost your job." "You can't even see your own kids." "I can see how that would be really frustrating."

Keep your voice quiet, slow, and soothing as you do this. Be careful not to come across as mocking. Be as sincere and authentic as you can.

Avoid Saying

Here are some phrases to avoid when talking to the subject:

"Calm down."- Saying this never makes anyone calm down. In fact, it's likely to have the opposite effect. Similar phrases to avoid include: "Relax.", "You don't have to get so excited.", "You need to get yourself under control."

"What's your problem?" - No one likes to be told they "have a problem." It won't make the situation better. It suggests that you don't understand.

"You're acting crazy."- Similarly, no one likes to be told they're crazy, illogical, or not making sense. Remember, it makes perfect sense to them. Stop trying to convince them it's "crazy" and start trying to see it the way they see it.

"Things can't be that bad."- Again, this suggests that you don't get it. Clearly, for them, things are really bad, so try to understand.

"You're not making sense."- Same as above. If they're not making sense, it means you're not managing to see it the way they see it. Important: Remember, when you emphasize you don't have to agree with them. In fact, it may be obvious to you that they are very, very wrong. That's not the point. When you empathize, you try to walk a mile in their shoes and see it for a few moments the way they see it.

Ask Questions

The "A" stands for "ask questions". Ask the subject questions to encourage him to talk and also to get a better understanding of the situation.

Better and Worse Questions

There are better and worse ways to use questions:

Open-ended questions are often better than closed questions. Open-ended questions usually require more than a one-word answer and can be good as conversation starters. Open ended questions begin with who, what, when, where, how, and why. Example: "Did you unlock this door?" The answer is either "yes" or "no". The open-ended version of the question is: "How did this door get unlocked?" Now the subject has to give you, at the very least, a sentence.

Be aware that "why" questions can sound accusatory. You can soften the sound of a "why" question by changing it to a different kind of open question. Instead of, "Why did you take the keys?" ask, "How did you end up with the keys?" or "What was your reason for wanting the keys?"

Try not to "interrogate" the subject. Avoid asking one question behind the other in rapid succession. This can make the subject feel as if it's an interrogation and will make them less likely to want to cooperate.

Summarize

S is for summarize. If you have put yourself in the subject's shoes and you have listened well, you should be able to summarize their issue.

When you summarize, you repeat back the facts—from the subject's point of view—and describe the emotion the subject is feeling.

Many agitated and challenging subjects will begin to relax if you do this well. They will sense that you "get it." They will decide they don't have to fight with you. They will often begin to let you help them. They may take whatever suggestion you offer.

This works because we all want to be understood. When someone takes the time to listen to us and really tries to understand where we are coming from, we are more likely to trust them. Sometimes, all an agitated person wants is to be heard. Once you demonstrate that you have heard them, they will willingly agree to leave the building, go with the police, or follow any other directive you give them.

Talk About Solutions

T is for talk about solutions. Once you have demonstrated to the subject that you understand, it's time to talk about how the situation can be resolved. Ask the subject to do something and/or explain what will happen next.

Use your judgment about what should happen next. Every situation is different. Some possible resolutions include:

- Ask the subject to leave the building.
- Ask the parties involved to shake hands.
- Ask the parties to go with you to the pastor's office to talk about the issue.
- Ask the subject to give back the property that does not belong to him.
- Ask the subject to go with you to the Security Office so normal church activity can resume.
- Ask the subject to let someone from the Medical Team talk to him.
- Ask the subject to put down the object he's been threatening people with.

- Ask the subject to sit quietly in the narthex until the police arrive.

Tell the subject what you want him to do. Ask him to cooperate willingly. Continue to talk slowly and quietly. Help the subject understand that what you're suggesting is the best thing he can do right now.

Tactics to Avoid

As you work to get the subject's cooperation, make sure you avoid the following:

- Shouting or giving rapid commands. Continue to talk slowly and in a low volume. Continue to move slowly—no sudden movements.
- Lying, tricking, or deceiving. Never trick the subject into giving up. You've worked hard to gain his trust. Don't abuse it. For example, don't tell him his children are waiting outside to see him if it's not true.
- Making promises you can't keep. Similarly, don't promise anything you can't deliver. For example, don't say, "I promise, the police won't keep you in jail overnight." That's not something you can control.
- Threatening. Obviously, threatening the subject also destroys the trust you've created.

Points to Remember

As you work through the steps in the verbal de-escalation process, remember that the subject is God's creation, made in God's image, just like you.

Be patient: The verbal de-escalation process takes time. Proceed slowly, always giving the subject time to think and figure out what to do. If he feels pressured, hurried, or stressed, he may never relax.

Respect the subject's dignity: Never stop affirming his worth as a person.

Accept his thoughts and feelings: Doing so is the key to making him feel understood and encouraging him to cooperate.

Maintaining Personal Control

Verbal de-escalation only works if the person doing it is able to keep himself under control. So, in this final section, we will look at why it's important to maintain personal control throughout the process and how to do it.

The Logic of Verbal De-Escalation

We have a perception that law enforcement and security personnel have to be tough guys and tough gals. But when it comes to verbal de-escalation, less is more. To be successful, you must let go of your need to act tough, to take no "stuff" off of anyone. Instead, adopt an attitude of humility or meekness. You want to: Be less authoritative. Be less confrontational. Be less controlling.

The more you stop trying to control the situation, the more effective you will be.

There are many passages in the Bible that speak to the issues of meekness and humility. Let's talk about two of them: Have someone look up and read Psalm 25:9. "The meek will He guide in judgment; and the meek will He teach His way." --Ps 25:9 (KJV)

Now ask someone to look up 2 Corinthians 12:10. The part you want to emphasize says: "When I am weak, then am I strong." –2Cor 12:10 (KJV)

Explain that Psalm 25:9 was written by David. 2 Corinthians 12:10 comes from a letter written by the Apostle Paul. But both express the idea that God will take over when we let go of our need to control. So, when faced with a threat that requires you to use the verbal de-escalation process:

- Always say a quick prayer.
- Purposely let go of your desire to be forceful or confrontational.

- Let God take control of your thoughts and actions.
- Remember: when you are weak, then you are strong.

Be Aware of Your Hot Buttons

Persons in crisis may try to taunt you: They may call you names. They may use foul or coarse language. They may invade your personal space. They may use bizarre or insulting gestures.

Never take anything personally: Stay in control of your emotions. Remain calm. Remember that the best way to calm someone is to remain calm yourself.

Talking back or demanding respect only inflames the situation: Resist the temptation to do that. Focus on putting yourself in the other person's shoes and understanding what he's thinking and feeling that's making him do these things.

Avoid Controlling Statements

Remember, your goal is to get the subject to willingly comply, and you get their compliance by taking the time to listen and understand. Controlling and demanding statements will not get you the cooperation you're after. They will instead encourage the subject to fight back or get angry or argue with you.

Avoid statements like: "Watch your mouth", "Be quiet,", "Show some respect", "Get away from there" or "Get out of the building, right now."

Close your training with a prayer.

References

https://www.usatoday.com/story/news/nation/2013/07/07/churches-boost-security-as-violent-incidents-grow/2495241/

https://www.nytimes.com/interactive/2015/06/18/us/19blackchurch.html

http://www.churchlawandtax.com/blog/2016/june/violent-incidents-at-churches-are-rising.html

https://psmag.com/news/research-on-shootings-in-churches

http://nebula.wsimg.com/dd349bdc053330df2c77c85ee591b805?AccessKeyId=16B07A2D0672906279DB&disposition=0&alloworigin=1

http://www.icpsr.umich.edu/icpsrweb/DSDR/studies/25561

https://bible.knowing-jesus.com/topics/Vigilance

https://dictionary.cambridge.org/us/dictionary/english/arson

https://www.merriam-webster.com/dictionary/arson

https://earthquake.usgs.gov/earthquakes/browse/stats.php

https://weather.com/storms/severe/news/flood-deaths-united-states-over-300-since-2015

https://weather.com/storms/hurricane/news/2017-atlantic-hurricane-season-one-of-busiest-september

https://www.usgs.gov/faqs/how-many-deaths-result-landslides-each-year?qt-news_science_products=7#qt-news_science_products

https://news.nationalgeographic.com/news/2004/12/1227_041226_tsunami.html

Appendices, Forms, and Policies

CHURCH SAFETY MINISTRY
SAFETY TEAM APPLICATION

APPLICANT

NAME	DOB	ADDRESS	CITY, STATE, ZIP

EMAIL ADDRESS	CELL PHONE	HOME PHONE

QUALIFICATIONS

- [ ] *I am a member or regular attendee of the Church*
- [ ] *I am physically qualified to perform the duties of a Church Safety Volunteer*
- [ ] *I understand Church Safety Volunteers are Not Employees of Church*
- [ ] *I have no disqualifying criminal convictions (Policy available upon request)*

REFERENCES

NAME	RELATIONSHIP	PHONE NUMBER	Office Use

LET'S GET TO KNOW YOU

Do you have any special qualifications or experiences relevant to safety or security?

What makes you interested in joining the Church Safety Team?

What other gifts and talents do you have to offer the Church and the Safety Ministry?

_____ Today's Date:_____/_____/_____
Signature   (Sign with Ink Pen)

OFFICE USE ONLY

Approval: ☐ Yes ☐ No | Clear Background: ☐ Yes ☐ No | Date: | Authority:

Church Safety Ministry   *Confidential*   *Application*

Appendices, Forms, and Policies

Church Safety Team
INCIDENT REPORT
Release of Information on Juveniles is Restricted

INCIDENT INFORMATION							
Campus	Incident Occurred	Service Personnel Contacted			Notified SST Campus Chief	Notified Church Leadership	
		Police	EMS	Fire			
Date:							
Time:							
Name of Reporter:					Phone:		

INCIDENT TYPE		
☐ Lost Child / Parent	☐ Medical Emergency	☐ Violent Physical Behavior
☐ Lost / Stolen Property	☐ Fire / False Alarm	☐ Terroristic Threat
☐ Damage to Property	☐ Suspicious Person	☐ Safety / Security Concern
☐ Other:		

PERSONS INVOLVED						
PERSON 1	Name:		Age:	Phone:		
	Street:	City:		State:	Zip:	
	Parent/Guardian:			Phone:		
PERSON 2	Name:		Age:	Phone:		
	Street:	City:		State:	Zip:	
	Parent/Guardian:			Phone:		
PERSON 3	Name:		Age:	Phone:		
	Street:	City:		State:	Zip:	
	Parent/Guardian:			Phone:		

DESCRIPTION ALLEGED PERPETRATOR					
DESCRIPTION OF PERSON				DESCRIPTION OF VEHICLE	
Height:	Hair:	Build:	Make:	Color:	
Weight:	Eyes:	Clothes:	Model:	# of Doors:	
Other:			Other:		

DESCRIPTION OF INCIDENT

SAFETY AND SECURITY TEAM MEMBER INFORMATION

Print Name (Safety Team Member)

Signature (Safety Team Member)   *Today's Date*

Defending the Flock

Church Safety Team
FOLLOW-UP REPORT
Release of Information on Juveniles is Restricted

REPORTING SOURCE				
Name of Reporter:		Position:		
Ministry / Event:		Phone:		
Street:	City:		State:	Zip:

BRIEF SUMMARY OF INCIDENT

RESPONSE / ACTION TAKEN

SUPERVISOR COMMENTS / INTERVENTIONS

MINISTRY LEADER INFORMATION

_____
Print Name (Staff Member)

_____   _____
Signature (Staff Member)   Today's Date

Church Safety Team
PATROL LOG
Release of Information on Juveniles is Restricted

SST STAFF / PATROL INFO.		CAMPUS / ACTIVITY INFO.	
Date	☐ Observation	☐ Facilities	☐ Grounds
Time	☐ Operations	☐ Service	☐ Mid-Week
SST Staff	☐ Incident	☐ Other:	
General Description			

SST STAFF / PATROL INFO.		CAMPUS / ACTIVITY INFO.	
Date	☐ Observation	☐ Facilities	☐ Grounds
Time	☐ Operations	☐ Service	☐ Mid-Week
SST Staff	☐ Incident	☐ Other:	
General Description			

SST STAFF / PATROL INFO.		CAMPUS / ACTIVITY INFO.	
Date	☐ Observation	☐ Facilities	☐ Grounds
Time	☐ Operations	☐ Service	☐ Mid-Week
SST Staff	☐ Incident	☐ Other:	
General Description			

SST STAFF / PATROL INFO.		CAMPUS / ACTIVITY INFO.	
Date	☐ Observation	☐ Facilities	☐ Grounds
Time	☐ Operations	☐ Service	☐ Mid-Week
SST Staff	☐ Incident	☐ Other:	
General Description			

Defending the Flock

Church Safety Ministry
SAFE ACCESS LOG

SAFE ACCESS INFO.	NAMES *(Please Print Legibly)*	INITIALS	PURPOSE
Date			☐ Deposit
Time			☐ Petty Cash
Ministry/Dept.			☐ Mgr Access
Campus			☐ Bank Dep.
SAFE ACCESS INFO.	**NAMES** *(Please Print Legibly)*	**INITIALS**	**PURPOSE**
Date			☐ Deposit
Time			☐ Petty Cash
Ministry/Dept.			☐ Mgr Access
Campus			☐ Bank Dep.
SAFE ACCESS INFO.	**NAMES** *(Please Print Legibly)*	**INITIALS**	**PURPOSE**
Date			☐ Deposit
Time			☐ Petty Cash
Ministry/Dept.			☐ Mgr Access
Campus			☐ Bank Dep.
SAFE ACCESS INFO.	**NAMES** *(Please Print Legibly)*	**INITIALS**	**PURPOSE**
Date			☐ Deposit
Time			☐ Petty Cash
Ministry/Dept.			☐ Mgr Access
Campus			☐ Bank Dep.
SAFE ACCESS INFO.	**NAMES** *(Please Print Legibly)*	**INITIALS**	**PURPOSE**
Date			☐ Deposit
Time			☐ Petty Cash
Ministry/Dept.			☐ Mgr Access
Campus			☐ Bank Dep.
SAFE ACCESS INFO.	**NAMES** *(Please Print Legibly)*	**INITIALS**	**PURPOSE**
Date			☐ Deposit
Time			☐ Petty Cash
Ministry/Dept.			☐ Mgr Access
Campus			☐ Bank Dep.

_____   _____
Church Safety Director   *Date*

Church Safety Ministry
SUSPECTED CHILD MALTREATMENT REPORT
Release of Information on Juveniles is Restricted

SUSPECTED MALTREATMENT TIMELINE								
Campus		Suspected Child Mal. Identified	Service Personnel Contacted			Church Leadership Contacted	Report Completed	
☐ PL ☐ SH			Police	EMS	Fire		Oral	Written
Date:								
Time:								
Requirement:		-	-	-	-	-	24 hrs	72 hrs

Did intake worker accept the oral suspected maltreatment report? ☐ Yes ☐ No

PEOPLE / AGENCIES INVOLVED	

RECEIVING AGENCY

Worker Name:	Phone:
Agency Name:	Fax:
Street:	City: State: Zip:

REPORT SOURCE

Worker Name:	Position:
Ministry / Event:	Phone:
Street:	City: State: Zip:

ALLEGED VICTIM

Name:	☐ M ☐ F Age: Phone:
Home Address:	City: State: Zip:
Parent/Guardian:	Phone:
Parent/Guardian:	Phone:

ALLEGED PERPETRATOR

Name:	☐ M ☐ F Age: Phone:
Relationship to Family or Child?	Resides with victim? ☐ Yes ☐ No
Home Address:	City: State: Zip:
Interpreter Needed? ☐ Yes ☐ No	Language Spoken?

ALLEGED VICTIM'S CURRENT HOUSEHOLD / FAMILY INFORMATION			
List all people associated with victim (except perpetrator - that info is listed separately above)			
Household / Family Member Name	Relationship to Victim	Age or DOB	Reside with Victim
			☐ Yes ☐ No
			☐ Yes ☐ No
			☐ Yes ☐ No
			☐ Yes ☐ No
			☐ Yes ☐ No
			☐ Yes ☐ No

ADDITIONAL FAMILY INFORMATION
(i.e. non-custodial or absent parent contact info, custodial arrangements, need for interpreters, language)

DESCRIPTION OF INCIDENT

SST - Suspected Child Maltreatment Report - Level 3   Confidential   Internal Use Only

Defending the Flock

_____

| RESPONSE / ACTION TAKEN |

| SUPERVISOR COMMENTS / INTERVENTIONS |

| SAFETY AND SECURITY TEAM MEMBER INFORMATION |

_____
Print Name (SST Staff Member)

_____
Signature (SST Staff Member)

_____
Today's Date

Made in United States
Orlando, FL
20 December 2021

12204896R00172